P9-BYZ-576

where's whitey?

where's whitey?

Kevin Weeks
&
Phyllis Karas

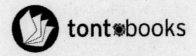

tont◉books

First published in 2010 by Tonto Books Limited

Copyright © Kevin Weeks & Phyllis Karas 2011
All rights reserved

The moral rights of the authors have been asserted

No part of this book may be reproduced or transmitted in any
form or any means without written permission from the copyright
holder, except by a reviewer who may quote brief passages in
connection with a review for insertion in a newspaper, magazine,
website, or broadcast

British Library Cataloguing in Publication Data:
A catalogue record for this book is available from
the British Library

All characters appearing in this work are fictitious.
Any resemblance to real persons, living or dead,
is purely coincidental.

ISBN-13:
9781907183164

Printed & bound in Great Britain
by CPI Antony Rowe

Ebook ISBN-13:
9781907183270

Produced up north
by Tonto Books

www.tontobooks.co.uk

This book is dedicated, with love, to Anna,
who has taught me what's important in life.

Kevin Weeks

To Toby Bondy, my sister, my best friend.

Phyllis Karas

Chapter 1
Joey, Lynn, Ma, 1986

When Jimmy calls to tell me he'll pick me up at the convenience store in an hour, I have a feeling something's up. Just the way he sounds, nothing specific, but my antennae are raised. Chances are, this is not going to be a relaxing ride to pick up a couple of envelopes.

Sure enough, when I get into Jimmy's dark-blue 1986 Chevy Caprice and see Stevie in the passenger seat, looking especially energized, his nostrils flared ever so slightly, I know my gut feeling is right on target.

'We're going to take a little ride to Lynn, Joey,' Jimmy tells me as I slide into the back seat behind Stevie, more comfortable with him in front of me. During the more than ten years I've worked with Stevie and Jimmy, I've never taken Stevie's unpredictability lightly; I'm aware how dangerous and violent these guys (both twenty years older than me) are, but I've always felt more at ease with Jimmy. Or at least more aware of how his brilliant Machiavellian mind works. Stevie is less complex: his answer to any problem, to any insult or slight, is a simple and unwavering one: Kill him. To Stevie, killing is more than just a part of the business – it's a pleasure he would rarely, if ever, deny himself.

But this early afternoon we head out of South Boston, north over the Mystic River Bridge and along crowded route 1A, through Chelsea and Revere to Lynn – three rundown cities with excessively high crime rates. Even though Revere and Lynn border on the Atlantic, with long stretches of attractive beaches, crime has managed to pollute the cities far more than waste contaminates the ocean.

Inside the Chevy, however, the closer we get to Lynn, the clearer the reason for our little road trip forty minutes out of Boston becomes. Always cognizant of the fact that the car might be bugged, Jimmy turns the radio on and says in almost a whisper, 'We're going to pay a little visit to Richie Lambodosi.'

As we drive across the Lynn way, which resembles one used car lot after another despite a few obscured views of the ocean, he explains the situation. It seems Richie's been coming up short a lot these days and Jimmy knows he's holding bets. Last weekend he had a friend of ours put in some large bets with him. When the office called Richie to take all his bets, two of those large bets didn't appear – and that's when Jimmy decided we would confront him.

We find Richie's house, a neat little single family on a cul-de-sac not too far from Union Hospital, and wait around the corner for him to come home. Once we see him steer his shiny new, dark-green Cadillac Coupe Deville down the street and amble into his house, Jimmy calls to tell him that he wants to talk to him from a phone booth outside the hospital.

'Sorry, but I can't come to Southie today,' Richie tells him. 'I got something going on, but I'll come in tomorrow.'

'No problem,' Jimmy says. 'We're right near your house. Just come outside and we'll pick you right up.'

Sure enough, five minutes later I move over behind Jimmy and Richie slides into the backseat beside me. In his early fifties, he's been in the business for a long time. Over the years, I've played a little poker with him and found him to be a likeable enough guy: a little loud, but a pretty decent card player.

'How ya doing, Joey?' he asks and smiles uneasily at me.

I nod, looking straight into his eyes. He's a short guy, kind of stocky, with thinning black hair, wide floppy ears, small narrow dark eyes and a bulbous nose. Today he's wearing loose-fitting dungarees and a yellow polo shirt and it's not hard to see he's not his usual easy-going self. After all, he'd have to be brain-dead not to be concerned when the boss shows up at his house to take him out for a little ride. No one who knows Jimmy's reputation would be pleased at this turn of events. Yet again, Jimmy switches the radio to loud just in case some overzealous DEA agents have been

2

successful in their typically futile attempts to install a bugging device in his car, then starts in with him.

'You've been coming up short,' he tells Richie, his voice pretty calm. 'You owe us $22,000.'

'People haven't been paying me, Jimmy,' he replies. I can see he's getting more nervous, abandoning any attempt to act natural, squirming a little in his seat, stealing glances towards the door to his right as if planning an escape. It's a cold November day but he's starting to sweat big time.

'You're a liar,' Jimmy tells him, his voice sharp and angry now, but still softer than the sounds emitting from the blaring radio. 'You had two bets last week: one for $2,500 on LSU on Saturday and another for $5,000 on the NY Giants on Sunday. Neither one was on your slip.'

He's staring straight ahead at the road in front of him but his hands grip the wheel tightly, the knuckles white and rigid. Wearing his trademark black leather jacket and jeans plus baseball cap and his eyes, as always, covered by sunglasses, Jimmys looks a good twenty years younger than his actual age (fifty-eight). Thanks to a religious schedule of exercising daily, there's not an ounce of fat on his 5'8" muscular frame and while he exercizes perfect control over his workouts, his temper knows no boundaries when riled.

'People have been placing bets but not paying me,' Richie says, stammering now, glancing even more longingly at the car door. 'I just wanted to make some more money to pay you back what I owe you.'

Jimmy pulls the car off sharply to the side of the road, a dead-end street close to what looks like a deserted leather factory, so forcing Richie up against the precious escape door that is all too firmly locked. Turning off the motor and gritting his teeth, he turns to face his prisoner.

'Where's my money?' he demands.

You can see the anger as one corner of his mouth curls up ominously and his face becomes a menacing shade of red. As he rips off his sunglasses and tosses them onto the centre console, his eyes are an icy shade of blue.

'I have problems,' Richie groans. 'My daughter Angela is getting married and I've no money to pay for the wedding.'

'We *all* have problems,' Jimmy tells him, his steely eyes fixed on Richie's face. He shakes his head as if to dispense with a pesky fly. 'But you've made a lot of money these past years so I'm asking you again: where is my money?'

'Just give me a little time,' Richie says, practically squealing now. 'I'll get it. I swear, I'll get it!'

His eyes still glued on Richie, Jimmy pulls out a two-inch barrel .38 and tells him simply: 'I want my money today or I'm going to kill you.'

'Then shoot me,' says Richie, his body slumped against the back of the seat, brushing against my shoulder.

I avert my eyes and stare instead at Stevie, who has turned round in his seat and is gazing enviously at Jimmy – wishing, I'm sure, that he could be the one administering justice. Then I scoot closer to the left; you'd have to be a fool not to see what's coming.

'You'll be doing me a favour, Whitey.'

With that, Jimmy says, '*Good*! Glad to help you out,' and shoots him through the right eye.

As Richie slumps in his seat, blood sprays across the rear window, some of it splattering onto my face. The funny thing is none of us flinches. After a while you just get used to the noise and the smell of the sulphur from the gunshot. I glance down at Richie and see a hole where his eye was. Already, his blood is beginning to slow to a steady trickle.

Luckily, the bullet exited downwards into the back seat so it didn't blow out the back window but it's still a mess everywhere, with blood and brains all over the car. Quickly, I push the body down onto the floor and tear off my sweatshirt, leaving my T-shirt on. I use my sweatshirt to wipe the blood from the window as best I can, saving the sleeve to clean my face.

Stevie just glances at the mess, winks at me and then turns to face forward as we start to drive away.

4

Driving down the Lynn Marsh Road, Jimmy pulls the Chevy onto an unpaved street that leads directly to a swampy area overgrown with weeds and discarded beer cans. It's clear from the way he's driving that he's been here before – and I doubt just to throw away a beer can. I jump out to make sure no one's around but I can see nothing except the distant tracks for the commuter train that carries North Shore residents to North Station. I'm certain that even if a speeding train were to come barrelling down the tracks, none of its passengers would be able to see us.

Stevie and I pull the body out, grabbing a leg and an arm apiece, and drag Richie about fifty feet away, where we dump him quickly and unceremoniously into the weeds.

Driving back to South Boston, Jimmy turns the radio back on. It's real loud again: this time Nat King Cole sings 'Ramblin' Rose'. Though my ears are still ringing from the pistol shots, my companions are in high spirits and can recount every detail of the earlier scene.

'Did you see the way his whole body started to shake when you asked where your money was?' Stevie asks. 'The poor bastard was too stupid to realize he was gone the minute he put his foot into the car.'

'It was like looking at a bull's-eye,' says Jimmy, obviously delighted with his handiwork. 'I got him right square in the middle of his eyeball. Perfect hit!'

'The blood spurted out like a fucking geyser,' laughs Stevie, shaking his head merrily. 'It was beautiful!'

'Sure was,' Jimmy agrees.

Stevie starts to laugh. 'Guess he didn't know you don't like to be called Whitey,' he says. 'Big mistake.'

Though I add a few words here and there, I'm content to sit back and let the other two complete their post-mortem. It's the part they really enjoy: if Stevie had his way, he'd be in the marshes dissecting the body right now. He'd make a great pathologist – or even a mortician.

All the way home, the mood in the car is pure elation. The two guys have spent the past hour doing what they love most: taking care of business in the most vicious manner available, nothing beats this for either of them.

As soon as we get back to South Boston, Jimmy parks the Chevy in a garage he's kept for years on K Street. He takes a navy nylon jacket out of the trunk and hands it to me. After I shove my bloodied sweatshirt into a bag he finds in the trunk, I put on the jacket and the three of us walk down Eighth Street to the Old Colony Projects, where my car is parked. I'm feeling pretty good, anticipating a quiet evening now that Jimmy's lust for blood has, for the time being anyhow, been sated. I figure we'll grab a nice dinner in Boston, probably just the two of us, or else he'll decide to go home and have dinner with Terry and her kids, in which case I'll go find Jeannie and spend the night with her.

I'm not feeling particularly remorseful over what's just happened in Jimmy's car: Richie was a player, he knew the rules, he gambled that he could break them – and lost. As for my role in his murder, I recognize that as an accessory, I'm just as guilty as Jimmy. It's possible, though improbable, that I might have done something to prevent the murder, but I didn't: Jimmy could just as easily have turned the gun on me, had I given him any reason to do so. I doubt he ever would but then I wouldn't take such a risk over someone like Richie. There are winners and losers in this game and Richie was in every way a loser.

Chapter 2
Whitey, New York, 1999

I'm working out in our New York hotel room when Cathy comes in with the news. It's just a few minutes after six and I'm about through with lifting weights.

'I saw it on the television,' she tells me, her voice slightly breathless.

She's wearing a fluffy yellow terrycloth bathrobe, her short blonde hair wrapped in a towel. Her skin is pink from the bath she took and as always, she looks fabulous.

'You've been named on the FBI's Most Wanted List, Jimmy: "James Whitey Bulger wanted for nineteen murders". My name's there, too.'

She stops for a moment and studies my face. I shrug and she goes on, her voice a little softer now: 'They also say you were an FBI informant, as well as the head of the South Boston mob.'

I'm not surprized: my contacts have been warning me for weeks that the FBI was going to list me. As for the informant shit, that's no big shock either – the surprize is that I hid it so well for thirty years. Now all that means is there's no one I can get in touch with – certainly not Joey – who I bet couldn't believe his ears. Too bad I never found the words to tell him myself – he deserved that.

I study her face. She's trying to play the game the way I like it, cool and collected. You have to give the woman credit – in so many ways, she's made for this life. I put down the weights and sit on the nearest chair.

'Yeah, no big surprize,' I casually mutter.

She folds down onto the floor beside my chair and leans her cheek against my leg. I'm sweating through my warm-up suit but that doesn't seem to bother her.

'How does this affect us?' she asks.

'Not much,' I answer. 'We've always been careful, there's nothing I'll do any different.'

She's quiet and I know what she's thinking. You don't spend almost every minute of the day and night with a woman for more than six years and not get to know exactly what's on her mind.

'Okay, things will be different,' I admit and she sighs softly. 'There's money out there.'

'A million dollars,' she says.

'Yeah,' I say. 'That'll count for something.'

'And your picture will be on that *Most Wanted* show all the time.'

'That, too.' I wish she'd let it go. Usually she knows when to back off, but this is different: it's her face out there on the bull's-eye, too. 'But I'm prepared for this – it's been six years since we took off. Hell, I hardly recognize you sometimes. We'll be okay, trust me. They're never going to find us.'

She positions herself closer and I feel her shoulders begin to relax against me.

'I know, Jimmy,' she tells me, 'but I get scared sometimes. I like our life the way it is, I don't want it to change and I couldn't bear to have anything happen to you.'

But I don't want to hear this. 'I've got to change and make a call,' I tell her, although with the FBI on the case, there's no one I can call right now.

Despite what I said, things *are* different: It's true none of this is a surprise, but it's still going to mean a major change for us. I stand up, maybe a bit too roughly, and she nearly falls over but I'm out of there and into the shower before she can say anything. When I get out, she's sitting on the bed reading some goofy paperback novel, the towel gone from her wet hair, her bathrobe tightly belted. The TV is on mute but I can see it's a news show.

'I'll be back in an hour,' I say.

She looks up and smiles.

'Sure,' she says and then glances back down at her book. She's smart, real smart – she probably knows there's no one I can call, that I've got to cut off all contact with anyone back home, but I need to get out of the room to think … by myself.

The hotel we've been staying at for the past two weeks is not too far from Times Square. It's the typical place I've always favoured: small, clean, no doorman but all the amenities we need and a clientèle that doesn't spend a lot of time checking out the latest headlines. Sure, I could afford to stay in the most luxurious hotel in the city but even before my face was plastered on FBI 'Most Wanted' posters, I was careful to avoid places with nosy doormen or guests who have the time and smarts to know what's going on in the world outside their door.

From now on I need to be extra-careful. Today's news might draw the attention of even the guests in this undistinguished hotel. For the next hour, I wander up and down the streets in and around Times Square, ignoring the crowds, the throng of traffic, the constant blasting of car horns and peddlers trying to unload carts filled with cheap knock-offs. Thinking, strategizing ... Already I'd made a plan for this day, which I knew would arrive but I need to think it over one last time before I put it into effect.

We've got to get out of New York. Not a good idea to fly anywhere, though. Better drive to a small town, like Louisiana, down south where the living will be easy and we can find a small place to rent for a few months and hang low. She'll like it there: people will be friendly and we'll fit right in – we're good at that. We'll take off tonight. Soon. I'm paid up for the rest of the week, so the desk clerk won't be concerned to learn we're suddenly leaving. Besides, I heard him say he himself was leaving for a new job tomorrow so his replacement will never have seen me – a stroke of luck right when I can use it.

As I'm heading back to the hotel, I think about what Cathy said: nineteen murders. Oh yeah, so that's what they think, huh? No surprize that Stevie gave me up for some of them. Nineteen was just the beginning but that doesn't matter. Not one of them, not even the women, is worth spending a second over. A bunch of them deserved to die. Hell, a lot of them were trying to kill me. Nineteen, thirty, forty, whatever ... they're all dead but I'm alive and walking round Manhattan, free as a bird.

As I approach the hotel, I have a fleeting thought: would I be better off without her? Maybe now. She's great company, she's smart and she takes good care of me, but things have changed and I need to consider every angle. When I get back to the room, her hair is perfect, she's dressed and packed ... and looking more beautiful than ever before. She's staring hard at me as I walk in and I think how easy it would be to do what I probably should.

'Let's go, baby,' I say. Then I grab my leather bag and her coach bag and head back out the door.

Chapter 3
Cathy, Tennessee, 1999

'Check the map,' he tells me.

We left New York eleven hours earlier and he's been driving through the night. A couple of times we stop to use restrooms and pick up some food, but he's as alert as if we took off just a half-hour ago.

'We're outside Knoxville,' I tell him and he nods. 'About twelve hours from Shreveport.'

'Can you go that long without checking into a motel?' he asks.

'Sure,' I insist, 'I'm fine.'

This is one of my favourite things: driving in the car with Jimmy, just the two of us heading somewhere new. The world races by our windows as we travel together, snuggled up like carefree lovers; no one in any of the cars we pass ever suspects who we are. There's an excitement to this life that makes me feel so completely alive. Before we left Boston, I spent a lot of time thinking about being on the run with Jimmy, but when I mentioned it to my twin sister Karen she thought I was nuts.

'How would you be able to sleep at night?' she asked. 'Any minute a policeman could come knocking on your door and take you away to jail or worse, kill you.'

I tried to explain that I never thought like that; that I had complete faith in Jimmy, that he was smarter than any cop we might run into, that he planned things so meticulously there wasn't any chance of a problem. But I didn't dare admit to her that ever since I'd seen *Bonnie and Clyde*, I'd imagined life on the run, with the man you loved, had a thrill you'd never find anywhere else. Sure, the ending of the movie was horrific but what a life they led. Of course Karen would've had me institutionalized if I'd ever told her that.

Maybe she would've been right. Perhaps there is something wrong with me, something that will never let me be happy with some ordinary guy who leads an everyday type of life: we could be living in a neat little house in the suburbs, raising a couple of cute kids. I knew from the beginning that Jimmy wasn't going to give me that kind of life but I still wanted him more than anything else. Guess you can't control your heart. I look over towards him for a long minute and somehow I just know, crazy or not, that I'm right where I want to be.

'Good,' Jimmy says and switches the radio to another news station (except for one mention of him, there's been nothing about Whitey Bulger on any radio broadcast). 'You'll like Shreveport,' he continues, taking a handful of organic carrots from the open bag between us and chewing thoughtfully. He looks so good today, dressed in his neat jeans and open blue-and-white striped shirt, the sleeves folded jauntily at the elbows – I never tire of looking at this guy. 'I scouted out a couple of possible places when I was there a couple of years ago. It's a friendly place – easy to get lost and have a good life.'

'Should be nice and warm for the winter,' I say. 'I like the idea of swimming in December, just might buy myself a new bikini.'

He nods, but he's not paying any attention to me: he's always lost in thought when he drives. I'm staring out the side window, imagining a nice sunny beach when he starts to talk again. It's like he's thinking out loud, talking more to himself than to me. 'I'm thinking maybe we should take a ride back to Boston,' he says, a mocking smile forming on his lips. 'I might want to pay a visit to some old acquaintances.'

'Would you really want to do that?' I ask, instantly excited at the thought of seeing my mother and two sisters. 'Even with the Feds looking everywhere for you – why risk going back there?'

'I have my reasons,' he says, his smile wider now. 'Maybe I can convince a few people to disappear and then the case itself will disappear altogether.'

With that he starts to laugh, a loud evil laugh.

Now I'm feeling nervous: I know what he means when he uses the word 'disappear'. Jimmy rarely tells me anything about business and he never discussed it when we were with Stevie or Joey but I'm not a fool: I know the three of them did dangerous and bad things together, but the less I know the better. That way I could never be implicated in any of their crimes but now I'm curious: 'What would you do, Jimmy? Give them money to take off?'

He laughs even louder. 'Yeah, something like that,' he says. 'I should have done it before.' At this he's no longer laughing, though he looks relaxed and pleased with himself. 'And I'll take care of that little problem when the time's right. But hey, forget it! It can wait. We'll just enjoy ourselves around here and do some more sightseeing.'

With that, I glance at him, wondering if there's anything that can unnerve this man. Somehow I don't think so.

'It might have been nice, though, to have seen some old friends, hey?' he asks, pulling out to pass the car in front of us to my surprise. Jimmy drives so slowly he rarely has to pass anybody; says the last thing he wants is a speeding ticket, but I worry we'll be pulled over for going under the speed limit.

'Like Terry?' I ask, instantly regretting my words but somehow unable to stop them from coming out. 'To see if she's ready to go back with you?'

He grips the steering wheel tightly and I know I've gone too far, but Terry's the one subject that drives me crazy.

'You're here now, Cathy, aren't you?' he asks coldly, his eyes staring straight ahead at the road.

'That's 'cause she got tired after two months,' I say, louder than I intended.

'I knew she would,' he tells me, 'but I had to give her the chance. We'd been together too many years not to give her that. You know all that, Cathy. Enough already.'

'Stevie,' I say, anxious to change the subject. 'Would you want to see him?'

'Oh yes, I'd definitely want to see him,' he says, his voice even, but ice-cold. 'Not that he surprized me: I knew he wouldn't be able to handle jail, that he'd give me up if they put him away. I told him all about Alcatraz and Leavenworth and Atlanta, but he wouldn't listen – he probably spat it out the first day we were informants. Like that was going to help his case, like they'd say he was innocent of any crimes he committed while an informant.'

He's silent for a long time, driving slowly again.

'Hell, we killed guys for doing what Stevie and I did with the FBI,' he finally proclaims.

And that's all he says until we get to Shreveport.

Chapter 4
Whitey, Louisiana, 2000

It's a warm late summer's evening and I'm driving down a two-lane highway outside Shreveport, Louisiana. There's a sense of freedom in driving that I don't get anywhere else; must be all those years in prison with the walls around me that makes me want to climb into a car and just drive. Anywhere.

Nothing's quite so good as heading to places I've never been before. Taking in all the sights: the landscape, the birds and dogs at the side of the road, Mom and Pop stores along the way, noticing the different ways people dress and talk. Wherever we go, there's something new to learn. Cathy won't stop asking if I'm tired, if I want her to drive. Like I'd let her behind the wheel. Hell, I never let Stevie or Joey do that. I'd never give anyone that kind of control over my life and certainly not now. If I'm going to get caught for a traffic violation, I'll know how to handle it behind the wheel.

The road's virtually empty tonight but I'm sticking to the speed limit. Cathy's beside me, jabbering about a movie she saw this afternoon – something silly about two guys and a baby. I barely follow what she's saying: my mind's preoccupied with what happened in the fruit store earlier that day.

It was probably nothing but I can't be positive. Cathy was busy checking out the peaches and I was picking out a couple of lemons when I noticed a woman staring at me. She wasn't obvious but I could tell from the way she moved her head slightly to the right as she pushed her shopping cart next to ours that she was more interested in the two of us than the organic fruit. Middle-aged, she was maybe forty-five and pencil-thin; nicely dressed, with a considerable amount of expensive jewellery on both hands. First, she glanced quickly at me, then a few seconds later towards Cathy. She got busy with some cherries, but I could see she was distracted. Cathy, smart as a fox, sensed something was going on and calmly pushed the shopping cart away. Less than three minutes later, the two of us were outside the store minus the fruit.

'Probably nothing,' I told her and she shrugged her shoulders as she got into the car and we drove off.

'I think you would have liked the movie,' she's saying now. I would have hated it and she knows it, but she's in her usual happy, good-natured mood and I see no reason to pull her out of it. So I nod and she goes on. And I finally put the fruit store incident out of my mind – it's not worth worrying about.

She's describing the cute little baby in the dumb movie when I notice a police cruiser in my rearview mirror. When the red lights beam onto the rear window, Cathy shuts up. I have no idea why the cop is pulling me over, but I'm ready for him. He ambles across to the car, a short, thin man in his late forties with thick black hair, who's probably been on the force twenty years or so.

'Driving kind of slow, aren't you, sir?' he asks in a thick Louisiana drawl. 'Is there something wrong?'

'No, officer,' I answer respectfully, 'just enjoying the summer night.'

'Sure,' he says and I notice a slight flicker in his eyes, along with a twitch at the right of his lower lip. He hesitates for a second and then says, 'Licence and registration, please.'

I feel Cathy stiffen but so imperceptibly no one else would notice. She acts relaxed around the law, following my motto that if you behave naturally, they'll suspect nothing. Leaning across her, I touch her leg lightly and open the glove compartment to take out the registration. I hand it to the cop and then pull my wallet out of my pocket, smoothly removing the Massachusetts' licence. Thomas F. Baxter, it reads, born November 15th, 1930.

I have no reason to believe my phony papers, established in the early eighties, have been compromized but something feels wrong. Call it intuition but it's a stronger feeling than I had in the fruit store: my adrenaline is racing and I'm loving the feeling that something's going to happen – and it's not me who's about to get hurt.

The cop walks back to his car and I touch Cathy's right wrist, possibly a bit too firmly, and stare hard at her.

'How you doing, Hon?' I ask.

'Fine,' she replies and I can see that she is.

As I watch the cop approach his car, I ease the .22 caliber automatic with its silencer out from under the mat and slide it between my seat and the controls. I hear an incoming call on the cop's radio about an accident with possible fatalities and through my rearview window see him lean down, grab the microphone and say a few words before replacing the microphone. As I watch him hurrying back towards me, my hand reaches for the gun, relishing the feel of cool metal. I try to read his face but there's no expression there. His left hand holds my licence and registration, but his right hand moves towards the holster attached to his waist. Cathy's perfectly calm: it's as if she knows she has to be ready for what may well be coming.

'I'm sure your papers are okay,' the officer says, dismissing me. He hands me back my licence and registration: 'Y'all have a nice night now.'

'Thank you, sir,' I reply. 'You have a good one, too.'

'I don't think so,' he says. 'I've just been called to the scene of an accident.'

'Sorry to hear that,' I say, as though I'm really concerned. I watch him get back in his car and make a quick U-turn, then begin driving back into the darkness myself. Meanwhile, Cathy squeezes my hand and sighs deeply.

I can't shake off the feeling that call saved the cop's life. Sure enough, the next day I discover my licence had been compromised. That jealous bitch Terry gave me up, revealing my assumed name to a pathetic rat who immediately alerted the law, hoping for a nice little reward. If the Louisiana cop had had time to check out my licence, he would've realized he was dealing with James Whitey Bulger, a fugitive named on the FBI's Most Wanted list for nineteen counts of murder. Seconds later, he might've made number twenty.

Chapter 5
Cathy, Shreveport, 2001

It's nothing new: the nightmares are as much a part of Jimmy as his blue eyes and lactose intolerance. Every night they come around dawn, plunging him into the depths of despair. He says they're the result of the LSD he took in the Atlanta prison as part of some CIA government-sponsored experiment: they wiped two years from his sentence and left his mind permanently injured. Since I never knew him before, I've no idea how much they changed him. He says he never had trouble sleeping before, never had any nightmares. It's pretty awful to think the government could fool around with prisoners' brains, treat them like animals. Not that I'd want to see any animal treated this way either. I left my two precious toy poodles behind when I took off with Jimmy and there isn't a day goes by that I don't think about them. A couple of times Jimmy has offered to buy me a new dog, but I know it wouldn't work with our lifestyle. He knows that too, but I appreciate him making the offer.

This night, Jimmy's nightmare is especially bad. For the four months we've been in Shreveport, they've been so much worse than usual. Don't know if it's the heat or something in the air, but I've lost count of the nights since we got here that he's woken up in a cold sweat, screaming and half out of his mind. A few years ago, I was listening to *Oprah* when they were discussing nightmares: this expert doctor said you shouldn't try and wake up the person having the nightmare, that it would be too much of a shock if you shake them awake. He said it was better to just keep on saying, 'It's all right,' real calmly and then wait for the person to wake up on his own.

The problem has always been when Jimmy's nightmares come when we're staying in a hotel. The last thing we want is for someone in a nearby room to hear screaming in the middle of the night and call for help. Jimmy's usually very careful about checking out our rooms before we settle in, making sure the walls are relatively thick, that our room is at the end of a corridor. And we always leave a radio on and I just make it louder if he starts to scream in his sleep. Many nights, he doesn't scream: he shakes violently, sweats and trembles like a terrified kid until the nightmarish scenes leave his body. It just about breaks my heart to see him this way and to know there's nothing I can do to help him.

Here in Shreveport we have our own house; it's not near any neighbours so there's no problem if Jimmy screams. But tonight he seems so tormented, I just can't stand it: I get out of bed and walk round the house, waiting for the screaming to subside. As always, he'll be totally exhausted when he wakes from the nightmare and will have a terrible time falling back asleep. Tomorrow, he'll sleep till two or three in the afternoon, which is no big problem since we have nothing special planned.

We've really enjoyed this town and met some nice people, who treat us as if we're just regular folk here to pass the winter. Even the local policemen are super polite, the way Southerners can be. Just yesterday, one of the policemen stopped the traffic to let Jimmy and me cross, saying, 'Why, hello there, Mr Thompson. Lovely day, isn't it?' Heaven knows, no Boston policeman would ever treat us like that, even if Jimmy wasn't involved in criminal activities.

I'm in the kitchen, looking through a few of my recipe books for something special to cook for tomorrow night when I hear Jimmy call my name. He's stopped screaming, but his voice is hoarse as can be. I race back to the bedroom and he's sitting upright in bed, sweat running down his face and soaking through his pyjamas. He looks awful, like he's seen a ghost. It's not as if he ever looks good after a nightmare, but tonight he seems much worse than usual.

'He's coming for me,' he says, eyes wide and bulging, his voice no more than a throaty whisper. 'Get the bat. Watch out, he's coming!'

I race over and sit on the arm of the chair, placing a hand on his chest, trying to shake him awake, but it's no good. He pushes me away, then yells, 'I said to watch out!' as I fall to the floor.

Jimmy often gets violent during his nightmares and I have to be careful that he doesn't lash out and hit me. Knowing what he's done in his life, I understand how violent he can be but he's never been that way with me.

There are times when I'm taking a long walk by myself and I'm in a strange mood when I find myself thinking about Jimmy and the kind of man he is and the terrible things he's done. Sometimes I wonder what I'm doing with him, if I'm out of my mind, but the minute I see him again I'm filled with so much love that I can hardly stand it. There's nobody in this world I've ever loved as much as I love this man and I know he loves me just as much. There have been other men in my life but none compare to Jimmy, certainly not as far as sex is concerned. Jimmy knows what I like, but it's more than just the sex: he's so smart and capable, generous beyond belief and he's afraid of nothing and nobody. Other men look cheap in comparison. No wonder Terry was with him for so many years: you can't walk away from this guy.

A month or two before I took off with Jimmy, I had this wicked cold that turned into double pneumonia. Jimmy wouldn't leave me alone for a minute. He took me to his doctor at Mass. General and made sure I didn't have to wait, even a few minutes. I saw the look on his face when I was having trouble breathing. He kept holding out my inhaler, gently reminding me when to inhale and exhale. I know he loves me and will always take care of me, just the way I love to take care of him, to cook and shop for him, to iron his clothes, even his pyjamas, just the way he likes them; to do everything to make his life as easy as possible. I decided years ago that some things, like the bad things I know he's done, are best left alone and not thought about.

Tonight, however, I'm worried sick about him. 'It's okay, Jimmy,' I keep repeating, as I sit beside him on the floor. But his arms are now swinging and before I can move, he hits me on the side of my cheek. I land on my back on the floor but he's still swinging at me. Suddenly he's off the chair, looking down at me and the expression in his eyes is beyond terrifying: I'm in trouble.

'It's me, Jimmy,' I plead, covering my face with my hands and rolling up into a ball. 'It's Cathy, baby. It's *Cathy*!' But he doesn't hear me.

'You fucking bastard!' he screams, bending down towards me. 'I saw what you did. I told you to stop, but you didn't listen. You'll listen *now*!'

The punch to my head hurts so much that I shriek out in pain but he still doesn't hear. He pulls my legs down, punches my stomach and all the wind goes out of my body.

'*No*, Jimmy!' I scream, but the next blow comes to my face and then all I see is darkness.

Chapter 6
Whitey, Louisiana, 2002

It's the last thing that I'm expecting. I'm taking a late-day walk down to Melvin's Landing on Cross Lake Boulevard to check on Mike Everett's boat. He thinks there might be a problem with one of the motors and he wants me to take a ride with him to see what's going on. Mike, his wife Suzie and their two boys have become close friends with Cathy and me since we've been in Shreveport. Actually, I bought Mike the boat just a few weeks ago – he was down on his luck and needed a bit of help. Cathy's crazy about Mikey and Timmy; I get a kick out of the little guys, too. Last week, I took the whole family to Water Town and we spent a full day there. Cathy and I didn't go on any of the rides, but we had a terrific time watching the four of them splash about, having a ball. Mike and Suzie might have run into some hard times recently but they're hardworking, decent folk and I can't think of a better way to spend my money than to help them get back on their feet.

When I get to the marina, Mike's still out shrimping and so I walk round the pier, making small talk with some of the other shrimpers and boat owners. So I'm talking to this guy named Louie, who takes people out on fishing expeditions, when a fellow comes up to see if Louie's free the next day to take him and a friend out. I nearly fall in the water when I see this guy's face; I'd recognize him anywhere: he's Mitch Ryan, one of my bookies from Southie.

I'm not surprised he doesn't recognize me – I hardly recognize myself sometimes when I see my reflection in the mirror. With the thin goatee and dark hair, I look nothing like my old self, but Ryan would probably drop dead on the spot had he realized who's standing no more than ten feet away from him. The last time I saw him, he was tied to a chair at the Marconi Club on Shetland Street in Roxbury. He thought he was going to die: he was saying his prayers, begging every patron saint he could think of for mercy.

The bastard deserved to die. Over the course of a few months, he laid off over $200,000 in bets with another office not connected with me. He had a coke habit, but that was no excuse. He'd committed an unpardonable crime, stealing off me. I should've killed him then.

'I'm giving you a pass,' I told him while Stevie stood in front of him, aiming a .22 caliber pistol right at his heart. Stevie wasn't happy with my decision: he loved a good killing and was looking forward to this one. Joey was calmer – it didn't matter one way or the other to him.

'Your mother was a friend of my mother's, that's the only reason I'm letting you go. You give back what's left from what you stole and pay me back every last cent of what you already spent. And if you ever steal one more cent from me, I'll kill you.'

Now here he is making arrangements for a fishing trip the next day. I can't stop looking at him. He's taken off some weight and still has all his hair, which is dark brown; he's tastefully dressed in chinos and a fancy cotton shirt. I notice he's wearing a solid gold Patek Philippe, a very expensive watch. Last I heard, he'd entered some rehab program, left the business and relocated somewhere down south.

When Ryan finishes his business and starts to walk, I follow him. I feel compelled to speak to this guy, there's no way I can let him walk away. As I approach him, the parking lot is pretty empty. 'Get in your car,' I tell him, sticking my hand into the pocket of my pants, like I have a gun there. He turns to look at me and I see the fear cover his face like a mask. It's been a long time since I've seen that look and it gets my adrenaline flowing. He's shaking, but somehow manages to get in the car and turn on the engine.

'Drive out of the parking lot, head straight down Main Street for five miles,' I instruct him. 'Then turn right and follow the coast road for another five miles.'

'What do you want?' he pleads, his voice shaking badly as he starts to drive. 'Take my money, my jewellery, my car … whatever you want.'

In response, all I say is: 'Keep driving.' It's been so long since I've exercized this kind of power and I've missed it. When we reach the end of the coast road, I tell him to turn into the marsh area. He's shaking so badly now that I have trouble remembering he was once a player and when he wasn't coked out, a pretty capable one, too. But he's been out of the business for a long time and probably has a family of his own: he's not anxious to die on this lonely stretch of marshes.

When I tell him to stop the car and turn off the engine, tears are running down his cheeks.

'I saved you once, Ryan,' I tell him. 'Who knows? You may get another pass tonight, buddy.'

He jerks his head towards me so fiercely that I think he's going to break his neck. 'Oh, sweet Jesus,' he ekes out. 'It's you, Jimmy, isn't it?'

'Yeah,' I admit, suddenly wondering what the fuck I'm doing.

'I'd never have recognized you,' he says, staring at me as if he's seen a ghost, somehow managing to tremble more than ever before. 'You didn't have to do this, I wouldn't have told anyone.'

'Oh, I know that,' I agree. 'You owe me too much.'

'I do,' he concedes, his head jerking up and down like a bobble toy. 'I owe you my life, Jimmy. I'd never give you up – I've owed you something for years. I always wanted the chance to even the score between us, give you what you deserve.'

He's babbling now like an idiot, desperate to save himself, but I say nothing, just let him go on. 'I've got money for you, Jimmy. Lots of money, millions and millions – and it's yours, all of it.'

I let him rattle on, talking faster and faster: 'I know how tough things must be for you, with the FBI list and all. And that shit about you and Stevie being informers.'

At this I reach out and grab him by the throat: those are not words I want him or anyone else to be speaking.

'I'm sorry, Jimmy ...' He groans as my fingers begin to squeeze the air out of his quaking throat. 'But I have millions,' he squeaks out in a barely perceptible voice. 'And it's yours, all yours.'

Those words get through to me and cause my fingers to separate at his throat. He slumps forward in the seat, puts his hands to his throat and begins to sob.

'I've got it, Jimmy,' he says, going on like he's never going to stop. Like the second he stops, I'll strangle him for sure this time.

I slam my fist against his jaw. Hard. Blood gushes out and he finally shuts up, terror closing his fucking mouth. In a few seconds, if I'm not careful this guy will drop dead from a heart attack.

'Okay, tell me how much you have,' I say, 'and where it is, and don't leave out one detail.'

He looks at me as if I'm crazy, and at that moment it's true: I want the money, but even more than that I want to kill him. I want to kill him, just kill him. He's begging me with his eyes as he did so many years ago in the basement of the Marconi Club. Only I think he understands that tonight there will be no second chance. Still, he hangs onto a tiny ray of hope. Dying men are like that, we all are. And I use that ray any way I can, like a truth serum; he'll tell me the truth about the money, he has no choice.

'It's more than three million,' he says, shaking so badly I can hear his teeth chattering. 'I'll give you half. No wait, I'll give you three-fourths of it. It's in a safety deposit box at the First National Bank, outside Baton Rouge. We can go there together. It's little more than three hours from here.'

And then he stops and he sees something in my eyes that lets him know he made a mistake, but this time there's no going back. It's over. And the colour slips from his face so quickly it's as if he's already stopped breathing. Could he ever have thought I'd walk right into a bank with him, with cameras and the chance of him making a scene there? Far too many unknown variables: he has to know I'd never take the risk, not for three million, not for five million. If he'd had it in a hide in his house, maybe I would have considered it – getting the money, anyhow.

In a flash, I reach with my left hand to grab him by the hair and pull his head back. With my right hand, I snap open the knife and stick it in the side of his neck, ripping it across his throat. He looks like a Pez dispenser, only it's spurting blood, not candy. All too soon he's dead, but I've never felt more alive.

It's after midnight when I get back to Cathy that night. The body's hidden perfectly in the marshes, the car's all cleaned up and I've changed into the spare clothes I always keep in the trunk. Thanks to the tides, it will be years before the body surfaces. Ryan was lucky: he'd gotten twenty-five years out of that pass, more than most people who steal off me.

Chapter 7
Joey, Boston, 2007

I'm lying in bed, my head filled with too many thoughts I want to banish, which prevent me from sleeping or getting out of bed, when the phone rings. Shit. I was supposed to call Johnny at 10.30 and it's almost noon. Clearing my throat, I grab the phone.

'Where the fuck you been?' he greets me. 'Don't you ever get out of bed, you lazy good-for-nothin' shit?'

The thought of Johnny Quigley sitting at his desk over at the local union office, stuffing his bulldog face with a jelly donut as he holds the phone makes me smile. But Johnny's always made me smile: ever since we met in the ring thirty years ago as teenagers, trying to bust each other's chops for the Golden Gloves. He was good, I was better – in the ring, anyhow. Unlike me, he learned when to put his fists down and lead an honest life, but Johnny's never held that against me.

'I've been busy,' I tell him. 'I got things to do, you know.'

'Yeah, you got things to do,' he repeats sarcastically, 'like sleep and fuck. Shit, Joey! I told you to come over here this morning and check out a job. You don't give a damn if you ever work again, do you?'

Somehow I resist the urge to slam down the phone, turn over and go back to sleep.

'I was over there yesterday and the day before, and the day before that,' I insist, keeping my voice even. 'Didn't do me one bit of good then. Don't think anything's changed in a day. You gonna tell me you got a job just waiting for me?'

Johnny hesitates. 'Naw,' he says, his voice softer now. 'Wish I did, buddy. I thought I had one lined up but this asshole came into my office this morning and told me to forget it. "Too big a risk," he says. Like you're really gonna bust up the place if they give you a shovel. But I might have another shot with another union: I'm expecting a guy from Somerville to stop over early this afternoon. I think it's worth your while to be here when he shows.

27

You know, like the two of us were just shooting the shit and I can introduce you to him. He's big in the union, think he might be your key.'

'Yeah sure, buddy,' I say, standing up and stretching. 'I'll be there within the hour.'

After I shower and get dressed, I head out. I've been living on the second floor of a three-decker on Savin Hill Ave since I got out. Figured it was better to live in Dorchester, where the cops don't know me as well. It's a decent family-type neighbourhood with some affordable housing left, even though the yuppies are starting to move in and hike up the prices. My apartment's a one-bedroom with hardwood floors and a small kitchen area. I set aside some money before I went away but funds are dwindling fast and I'm desperate to make some dough.

As I walk by Donovan's Restaurant at the end of Savin Hill Ave, one of the kitchen help is carrying in a crate of vegetables. I grab the crate from him and carry it in. The joint has the best steak tips around.

'Thanks, Joey,' he says. 'Come on in and let me make you a hamburger.'

'Thanks, but I'm late for an appointment,' I tell him. He smiles and nods. A few months ago, he offered to help me get a job there, but there's no way my probation officer would allow me to work in a place where liquor is served.

At Store 24, I pick up a surprizingly strong cup of coffee and chat with Carla, the manager, for a few minutes.

'I could use some help this weekend, if you're available,' she says, as I hand her a buck. 'I'm moving into another apartment in my building. I'd be glad to pay you for your time.'

Carla's got two strong teenage sons who can help her all she needs, we both know that. But she's a kind lady, a single mom who's had more than her share of bad luck yet managed to raise four good kids and she's lonely. It wouldn't be a good idea for me to get too involved with her personal life.

'I'm not around this weekend,' I lie, 'but if you end up needing some help next week, just let me know.'

She nods as I take off and drop into the Pot Belly Deli for a blueberry muffin. The guy behind the counter has only been working there a few weeks. He's a tall, skinny redheaded kid, around eighteen, and I can tell by the way he nervously hands me the muffin that he already knows my reputation.

'How you doin'?' I ask and he practically drops the dollar bill I give him, unable to answer me. Nothing I can do about that. In time, like everyone else around the neighbourhood, he'll learn to relax around me. The last thing I want is any trouble. Not that I'd avoid it if someone came into my space, or threatened me or my sister Rosie or my niece Lucy, but all I want now is to make a living and lead a quiet life: I've had enough excitement to last me a lifetime.

This afternoon's meeting is pointless. I've been out for nearly a year now and my job prospects are the same as the day I walked out of prison: lousy. Johnny's been trying hard as he can to find me some work. So have Mickey and Chopper, but it's like banging your head against a metal door. One guy will say, 'Sure, we got plenty of work. Come on down and sign the papers.' And then, like clockwork, an hour later I get a call saying things turned out to be a little slower than they expected and they'll call me, for sure, when it gets busy again.

I know what happened: the poor schmuck mentions my name to his supervizor and the guy takes a fit: 'Joey Donahue, the mobster? Are you *crazy*? That guy was James Whitey Bulger's deputy! The two of them were killers. He'll be busting up anybody who looks at him cross-eyed. Too big a risk, forget it.'

The fact was that I was the last one to cooperate with the Feds after everybody else made their deals. Giving up Stevie and Jimmy and a few corrupted police might have shortened my life sentence to seven years, but it did nothing to convince anyone I I was through with crime.

Then they wonder why parolees end up back in jail: when no one will give you a chance, you go back to the only work you can get – crime. And the opportunities are everywhere I look, but each day I tell myself, 'Today I'm not going to commit a crime.' It ain't been easy, but so far I've kept my nose clean.

To get to Johnny's Union Hall on Freeport Street in Dorchester I walk through two used car lots, both framed by waving triangles of red, white and blue flags, each filled with fifteen to twenty cars in varying degrees of disrepair placed next to more impressive bargains, ranging from $200 to $10,000, though one boasts a 2004 Mercedes in 'perfect condition' for $22,500. Just for the sheer heck of it, I take a quick look at the Mercedes, a shiny black one that looks pretty good to me; reminds me of the 1998 beauty I once owned. I walk away quickly, thinking of the 2003 Toyota Corolla I now own, whose payments are increasingly harder to meet.

'How you doin', man?' a black salesman at the second lot calls out to me. 'Gettin' tired of walking? I've got an almost-new Mercedes you'd look great in.'

But I keep on walking, thinking what a lousy job he's got. Then again, he's got a job.

It's a rough and slightly run-down, racially mixed neighbourhood, the streets neither dirty nor clean, more business than residential, the perfect setting for a Union Hall. The sounds of cars whizzing by on the nearby expressway form a steady rhythm, as much a part of the neighbourhood as the lucky bastards who've snagged jobs. Forcing myself to feel more upbeat, I pass a serve-yourself Mobil gas station with a two-bay garage. Again, I look at the kid manning the garage and feel a shiver of envy: I know more than enough about cars to handle that job but I doubt it could ever be mine. The Rent-A-Tool place beside the gas station is nearly empty, as is the small place selling subs, Tony's Subs and Pizza, next door.

Two men dressed in painters' overalls emerge from the Credit Union as I walk past and one looks at me a minute too long. I meet his gaze and he drops his, but I see the flicker of recognition before he does so. He draws his face closer to his friend, nodding in my direction. I can just imagine the conversation: 'That's Joey Donahue. You know, the guy who worked with Whitey Bulger.'

30

For a moment I consider grabbing him by the shoulder and saying, 'Yeah, it's me. You got a problem with that, man?', but I keep my fists in my pocket. Do I give a shit if this guy notices me? My photo was all over the place when I was arrested and I hit the papers plenty after I was released from prison.

Finally, I walk into the Labourers Union Hall, a one-storey building with a waiting room and several offices. When I reach the waiting room, Johnny's secretary Doris tells me he's down in the supply room straightening out some kind of a mess. She's pencil-thin, with shiny black hair that falls neatly down her back. Doris got married when I was away and had a baby named Patrick, whose photos are all over her desk. Patrick's also got long black hair and he's about four. Her husband's short and skinny, wears a Patriots sweatshirt and a Red Sox hat. He's standing there, smiling dumbly, but he's probably a nice guy and a good father. It's funny how a person's life – and desk – can change in six years.

'Nice jacket, Joey,' she says, checking me out. 'Even in jeans, sweater and leather jacket, you look put together. I just wish you could get your friend Johnny to straighten up his act – or at least to lose some weight. I'm sure you work out every day, don't you?'

At this, I can't help smiling. I wouldn't put it past this lady to question me about my sex life.

'Yeah, I still run a few miles every day.'

'Few miles?' she asks, shaking her head and smiling at me. 'I have a feeling it's more like *ten* miles. Right?'

'Sometimes …' I shrug, embarrassed.

She laughs and stares at me again, resting her chin on folded palms. She's a good-looking woman with big black eyes that match her hair and a warm, easy smile. Her foolish husband is one lucky yuppie bastard.

'*Sometimes*?' she repeats. 'I'd say every day. My sister Alicia lives on the same street as you and she sees you every afternoon, just before it gets dark, running around the neighbourhood. Says you're gone at least an hour.'

I have no idea who her sister is, but I'm about to ask when Johnny shows up.

'Well, well, what a surprize,' he says, his white shirt open at the collar, wrapping a thick arm around my shoulder in his usual one-armed bear-hug greeting. The little bit of light-brown hair he's got left is brushed into its usual dumb-looking combover. 'It's still daylight and look who's up and running!'

'Speaking of running,' Doris begins, but Johnny cuts her off. 'Not now, boss lady,' he tells her and leads me into his office.

'That woman never stops,' he says, loud enough for her to hear. 'It's not bad enough I hear it from Marilyn, but I have a second wife sitting outside my office every day, harping on at me to get in shape.'

As I sit down in the chair opposite his desk, he looks me over. His radio is on an Oldies station and 'Mack the Knife', of all songs, is playing softly. I notice the photos of Marilyn and the two daughters on his desk. Pretty girls, but already heavy like their parents.

'You putting on a few pounds yourself, buddy?' he asks.

'A few,' I admit.

'You sure were thin when you got out,' he observes.

'Yeah, nothing like lousy food and nothing to do but read to shape you up. I highly recommend it. Actually, I'm thinking of giving it another try real soon.'

Johnny stops smiling, so I shake my head. We grew up together in the Projects, but he's straight as an arrow. When I was with Jimmy, Johnny and I never talked about it. We hung out when I wasn't hanging with Jimmy, even took a few trips with Chopper to Aruba and Vegas, and when I went away, he came as often as I'd let him. He even sent funny cards and wrote a few letters, which was a big deal for him. Chopper always said I was two guys: the bad guy and the good guy, but he and Johnny only knew the good guy. But it wasn't as if I tried to hide what I did with Jimmy from my friends: this was business and they weren't involved. Johnny was always a loyal friend and there was nothing I wouldn't do for him. Only now, it's me who needs the help.

'Just joking,' I say and he relaxes.

I'm only there for about ten minutes before Doris lets Johnny know that Billy Sampson is here.

'That's our guy,' Johnny tells me, as he gets up to greet Billy.

The two talk outside for a few minutes and Billy, who's every bit as fat as Johnny but has to be at least ten years younger than both of us, is all smiles when he comes into the office and shakes my hand (he's got a weak handshake for someone who must weigh well over 200 pounds). He has a rounded, soft face, surrounded by thick brown hair that falls over his glasses and an easy open smile. Billy is dressed almost identically to Johnny, in a white open-collar shirt and dark-blue slacks.

'Johnny's told me a lot about you,' he greets me, his smile just slightly nervous, 'and I've heard a bit myself, too.'

'I'm sure you have,' I say, doing my best to offer my least intimidating look.

It's funny but when I was with Jimmy everything was about impressions and making sure you always stared down your opponent or victim: you had to look in shape and never show any signs of weakness. In my new life, it's all about impressing would-be employers with a regular-guy look: 'Don't worry about me,' that look is trying to say. 'I wouldn't hurt a flea.'

Whatever I'm showing appears to be working because Billy spends a good half-hour with Johnny and me. He appears more relaxed now, talking about jobs in his union and some of the guys he works with. I'm feeling more hopeful than I have since I got home. When I get up to leave, Billy takes down my number and assures me I'll be hearing from him. Johnny's smiling proudly, like his kid just hit it outta the park at a Babe Ruth game, and I walk out wondering exactly when I'll start and what I'll be doing.

'Looking really good, Mr. D,' Doris murmurs as I pass her desk and I can't stop myself from wondering how good she would look out of those clothes and in the sack.

It takes three days for Billy to get back to me. I know from the second I hear his voice that I was a fool to have gone out and used my last hundred bucks to buy a new CD player.

'I can't understand it, Joey,' he tells me. 'I had it all set, but someone squelched the deal. I wish I could find out who it was so I could talk to him myself, but it's this big confidentiality thing. I'm really sorry, kid. All I can say is I'm going to stay on it. Let's just give it some time and I'll try to push it through again.'

'Sure,' I say, as if it's no big deal, 'I understand. Thanks for your help.'

'Hey, I'm not through yet,' he insists and we hang up.

I'm not altogether surprized when my fist shatters the wooden bowl that Rosie bought me the other day and sends the fruit she arranged in it flying all over the floor of my small kitchen.

Chapter 8
Joey, Saugus

When Bobby calls and asks me to meet him, I don't hang up. This morning when I got up and for the first time since I've been out, I couldn't mouth my usual mantra: 'Today, I'm not gonna commit a crime'. So when I get the call, I have a strange feeling, like something's about to happen – and Bobby's the one who will make it happen.

In fact, he's been after me to work with him for the past few months but I've given him the brush-off, just the way I've done with lots of other guys who've approached me about getting back into the business. I've known Bobby since we were kids hanging around the South Boston Boys Club. He did a little bit of drug dealing for me and Jimmy, but was never a big player. I've always liked him: he's no bullshitter and he stood by me when I went away, keeping in touch with Rosie and Lucy, helping out any way he could.

And it's my help Rosie needs now. I was there last night and I only wish I had money to give her: not that she asked, not that she ever would. Before I went away, I had her and the baby and her shit-for-brains husband in a nice little house in Newton, but when things went bad for me, I couldn't afford to keep her there. The tiny place I got her into in Southie is clean, but the furniture's old and showing its age. It's on the first floor of a three-decker on the corner of F and Silver Street, one block from West Broadway. The whole neighbourhood's in a state of decline: thirty years ago, when I was growing up there, it was a thriving commercial area filled with well-kept stores, family restaurants and movie theatres, places where you could shop for clothes or curtains or hardware, and eat and have some clean fun.

You could walk into Woolworths and buy a turtle or a parakeet, or sit down at the counter and have a hot fudge sundae or a banana split. As you walked along the streets, you'd see mothers pushing their English coach carriages and wicker strollers with groceries packed in alongside the kids as they stepped into Brigham's for an ice-cream cone or to cash a cheque at the South Boston Savings Bank. Now all you see are Dollar Stores, Goodwill and a Radio Shack – small impersonal stores, where they do anything but help – and a lot of fast-food places, like pizza joints and Chinese restaurants. When you want to shop, you drive to the nearest mall or supermarket, but if you live in the Projects and don't own a car, you spend your dough in the dollar shop.

People walk quickly with their heads down, unfriendly and nervous. The demographics of the neighbourhood have changed: More blacks and Hispanics have moved into the Projects while yuppies have bought real estate and driven the housing prices up; people who've lived there for generations can't afford the rents anymore. Lucy's seven now and real cute, but you can see she hasn't had a new piece of clothing in way too long. I try not to think about how smart Rosie is and how much hope I had for my baby sister's future.

I know Rosie does the best she can with what she has, but with Lucy's bad asthma, the hospital bills keep piling up; things got much worse for her the six years I was away. Her junkie husband has been in and out of jail for bullshit stuff since the day they married. He's a moron: he gets into fights, all when he's drinking, one assault-and-battery charge after another. I hate the neighbourhood and I want to see Rosie in a decent place where Lucy can play outside and not find needles and empty bottles all over their yard. If Bobby's got a good score in mind, today I'm ready to hear it. Just one score, a big one. Then I'll have enough to buy that convenience store in Braintree and get Rosie into a nice little house over in Weymouth, like where we lived when she was growing up.

Just before I leave to meet Bobby at Joseph's Bakery and Deli in South Boston, he calls to say he'll be an hour late. Since I'm all ready and the bakery's around the corner from Jeannie's place, I decide to drop over there. I've been dating Jeannie on and off for the past twenty years and I'm as comfortable with her as I've ever been with any woman. She's a pretty, smart lady who could easily find herself a marriageable guy but she's always understood I'm not the marrying type. Whenever I mention that, she says, 'I'd rather have you for a few nights here and there than any other guy forever.' Even when I went away, Jeannie stuck by me.

A lot of women get some weird thrill from hanging around with bad guys like Stevie or Jimmy or me, but Jeannie isn't that kind of woman. She's satisfied with a quiet dinner in Maria's, the Italian restaurant in Southie we like. It's nothing fancy, just six tables and a menu that changes every day depending on what Maria feels like cooking. To Jeannie's credit, the sex couldn't be better … for both of us. And she never asks a lot of questions or tries to get into my head. Like I told her once, 'There's not a lot going on in there.'

When I said that, she looked at me funny and said, real soft, 'There was before everything happened to Rosie.' I didn't answer her and she never brought it up again. That was good because if she had, I'd never have seen her again, but this morning, for some strange reason, we end up talking about Rosie. Mostly, it's me saying how I let my little sister down, how sick I am of the life she leads and what high hopes I had for her when she went off to UMass, up in Amherst.

'You've always protected her from anyone hurting her,' Jeanie says, when I finally shut up, 'but you can't protect her from herself.'

'She never had a chance with Ma dying when she was so young,' I say.

'She had plenty of chances,' Jeannie insists. 'You did everything humanly possible to make sure that kid had a decent chance at life.'

I'm sitting at her kitchen table, with its bright red-and-white cotton tablecloth, having a cup of tea and she's standing behind me, rubbing my neck gently.

'Rosie was two when Ma died,' I remind her. 'What did a seventeen-year-old boy know about raising a little girl? I should've found her a decent home.'

'That's bullshit, Joey!' Jeannie drops her hand angrily. I put out a hand to steady her, so she lands in the chair beside me. Why the hell did I bring up Rosie in the first place? The last thing I want is to talk about what it was like trying to take care of a two-year-old, begging neighbours and a sick old aunt to help me out. Some things are best left alone: Rosie's pathetic childhood is one of them. But Jeannie's all fired up: 'I get so sick of you putting yourself down like that. You found the best daycare possible for that little baby, gave up any chance of a decent life for yourself to get money to pay for that daycare,' she goes on, back on her feet now, hands on the hips of her tight jeans, green eyes blazing.

'Shit, you sent her to the best private schools and would've sent her to any college she wanted. Please don't try to bullshit me into believing that Rosie's problems were your fault. She had a choice and she made it, and now she's living with it the best she can. Christ, Joey, you went to work for Jimmy to make better money for her! What other sacrifices could you make?'

Jeannie's a small woman, no more than 5'2" and less than 100 pounds, but she's no pushover. When you rile her up, her temper's as fiery as her long, curly red hair.

I'm out of there before she can say another word and I'm not surprised when she doesn't come after me. I wouldn't come back, anyhow. Rosie's been off limits for years: if I want someone to analyze my life, I'll go to a shrink. Disgusted with myself for causing this mess, I kill the twenty minutes left before my meeting with Bobby trying to cool my jets with a long walk along the causeway of Castle Island, the same spot where Jimmy and I always walked and discussed business. It's a beautiful, late-fall morning and the circular harbour walk, the Sugar Bowl, is filled with retirees dressed in windbreakers and hats. They walk at a slow pace, enjoying the great weather, along with young mothers jogging purposefully at the back of their strollers and grandmothers slowly pushing baby carriages. A few are gathered round Sullivan's take out-only snack bar, sipping coffee or grabbing a hotdog or onion rings. Three gray seagulls squabble noisily for the crumbs left on the one empty table. Overhead, jets fly by, heading into Logan for a landing. Out on the ocean, two large, silent container ships, their metal storage units clearly delineated, sit waiting to unload. There's no view of Boston Harbor or the airport like the one you get walking along this 22-acre stretch.

The enclosed lagoon along the harbour walk shimmers in the sunlight, its sandy beach deserted, void of the crowds who inhabit it during the summer. This past summer I took Rosie and Lucy there several times and I can still hear Lucy's happy shrieks when I played with her in the water. Rosie perched nervously on a beach towel, carefully watching for any accident that might befall her precious little girl. At twenty-nine, she's still great looking and I noticed several guys giving her approving once-overs that day – if only I could turn back the clock and eliminate that miserable bastard of a husband from her life.

I try to push the thought away, but it's no good and my mind fills with memories of Rosie and her wedding. Nineteen and pregnant, she had just completed her freshman year at UMass and the whole world was in front of her. I tried to convince her to get an abortion but she wouldn't hear of it. 'Timmy's a good guy,' she kept on telling me and I wanted to believe her, even though I knew he was a useless piece of shit who couldn't hold his liquor. At first, he proved me right when he told her there was no way he was going to marry her, but after one short visit he saw things slightly differently and gave her the little ring, which I bought.

I did a quick score with Jimmy and got enough money for a pretty white dress for Rosie and a small, but nice wedding at St. Augustine's, down the street from the house where I'd grown up. Except for Tim's mother and sister, an aunt of ours and two neighbours, there were just a few girlfriends of Rosie's, Jimmy, Jeannie, a couple of my friends and the priest at the ceremony. Rosie, three months pregnant then, still looked gorgeous, like something out of a bridal magazine. With her jet-black hair and huge blue eyes, she literally floated down the aisle like a vision. Even Jimmy couldn't get his eyes off her.

When I walked her down the aisle that day, I knew the marriage wasn't going to be a good one and it was all I could do not to pick her up and race out of the church. But Rosie always had a toughness about her: chances are, she would have planted her small feet on the church floor and nothing I could have done would have removed her from the spot. When I think about what's happened to her after that wedding, I get physically sick. Losing the baby a week afterwards was bad enough, but deciding to stay with Tim nearly killed me. All those years he was in and out of jail, always begging for my help to get out, swearing to clean up his act this time for sure. For my sister's sake, I did as he asked: paid the lawyers to get him out so he could come home for six months at the most and then end up back in a cell again. Drugs, alcohol, they were all that piece of garbage wanted, but still she loved him ... and went through three more miscarriages before Lucy was finally born. She could have had anyone and she stayed with Tim. Why? What did I do wrong to make her like that? As the beach fades in the distance, I finally stop thinking about Rosie and concentrate on my upcoming meeting.

By the time I get to the bakery, it's a few minutes before noon and Bobby's already sitting at a table, making his way through a thick roast-beef sandwich. I order a cup of coffee. Bobby's a big guy, well over 6' and a good 250 pounds. He was always big, yet surprizingly quick on his feet and pretty good in the ring. He'd give me a good workout, even though the result was pretty much the same. Usually, I got the better of him: he might have been bigger than me and faster, but I was quicker.

He reaches across the table and with a mouth full of roast beef, grabs my shoulders in an affectionate hug. 'So glad you're here, Joey,' he says, then gets right to the point. 'It's a real simple deal: this guy moves like 50 pounds of pot a month. He keeps a lot of cash in his house in Saugus, in a hide in his bedroom closet. He probably has 150 grand in cash there.'

'How do you know?' I ask.

He says, 'This kid I know gets his stuff off him. He's been in his house and seen his hide. It's a piece of cake, Joey. I've been sitting on it for a few weeks now, just waiting for the right time. I could do it alone, but I'd rather have you on board. So what do you think, buddy? Are you in this time?'

I'm ready to say yes, but somehow I can't mouth the words: I want to tell him I'm in, but instead I stand up. Memories of my jail cell, all those days just sitting there, counting the seconds, waiting for one of the guards to hassle me over nothing or an inmate to try and cause a problem, come racing back. I can't go back there. So I put down a ten-dollar bill and shake my head.

'I'm here if you change your mind,' Bobby says and I tap him lightly on the shoulder and walk away.

That night, I lay in bed staring at the ceiling, wondering in turns whether I'm the most stupid or the smartest guy in the world. The score sounded so easy: it would have netted me just enough cash to start my own business, no more begging anybody and everybody for a lousy job. Now, I'm back to square one.

For nearly a week, I sit around and do nothing but twiddle my thumbs and watch crappy television. Johnny and Chopper call and try to get me to play poker, but I refuse: I'm lousy company for anyone. Even Rosie and Lucy get on my nerves and I can't even force myself to call Jeannie and make amends for the other night.

A week after I met with Bobby, I call Larry Houlihan. I never could stand the guy but he owns a string of apartment buildings in Southie and I've heard he's looking to renovate them.

'How you doing, Joey?' he asks, when he takes the phone from his secretary.

It kills me how many of these guys have secretaries and more money than I can ever hope for these days. When I was with Jimmy, I could buy and sell them all but it's a changed scene now. Just about everything I ever made with him, I spent as fast as I earned it – the rest went to Rosie and then my lawyers.

'Okay,' I answer. 'Thought maybe I'd come in and speak to you about your apartment buildings. Maybe you could use a little help getting them in decent shape?'

His laugh rips through me like a scissors. If I were near him, I'd wrap my hands round his throat and squeeze till his face turned purple.

'Didn't know you were into putting things together, Joey,' he says, barely attempting to hide the sarcasm in his voice. 'Thought ripping them apart was more your strength.'

I don't waste another second. Chopper warned me to stay away from him, but I didn't listen. Now I've given him a great story to spread around town. I hang up and call Bobby.

'I'm in,' I tell him.

'Nice,' he says.

We case the house for a couple of days. The guy's out every night and has no one else living in the one-family home with him. It's an okay neighbourhood, fifteen miles out of Boston; nothing special, with a mix of one- and two-family homes. None of them have front lawns, but rather blacktopped areas where they park their cars. It's not too far from the Saugus Iron Works, now a national historic site, with its seventeenth-century blast furnace and working waterworks, an over-reaching metal dinosaur with pipes and bridges arched upward and within walking distance of a long and narrow, one storey nursing home and a strangely fancy-looking Dunkin' Donuts. There's nothing else going on in the neighbourhood to cause us any problems.

The night we do the score, it's easy. Around midnight, we park the car a block away from the house and walk down to it. Bobby enters by a side window and opens the back door, then I come in. There's a smell, like someone recently cooked onions. We go right to the closet at the back of the hall and pull the panel away to expose the hide. Inside are two bundles of $5,000, wrapped in rubber bands on a black zipper bag.

I glance at Bobby and say, 'What the fuck? You said there was supposed to be $150!'

He says, 'I don't know, maybe he moved it.'

I stash the money in a small black bag and say, 'Let's get out of here.'

We walk back to the car and as we get in, we're surrounded by FBI, guns drawn, telling us to freeze. They're all wearing blue windbreakers with yellow lettering on the back.

'Joey, you're going away for good this time,' one of them tells me. The minute I hear my name, I know I've been set up. Fuck, fuck, fuck ... I feel my stomach fall and the lump in my throat makes it hard to breathe but I catch myself quickly. The last thing I'm gonna do is let those bastards see what they've done to me.

I look at the biggest bastard of them all and he can't meet my eye. They handcuff and put me in the back of a Crown Victoria. As they do so, I keep my head down to avoid their gaze. Once again, I'm caught in a trap, like an animal, with every piece of my freedom gone – this time, I'm sure, for good. Meanwhile, they don't handcuff Bobby as they put him in another car. No surprize there.

As we drive away, all I can think is how stupid I've been; how I deserve to have my life destroyed. I went against one of my own cardinal rules: anytime someone comes out of the clear blue to me, someone who hasn't been around me for a while, I always wonder what's happened to them. I think it over carefully and try to figure out why they're coming round to me now, but the thought of 150 grand overtook my own cautious approach. It doesn't take a genius to work out what's just happened: Bobby was in some kind of a mess. He's always done his time in the past but faced with something bigger, he gave me up. And I was too stupid to realize what he was doing until his goons stood in front of me, waving the chains in my face. Since the day when I was released, I've known the government lawyers, unhappy with my deal, were keen to violate my parole, to find a way to get me back behind bars ... and I couldn't have made it any easier for them.

So I sit there, a bug caught in flypaper, as three agents (two comfortably seated in the front seat and the third beside me) drive me into an underground garage with thick, gray concrete pillars separating the cars. No one says a word as they park the black Oldsmobile and pull me out, hands still handcuffed tightly behind my back, and lead me to a locked door, on which one agent presses some numbers to open it. When we reach a bank of elevators, the same guy presses the button and an empty elevator at once appears, which takes us to the fourth floor. It's funny how I haven't seen one human being except for those three agents since they got me out of the car nor heard a single word spoken. Also, it's beginning to feel a little weird that they don't simply charge me and deposit me in a cell.

Still silent, the agents deliver me to a stuffy, windowless conference room with a long wooden table and ten chairs neatly positioned around it, all facing a TV monitor. There's a pitcher of water and a bunch of glasses in the middle of the table. The agents push me into a seat at the head of the table, sit down and finally start talking to explain the situation, pure and simple. There's a deal to be made here: two of the agents are real professional about the whole thing, while the other one's a total fuck up, falling all over himself to show how tough and important he is.

The guy's name is Murphy and after five minutes with him, I'm wishing I had a .45 in my hand and could blow his fucking head off. He's in pretty good shape, probably around my age (late forties), with thick black hair, lips set in a permanent scowl, beady little eyes and a mouth that doesn't stop. 'Your buddy gave you up, plain and simple,' he tells me, as if I didn't already know. 'He got grabbed six months ago for dealing cocaine – the Feds caught him with two kilos. A three-time loser, Bobby was going away now for twenty to thirty years. When we mentioned our little deal to him, he was only too happy to help out.'

'Let me explain …' The black agent (nametag Bill Rogers) interrupts big mouth. Completely bald (maybe he shaves his head?), he looks as if he lifts weights for a living. All three agents wear suits and ties, but this guy's tie has some sort of golf theme on it. 'So, you've got something *we* want, Joey … and we've got something *you* want.'

But he can barely get the words out before Murphy shoots his trap off again: 'You're supposed to be a real smart guy, so let's give it to you straight! Either you tell us where your old boss

James Whitey Bulger is, or you're going away for the rest of your life. That's the deal, kid. Take it or leave it.'

By now I'm breathing so heavy you might hear me outside the building on Washington Street. Whoever could have concocted such a plan? Grab Joey and he'll lead you to Jimmy. I stare at Big Mouth and he's got such a shit-eating grin on his face, like he just swallowed the canary. It's a good thing I'm handcuffed or I'd rip the bird out of his fucking throat. All three guys are staring at me like I'm in the electric chair and they're about to pull the switch. I close my eyes and all I can think of is Jimmy. Christ, the guy turned out to be an FBI informant just like Stevie! Had he ever sat in this same room, at this very table, spitting out the names of our associates for these jerks? How did that feel? Was it any different to what's happening to me now? It must be: nothing could be worse than being a goddamned informant for twenty-five years.

'Take it easy, Murphy,' says the third agent. When I open my eyes, I see his nametag is Matt Berman. This guy's favourite restaurant has to be McDonald's. He looks around the same age as the other two agents, but there's something boyish and good-natured about him: they're having a great time playing good cop, bad cop with me. 'We're not so sure you know where Whitey is,' he goes on, smiling at me as if he's sorry about this whole mess, 'but you probably have a better idea than anyone else, so we'll set you looking. That's the whole deal, Joey. You think about it for a little while and we'll discuss it some more then.'

As they leave the room, I keep my eyes focused on the floor. I'm no longer angry, only filled with a self-loathing that makes me want to puke. What kind of a fucking mess did I get myself into? There's no way I could ever lead a worldwide search for Jimmy and if I refuse to even try, then I'm gonna spend the rest of my life in a cell. And it's just what I deserve: I have no one to blame but myself ... and no way out.

Fifteen minutes later, two new agents arrive to deliver me to the Federal Courthouse. Not a word is spoken: I can't force my eyes to look at them. Again I'm taken by elevator to an underground location full of cement and tall poles, but devoid of people. We walk for a few minutes then pass through an enormous door into a corridor of empty cells, where my handcuffs are removed. A small metal door opens and I'm placed in a cell with a single metal cot attached to the wall, one blanket, one sheet and a pillow piled onto the yellowing mattress. There's a metal toilet and a metal sink. The door is closed and I'm now alone. Though I struggle to fight it, despair crawls over me like a thick fog and it's hard to breathe. I sink onto the cot, head in my hands, trying desperately to dispel the haze, to focus on what's happening. There has to be a way out of this mess and somehow, if I just keep my mind focused, I'll find it.

How, I ask myself over and over, can I find Jimmy? Hell, all those scores we did together: all those guys we destroyed, the lives we ruined or ended when we were working together. Every small detail planned, we never made a mistake – like clockwork, just the two of us. So many memories come flooding back: Johnny the poor kid, chained to a chair and pleading for his life, mumbling prayers to every patron saint he can remember from schooldays. All the while Jimmy stood over him, that glazed look in his eyes, a gleeful smirk on his lips, drawing information from Johnny and making him repeat in his parched voice the name of the street where he'd hidden the lousy $35,000. Then comes the dull sound of Johnny's chained feet on the stairs as he follows me downstairs 'to take a dirt nap' and the loud snap of the gun as the bullet enters his skull, the roll of the body down the last step and then it's over.

In a state of pure pleasure, Jimmy heads upstairs, energized by the murder in a way that nothing else in this world revitalizes him. He's anxious to lie down and revel in the joy of this, his most recent accomplishment. But for me, the work is just beginning.

Hours and hours after the poor sucker (whose crime incidentally was to attempt to cheat Jimmy out of $35,000) was put out of his misery – his life in the end worth less than that sum, I am still digging through the basement floor to hide yet another bloodied body beneath the sand and rocks.

Memories of so many scores, some in which we ended up millions of dollars richer, others covered in the blood of still one more victim. So many victims whose crime was to attempt to give themselves up to the very same men now asking me to hand over my former partner-in-crime. How can I do this, how can I turn against Jimmy? I ask myself over and over, as I lie on the cot that could be my bed for the rest of my life, unable to sleep. Jimmy, I understand, has turned out to be an FBI informant himself, but that doesn't help me: he's still my friend. Besides, who knows what forced him into the life of an informant?

Hours later, I have no answer: just more memories of the past, cold facts about my present. As I stand and look beyond the bars, I can see the other cells are empty and it's obvious they don't want anyone else to see me. Apparently, no one knows about the deal, but that doesn't make me feel any better. No matter how hard I try to think clearly, I blame myself for being here, for being a sucker … but I also blame Jimmy and Stevie for betraying everybody. And now because the Feds want to clean up their act, I'm the sacrificial lamb. Once again, I'm fucked. There's no way I can play the game with these agents – the only place I'm going is right back to where I was a year ago. As I pace round the cell, it's as if I never left prison: feelings of claustrophobia, of helplessness, despair at the idea of never getting out and rage at my own stupidity overwhelm me. Locked up again like a caged animal, I want to bang my head against the metal bars until I pass out. Finally, just before dawn I'm able to turn off my thoughts and roll over in the bunk as I've done a thousand times before and force myself to sleep.

In the morning, they take me from my cell, handcuffed and shackled, and I'm led to a conference room to meet my lawyer. I'm anxious to see Tom Raftery, figuring he's the only hope I have in this fucking mess. He did the best he could with my racketeering case and the six-year sentence was the shortest we could have hoped for (with the RICO Act, I might have gone away for a lot longer). When I walk in, he says, 'I don't know what to tell you, Joey, but this isn't going away.'

He's a husky guy, the Brian Dennehey of the legal world. His dark suit is a bit rumpled, but he still looks too large and important for the windowless, stuffy room that's barely big enough for the two of us and lit by a too-bright overhead fluorescent light. There's an unpleasant scent of sweat in this room that Tom's designer aftershave won't mask. The metal table is cemented to the floor, unlike the two metal chairs we're sitting on. Tom has his usual yellow pad in front of him and despite his tan, he looks tired and uncomfortable, exactly the way I feel.

'But it was such an out-and-out set-up,' I say. 'There's nothing we can do about that?'

This time he shakes his head and says, 'They've got you right in the act. We can't refute the facts. It stinks, but it's all within the law. Either you give them what they want or you're going away for at least thirty. And probably more, since it's a violation of your parole.'

'They really think I know where he is?' I ask, feeling yet one more punch in my stomach.

At this, he nods: 'You're the most obvious person. So, do you?'

As always, he's a straight shooter.

'No,' I reply. 'Not really.'

'*Not really*?' he repeats. He puts down a pen, removes his glasses and stares at me, biting his lower lip. I've seen that intense look before: he wants me to talk, to tell him the truth – which I have always done and intend to continue to do so. 'What does *that* mean?' he finally asks.

'I have ideas about where he might be,' I say, meeting his eyes directly. 'And how he's staying on the run for so long, we talked about it plenty over the years. But I haven't seen him in over seven years, since before I got arrested. I saw him five times in all since he took off. The last was when he and Cathy were in New York. But you know all that, it's all documented in my testimony.'

'And you haven't heard a word from him since that last time in New York?'

'No, and I wouldn't expect to either. Not after Stevie announced they were both FBI informants.'

48

'Then you do what you can to help find him,' he tells me. 'I have no idea what'll happen if you don't come up with him, but I'll try to make out an agreement that protects you either way, so long as you make a serious attempt to find him. They'll finance your search and watch you every step of the way.'

I nod, beginning to accept the realization that the die has been cast. What looked so hideous in the blackness of last night seems obvious now: I have no choice but to do what these bastards want.

'And a million dollars if I find him, right?'

'I'm not sure they'd let you have it without a fight but that's what I'm here for.'

'And that's what you're so good at,' I say.

'Oh yeah,' he answers wryly. 'I'm so good at it you're back under lock and key, but hopefully not for long. What will it be like for you, if you do find him?'

'I can't begin to imagine it,' I say. 'I'm still finding it hard to believe he and Stevie were FBI informants the twenty-five years we worked together. I was helping them kill guys for what the two of them were doing. I can't undo what I did, but things would have been different if I'd known I was working *with* informants, as well as against them.'

But Tom doesn't say anything, he just stares at me.

'It won't be easy for me,' I continue (Tom's laconic way always makes me feel free to tell him things I'd never tell anyone else). 'It would be easier if I could hate him. He was a homicidal maniac, yet he was my friend as well as my associate. We did things to men that make me shudder now, but we also shared a hell of a lot of good times during those years. I'd be lying if I said I didn't like the guy. Maybe you should just plead insanity for my case.'

Tom offers me a rare smile. 'Where would you start looking?' he asks.

'Not around here,' I say. 'He's long gone from the East Coast and after 9/11, he couldn't travel in and out of the country as freely as before, but he'll still figure out a way to do it every time he wants. It's going to be next to impossible to find him. The guy is brilliant – he thought out every little detail of each score we did with a fanatical genius, he left nothing to chance. When he took off, I knew he was gone for good, that he'd outsmart anyone who tried to catch him. Suddenly, that's my job. I've been trying to find a lousy job for a year and now I have this one handed to me! I'm not smarter than Jimmy – I don't know anyone who is. Shit, Tom, not only can I not do it, I don't even *want* to find him!'

'I don't envy you, Joey,' he says, shaking his head sympathetically. 'The Feds are under the gun to find Whitey Bulger and they're desperate enough to consider you their only chance. They know you've been away for six years and they've tracked you enough to know you haven't been in touch with him this past year but they're still willing to pin their hopes on you. No one knows Jimmy better than you.'

'He's too smart for anybody to know him that well,' I reply. 'He's incredibly disciplined – exercizes daily, still ripped, I'm sure; eats healthy and doesn't drink, has no vices to speak of except for his temper and his love of murder, but even that's probably under control. 'He has enough money stored away to stay out there for years. I'm sure Cathy's still with him, helping him in a ton of little ways. He's in his seventies now, an old guy with a face that could blend into any crowd. I saw the way they manoeuvred around New York. No one gave them a second glance, they look like your typical little retired couple.'

Tom shakes his head. When he stands up to leave, we shake hands.

'If only I could have found work …' I start to say, then stop.

He begins to walk away and then turns around.

'Any chance he's dead?' he asks.

'Naw,' I say, wishing it with all my heart. Better yet, that I'd never met him and messed up my life so badly. 'I'd know if he was.'

'How?' he asks.

'If he died, Cathy would find a way to get in touch with me,' I tell him.

'And if she's gone?'

'He'd get to me. And don't ask about the two of them – if they were both dead, we'd all know about it.'

He offers me no more than a deep sigh as a guard comes to lead me out of the room and back to my cell.

Within an hour, I'm in a large conference room. Sitting around the long U-shaped table are the three FBI agents that I met the day before. And they're still playing their good cop/bad cop routine, not one second wasted in getting down to business.

'Look,' says Berman, leaning across the table with an 'I-don't-want-to-have-to-hurt-you-so-let's-be-friends' look plastered on his full face, 'I know this isn't easy for you, but we all want the same thing: to get you out of here. You have no choice here, so let's just get going.'

Roger's even nicer, saying: 'You're the one person who can help us here and we're going to be more than grateful for your assistance.'

'Get to the point, will you already?' I say. 'Explain what I have to do to get the hell out of here.'

'You want to know the deal?' asks Murphy. I don't say a word, just stare straight through him. But he doesn't see this any more than he notices his co-workers' glares; he's too busy letting me know how important he is. 'You're going to find Bulger for us. We'll give you what you need to do this but if you screw with us, we'll go after everybody you know and love back there. We have all kinds of ways of making lives miserable – they don't even have to commit a crime, trust me. And that includes everybody. Now here's the best part: I'll be with you every step of the way. We'll be joined at the hip so I'll know exactly how hard you're looking for your old boss. Understand the deal now?'

Though I can taste the adrenaline in my mouth, I force myself to swallow the rising anger: I don't say a word, I just stare at him. I'm surprised he doesn't register any signs of fear, but merely stares back at me.

'Let's just calm down a bit here,' says Berman, looking uncomfortable.

'Yeah,' Rogers agrees. 'There's no reason for this to be any more difficult than it is. We'll make sure you have the resources you need – you'll have access to all we know after he took off. You can go anywhere that makes sense to you.'

He offers me a slight smile as if we're discussing plans for a night on the town.

'So when do we get going?' I ask, directing my question to Berman and Rogers. 'The sooner, the better for me.'

Murphy gives me a puzzled look. I know what he's thinking: If I let him loose, he'll go right for me. But he doesn't hesitate: he takes a key from his pocket and unlocks my handcuffs and shackles.

'Get your stuff together, tell your sister and friends you've got a job out of town and come to my office, room 718, tomorrow at nine. We'll start then,' he tells me. And without the slightest show of concern, he turns around and walks out of the room.

I rub my wrists and stretch my legs a bit, then glance at Berman and Rogers, who nod approvingly.

'We'll be keeping an eye on you till then,' Rogers tells me, almost apologetically.

With this, I shrug. They take me out to the elevator and down to the garage, then drive me to South Station to grab the train. In the car, Berman says, 'Don't worry about Murphy – he's been in the office all these years and this is his first chance to make a name for himself: he'll get a grip on himself.'

Walking towards the train, I feel just as trapped as when I was handcuffed and shackled. After all these years, once again the only person who can get me out of this fucking mess is Jimmy – and he will.

Chapter 9
Murphy, Boston

I sit at my desk, trying to concentrate on the paperwork in front of me, but I can't read a word on the sheets: all I can see is the look on that miserable criminal's face when I let him know what he was up against. I've dreamt of our meeting for so long that it was as if I'd already lived through it when it actually took place. Joey Donahue, Whitey Bulger's second-in-command, is under *my* command now. The powerful, feared chief lieutenant of the Bulger mob has been forced to become my lieutenant and to find his former boss.

Months and months of planning, all my work with that pathetic little drug dealer to get him to do exactly as I wanted, to say the words just as we'd rehearsed over and over … it was a miracle the fool came through for us. But hey, he did it all right: led the victim right into the cage, where he nibbled at the cheese before I slammed the door right on his fat ass. And it'll be a good long time till he tastes freedom again: he thinks he'll be free once this is over, but I wouldn't bet on it. I'll do everything in my power to make sure it doesn't happen. It might just be that I need to kill him along with Whitey Bulger, something I wouldn't hesitate for one second to do. And if Joey makes it, he's not going anywhere: career criminals like him deserve to be in jail for the rest of their lives. If this was my case, I'd make sure he *died* in jail.

I saw that look on his face, like he wanted to place his hands around my throat and put me away. But he didn't, he knew better: I haven't been working my ass off in the gym every night for nothing. And he's supposed to be so smart. Everyone kept telling me how brilliant this Donahue was. Yeah, well he wasn't smart enough to outsmart John Murphy.

I'm dying to call up Mia and let her know just what her ex-husband has done but I realize that wouldn't be smart, not now anyhow. But once this operation is over, she'll be the first to hear. By then, everyone will know that FBI Agent John Murphy brought in James Whitey Bulger, the elusive master criminal on the run for ten years. I'll be on *America's Most Wanted*, for sure – and every major news channel in the country. Hell, in the *world*!

I can't wait to see how Rogers and Berman handle all this. For years, I've sat twiddling my thumbs while they get the plum assignments and I stay behind doing shit jobs – and all because I messed up one kidnapping assignment ten years ago. It wasn't even my fault: I never got the memo about the mother being clear of all culpability so I went after her a bit too strong. It didn't mess up the operation, we found the kid but from then on, I was a zero, a desk jockey. Two years away from retirement, I'd been forced to look back on my career as a big zero.

I'd had such great hopes when I graduated from Quantico in 1984 and arrived at the Bureau a year later. Things might have worked out so differently if it hadn't been for that damned kidnapping glitch. Then it was like a door had been locked tight so there was no way into the building for me. Until this came my way, no one was willing to give me a chance to prove it wasn't my fault.

It was an incredible stroke of good luck when the door was open one day and I'd overheard them discussing the Bulger case. 'Who can we spare?' Tom Walker asked a few of his cohorts, but everyone mentioned wasn't available. All the other agents were working on important cases: Agent Edelman was on a drugs case, Andrews was working on the bank robbery task force, Bostley was on a terrorist task force, like half the force. Man, 60 per cent of the Bureau is assigned to terrorist cases under Homeland Security these days. Every other name brought up was on a legit case and the last thing they wanted was to assign someone they might miss. Everyone knew it was just show, acting like they really gave a shit if Bulger was found, ten years after he went missing. But the minute I heard his name, I knew it was my last chance to prove everyone was wrong: that I wasn't a loser, no matter what my ex-wife or my fellow agents might think. I could take this ball and carry it all the way across the field: it was *my* case.

For a few days, I waited patiently: hanging around Tom Walker's office, dropping off papers, making sure he noticed me and sure enough, it happened. Late one afternoon, he knocked on my door and said, 'You got a minute, John?' I smiled confidently and nodded, pushing aside a bunch of useless papers. And when he asked if I was willing to take a shot at the case, I looked thoughtful for a few minutes before saying, 'Sure.'

When there's a knock at my door now, I know before it opens that it's Rogers. 'Got a second?' he asks as he walks in. Something about the guy makes me feel sick: I know he got where he is because of the colour of his skin and he knows I know that.

'Sure,' I say, waiting for him to begin his schpiel.

And he doesn't disappoint. 'Looks like the chemistry between you and Joey Donahue sucks,' he says. 'Think maybe we need to rethink this deal.'

But I'm ready for this. 'I had a long talk with Tom Walker this morning,' I tell him and love the way his expression changes. Talk about chemistry, there's never been any good chemistry between Walker and himself, and unlike the days of Bill Masters, since Walker took over our office things haven't been quite so rosy for Rogers.

'Tom says I'm handling everything perfectly. Thanks for your help but I don't think I need it,' I tell him.

With that, I pull a sheet of paper out from the pile on my desk and begin to mark it up. Rogers leaves without another word and I can't remember feeling this good in more than ten years.

Chapter 10
Joey & Jeannie, Boston

Before I go to Rosie's, I call Jeannie. I can tell from the minute she answers the phone that she's gotten over yesterday. That's the wonderful thing about Jeannie and probably the only reason she can put up with someone like me: she gets mad real fast and furious, but when it's over, it's over. Unlike the rest of us Irish, she doesn't hold grudges as sacred ornaments never to be thrown away.

'Come on over,' she says. 'I've been worried about you.'

I'm there in twenty minutes and she's busy cooking me a steak-and-potatoes dinner. Between Jeannie and Rosie, I could never go hungry.

'I just had a feeling something was wrong,' she tells me as she keeps an eye on the grill. 'Tell me I'm wrong.'

'You're right,' I tell her instead, 'but I don't want to talk about it. All I can say is that I'm going away for a little while but I'll keep in touch while I'm gone. And I'd appreciate it if you'd stay in touch with Rosie and Lucy while I'm gone.'

'Are you going back to jail?' she asks, to which I shake my head. I see the worry in her face but I don't say another word, wondering yet again why this woman could possibly want to bother with me. She stares at me for a few minutes longer, then sighs and returns to the steak. Jimmy was so right when he said criminals shouldn't be married: the best thing I could do for Jeannie would be to turn around, walk out of her life and never see her again. Eventually, she'd get over me and find someone who could give her all she deserves. But I don't do that: instead, I pour the wine, put some salad in our bowls and wait patiently till she cuts the steak and performs her finishing touches on the mashed potatoes.

We talk little during the meal, which is fine with me. I'm starved and the steak is perfectly done: barely pink, just the way I like it. It's only when we're through with dinner and the kitchen has been cleaned up and we're sitting on the couch, having tea that I tell her: 'I will call you as often as I can.'

'And I can't call you, right?' she says.

'Right,' I say.

'I was just getting used to having you back,' she murmurs. 'It was even good to fight with you.'

'Jeannie, you know you don't have to …'

'Stop, Joey,' she says, gently placing her fingers on my lips. 'I know what I *don't* have to do, but I'm doing it, anyhow. I'll be here when you get back and I'll keep a close eye on Rosie and Lucy and that asshole husband. Who knows? Maybe a miracle will happen and you'll get back before he gets out of jail.'

She smiles the sad smile that always gets to me and I put down my cup and reach for her. And I try very hard to make her as happy as I can, to explore every inch of her body, until the smile I ache to see appears on her lips. Then she works her magic on me until I can think of nothing except how perfect this woman is and, for a brief moment anyhow, how fucking lucky I am.

Chapter 11
Joey's Assignment, Boston

At ten to nine the next morning, I show up at room 718. Murphy sits at his desk, studying a bunch of official-looking documents piled high in front of him. The desk, along with his entire office, is a mess: large boxes scattered all over the floor, some half-open, with pieces of clothing and blankets and small household items such as lamps and pots and pans spilling out of the cartons. At first glance, I recognize a small bronze lamp that was in Jimmy's living room as well as his white teakettle. Murphy himself looks as muddled as his office: his thick dark hair is heading in several different directions, there's black stubble on his cheeks and chin, and I'm pretty sure he's wearing the same pants and shirt that he was in yesterday. Only now they look as untidy as the rest of the place. If I was as smart as these FBI guys, I could figure out this guy went right to his office after our 'meeting' yesterday and hasn't moved since.

When I knock on his already-open door, he looks up and notices me, giving me the same look I'm giving him, like I'm the last person in the world he feels like spending time with.

'Come in,' he says gruffly. He glances at the clock on his wall. 'You're early.'

'I'm always early,' I tell him, looking for a spot to sit down. The two chairs opposite his desk are littered with papers and the small couch at the other end of the office is indistinguishable beneath the cardboard boxes covering what I think is some sort of ugly dark-blue fabric. A quick glance around the office shows me there are no signs of any personal life. Not that I can imagine this asshole having any sort of life. There are no family photos, no diplomas, no snapshots of famous people, no golf ashtrays or tennis letter openers: it's a dark, depressing little office, way too cluttered for my taste. No way could I survive one day working here, but it seems a perfect home base for this guy.

Murphy gestures towards a small chair to the right of his desk with only the minimum of clutter. I walk over, remove one small unopened box and sit down.

'I've been going through all the files the bureau has on Jimmy,' he tells me, putting his papers down on the desk. 'I've got everything here from his condo in Squantum, magazines, military books, videos of World War II and Vietnam ...'

'I've seen it all,' I say, interrupting him.

He shakes his head. 'Yeah, *of course*,' he agrees nastily, 'but we're trying to look at it for clues as to his *present* location.'

He gestures towards the clutter on the floor surrounding his desk and my chair. 'We're convinced somewhere, under all this stuff, is some info that's been missed by previous searches. Maybe you could try and shed some light here, let me know what you think is important – *if* you wouldn't mind, of course.'

I'm not sure if the guy is trying or if this just comes naturally, but I've never met anyone so annoying, or so sarcastic. Not even in prison or during my years with Jimmy.

'Let me see what I can find,' I say, then reach down and pick up a carton filled with books and papers.

For the next three hours, I say as little as possible, concentrating instead on all these items and each one brings back some memory that I swallow. But Murphy doesn't make it easy for me: every time he sees me holding a book or a paper or an envelope, he feels the need to say something. 'Do you recognize that book ring?' he asks, and I shake my head. 'You *sure*?' he continues, and I shake my head again. 'I can't believe you never saw that book before,' he sighs and I give him a third shake. This goes on and on: it's almost impossible for me to concentrate on anything with his endless, inane questions. And it's getting easier and easier to understand why Jimmy's still on the run – and why, without some serious help from me, he'll most likely never be caught.

At one point, I'm spending a few minutes checking over a book about Ireland when Murphy just about falls out of his chair with enthusiasm. 'I saw a couple of other books about Ireland,' he says. 'What's your feeling about that country as a haven for Jimmy and Cathy? Could you imagine him being there for a year or two?'

But I simply shake my head, saying: 'Jimmy's not in Ireland – he knows you'd be looking for him there.'

He glares at me, before saying: 'Oh yeah? You're so sure of that, huh?'

I nod and put the book back, then reach for another stack of papers.

'You do understand what your purpose here is, don't you?' he asks in that arrogant tone perfected after years on the job. I try to read, but he's still mouthing off. 'It's not to be cute or smart, it's to help us find your former boss. And if you can't do that, then let's stop the charade right now. Understand?'

'Yeah,' I say, keeping my voice low and even, something I know infuriates him. 'It's what I'm trying to do, but the fact that you won't stop bothering me makes it hard. Maybe if we worked in separate places and reported back to each other, we'd have a better chance of getting this done.'

'You're not going anywhere,' he tells me. 'In case you didn't understand your "assignment", you and I are one tight little team and we'll be together night and day until we've successfully completed our job. If you have a problem with that, we'll just have to end our little relationship now and send you back where you came from.'

It's not easy but I manage to swallow my rage and get back to the job. Later that afternoon, Murphy finds a book on Mexico, with lots of pages turned down. 'Now here's something that's worth looking at!' he says excitedly. 'Looks like he's given this place a lot of thought, might be worth checking out.'

'Nah,' I say, shaking my head, and return to some papers I'm reading: an FBI inventory of Jimmy's house in Squantum. 'Not worth checking out.'

'Are you bullshitting me?' he says, shouting now. 'Trying to steer me in the wrong direction again?'

'Jimmy's already been there – that's why he had the book. Stevie suggested it and Jimmy figured Acapulco would be a good vacation spot, so they went. But Stevie had other plans, like looking for the new boyfriend of his girlfriend; wanted to find him and kill him. Jimmy came home disgusted, said they never had a chance to relax. Stevie was nuts all the time, trying to track down that guy. Never found a trace of him.'

Murphy looks at me long and hard: 'I say we head for Mexico,' he says firmly. 'I'll take care of the details.'

'Whatever you want, boss,' I say. 'It's your dime.'

He stares at me with his beady little eyes, before saying, 'Get your bags packed and be back here by five o'clock this afternoon.'

'Whatever you say,' I reply, but I can't help smiling, which is the worst thing I can do.

'You think this is some big game, don't you?' he shouts, moving closer and spitting his words in my face. I shove my hands in my pockets so he's safe – for the moment, anyhow. 'Well, you're outta here now and it won't be to Mexico. I'm gonna violate your ass faster than Stevie could remove the teeth from one of your dead victims!'

Before I can say a word, he's outta there, probably heading into Rogers' or Berman's office to start the paperwork to violate my parole and toss me back in prison for armed robbery.

I pick up my jacket and walk quickly out of the office, shoving a couple of Jimmy's old magazines into the lining. I figure I'd better go see Rosie and find out what's going on before I get thrown back in a cell. As I'm driving over there, I'm not even angry: from the beginning, I knew the arrangement with that moron would never work. Mexico? Yeah, really! The perfect place to look …

When I get to her house, Rosie's exhausted. She's been up all night with Lucy, who was running a high fever.

'I finally took her to the emergency room around four,' she tells me, as I pick up the poor little tyke and feel her forehead (it's warm now but no longer burning). 'It's her asthma again.'

'Why'd you wait so long?' I ask. She shrugs and I already know the answer. With no insurance it's a long, lousy wait at City Hospital ER, something Rosie would do anything to avoid. 'You tried to call me, right?' I ask, but she looks away.

'Don't worry about us so much, Joey,' she tells me. 'I didn't need you to go with me: we're okay, they gave us the new inhalers and she's better now. I hate you worrying about us all the time. Just promise me you'll stay for supper – I made a terrific marinara sauce.'

'Sorry,' I say, because there's nothing else I can tell her. I'm no different to her shit-for-brains husband, who would have been out drinking if he hadn't been in prison. She's alone as any single mother can be. Lucy leans into me, resting her little head against my shoulder. As always, her beauty mesmerizes me. She looks just like her mother at that age though she's smaller than Rosie was at eight. It's killing me because I'm going to have to leave her and her mother for a lot longer than last time but I haven't the heart to tell my sister what's happened to me.

'Sure,' I say, when Rosie leans over and kisses the top of my head. 'I'm starved.'

After Lucy and I play a few of her games, Rosie asks me to read her a story. Usually, she's the one who reads the stories, but tonight I can see how worn out and frail she is so I agree immediately. Once I get a few of Lucy's favourite little books out of the big pile Rosie has set up in the corner of the living room and settle onto the couch with Lucy snuggled up beside me, I take off my jacket. And that's when I see the magazine I put there. It hits me right away: *Yachting* magazine. There's a cover story on multi-hulled boats: catamarans and trimarans, Jimmy's favourites. I pick out the story that Rosie told me Lucy used to love, 'The Little Engine That Could', and read the kid's book with so much enthusiasm that Lucy giggles all the way through.

That little engine is not the only one that could.

At 8.30 that night, I call Murphy at his office and tell him I want to see him. I know he'll be there: he's obsessed with the case and I don't imagine he has anywhere else to go. I figure he spoke to Berman and Rogers to kill my deal so I tell him I have a hunch and want to talk to him. He tells me to come on over and he'll have the night security guy escort me to his desk.

Sure enough, when I get to room 718 he's slouched over the desk, head on his arms, a pile of papers beneath them and sound asleep. He hasn't shaved, changed his clothes or combed his hair. There's an open box with a half-eaten pizza on the floor beside him and a couple of empty Styrofoam cups with coffee stains. If the guy didn't make me sick to my stomach, I might feel bad for him.

I'm standing by the open door for a good five minutes before I lightly tap on it. In one second, he's wide awake and glaring at me. 'What the fuck do you want?' he asks. There's no fear in his voice, which doesn't surprize me at all. In no way is he afraid of me. Considering what he's threatened me with, you might think he'd have the good sense to be watchful of my actions. After all, thanks to him I'm a desperate man. But he's standing up now and despite his dishevelled appearance, he looks ready to take me on if I want a fight (I don't).

'I came across something I think might interest you,' I say, handing him the yachting magazine. 'Jimmy always talked about getting a trimaran and sailing to the islands in it. I can imagine him buying one and either living on it off the coast of Florida or the Carolinas, even sailing to the islands. Cathy's a good first mate, so together they'd have no trouble going wherever he wanted.'

He looks at me dubiously. I'm sure he'd far rather throw me back in the can than believe me but then again, he wants Jimmy bad. I just stand there and crack my knuckles. He cringes slightly at the sound, but keeps his eyes on my face.

'Sit down,' he finally says and I know I'm not going back to jail, at least not yet. 'Where would he buy the boat?' he asks, as he tosses some papers onto the floor from the small chair I sat on that morning.

I pick up the calendar on his desk, look it over and put it back in the middle of a clump of papers. 'The San Diego Boat Show will be going on sometime early next week,' I say. 'Jimmy always went whenever he could. That would be as good a place as any to start looking.'

He nods, then turns to his computer. For a few seconds, he plays around with it and then announces: 'The boat show begins in two days. It's held at the San Diego Convention Center and runs for three days. I'll be there ... I'll let you know tomorrow if you're going there or to Federal Prison.'

I stand up and head for the door. I'm almost out of the office when he calls my name.

'You had a reputation around town when you were younger for being good with your hands, especially in the ring,' he snarls. I keep on walking without turning round. 'Looking at you, you don't look like you *deserve* that reputation.'

I turn around, not sure if I've heard him correctly. He makes sure I have.

'*You* heard me,' he says. 'Maybe someday you'd like to prove me wrong.'

I stop over at Rosie's before going back to my place but I'm none too happy to find her excuse of a husband sleeping in his car outside the apartment. Last night I had a sick feeling that he might be out, but didn't have the heart to ask Rosie and have my suspicions confirmed. The timing couldn't be worse. I knock heavily on the car window and he wakes with a start. He opens his eyes long enough for me to see they're bright red before he closes them again. I rap even more heavily a second time and he opens the window a small crack.

'Get the fuck out of here!' I tell him. He looks at me as if he's not quite sure who I am, but then I see the recognition in his eyes. He's drunk, but not enough to get out of the car and confront me. It takes an effort but he puts the key in the ignition and takes off.

When I walk into Rosie's apartment, she's washing some clothes at the kitchen sink. She takes one look at me and says, 'You saw that creep, huh?' I nod. 'He's gone now?' she asks, to which I nod again. 'Thanks, Joey,' she says. 'Now he knows you're around, he won't come back. Besides, you know Timmy: he'll be back in jail in no time.'

'Why didn't you tell me he was out?' I ask, but she shrugs her shoulders. I want to tell her that she has to divorce him, that he'll be in and out of jail, drunk and on drugs all his life. Instead I say nothing – I've said it all a million times before.

'Actually, it's me that's taking off for a little while,' I tell her. 'I've got a good chance to make some money working in construction and I have to take it. Heaven knows, I haven't had any other chances. I won't be gone long, I promise, and I'll stay in touch every day.'

She smiles happily: you'd think I'd just told her I won the lottery. 'That's *great*!' she says, throwing her arms around me. 'I knew something good would finally happen.'

'Thanks,' I tell her.

Then I find Lucy curled up on the couch watching a video of *Between the Lions*. I give her a big hug and a book I picked up at the corner drug store. 'How about I read you a bedtime story?' I suggest and she gets up and grabs my hand. She's pretty much asleep before I finish the second page of *Five Little Princesses*.

'I'm going to be away for a little while,' I whisper in her ear as I tuck her in. 'You be real good to Mommy while I'm gone.'

And she promises me that she will. As I walk out of there, I have a sick feeling in my gut. Afterwards, I call Chopper and tell him the same lie that I told Rosie and ask him to keep an eye on Rosie and Lucy, to make sure her piece-of-shit husband stays well away. He promises me that he will and when I finally fall asleep, I feel a little better.

Chapter 12
Murphy, Downtown Athletic Gym, Boston

The next morning I call Joey at 7.30 and tell him to appear at FBI headquarters in an hour.

'Pack a suitcase,' I instruct him.

'Yeah,' he says.

'You want to know where you're going?'

'No,' he answers.

I decide to give the guy a break: 'Then let me just say you can bring your own clothes.'

He lets out an audible sigh of relief and I add: 'Don't get too excited, Joey! You'll need to pack earplugs. I've been told that I snore like a drunken sailor.'

He says nothing, simply hangs up and I'm disgusted with myself for trying to be Mr Nice Guy. It won't happen again.

At 8.30, I'm waiting for him in the entrance, a gym bag on one arm and a carry-on bag on the other. He looks at the black sweats I'm wearing, but says nothing.

'Follow me,' I say. 'We're heading for the gym – we've got a little time to kill before our one o'clock flight.'

He follows me without saying a word. We both understand I'm in charge ... and that he thinks I'm a pathetic moron. Well, he'll be singing a different tune real soon. We walk down Washington Street for about ten minutes to a downtown gym. I'm so wound up that I have to keep myself from practically skipping down the street while he stays a respectful few feet behind. But he knows if he so much as moves from that position, I'll be on him like flies at a picnic spread.

He's still right behind me as we arrive at the Downtown Athletic Gym, an expensive state-of-the-art gym complete with racquet ball, weight rooms, steam rooms, spa facilities, everything. I know what he's thinking: the perfect gym for yuppies who want to show off their manhood. And he's right: it's so sanitized that it doesn't smell of sweat but it does have a boxing gym. Maybe now he understands what's going on.

I sign us in with a big greeting for the athletic-looking brunette at the desk. She smiles at me, the usual half-serious look she gives me every day that I'm not sure how to read. I just don't know if she's saying, 'Oh, it's you again,' or, 'I'm out of my mind with joy to see you this morning.' Either way, it must be obvious to Joey that I know the place well.

When we get into the locker room, I quickly open my locker and hand him a pair of sweatpants, a T-shirt with the name of the gym printed on it and some gloves.

'Why don't we kill a little time and jump in the ring?' I ask, attempting to sound nonchalant but missing the mark and probably coming across as a silly little kid who can't keep the excitement out of his voice. 'We'll call it good guy versus bad guy. You know, just to get the two of us warmed up before our long flight. Figured it would be a nice way for us to get to know one another, see what the other one is made of.'

He just stares, like he's struggling to get a handle on me. I've no idea what he sees, probably a wimp who puts on a suit each day and sits behind a desk doing nothing. But in a few minutes, he'll see exactly how tough I am.

'Sure,' he answers. As if he has any choice.

'Perfect,' I say and fifteen minutes later, thanks to the corner man I've provided, we're all taped up, wearing Downtown Athletic Club T-shirts and facing each other in the ring. I've even hired a referee, who also happens to be my trainer. Joey looks as if he has no idea how to act with me so I just move around, throwing jabs and right hands, while he bobs and weaves, probably trying to get the feel of the ring. After all, from what I've figured out, it must have been about fifteen years since he was there.

The first round we just dance around each other. I'm feeling pretty good, light and nimble on my feet, executing decent foot skills. What's more, I'm getting a lot of use out of my quick jab. He's not doing much, just sort of studying me, but then he starts to move in, cutting the ring down on me. To his obvious surprize, I start executing good hand speed, throwing punches in combination: left jab, straight right hand, left hook … I know I'm mechanical in the ring, not a natural boxer like him, but I've learned a lot from taking cardioboxing with my aerobics instructor, along with shadowboxing. Even had my own boxing instructor for a while, a terrific guy who kept telling me to watch out for a fatal flaw in my tactics: that I don't finish my combinations with a left jab. But I've been working on that and I'm feeling pretty damn good at the end of the first round, which belongs to me.

When Joey comes out in the second round, he starts pressing the action more, hitting me some left hooks to the body. I take the second round but not in the same easy fashion as I did the first. After the round ends, I call out to him from across the ring: 'I thought you were good, Donahue. I thought you'd present a challenge. I'm disappointed!'

He says nothing, simply turns away and takes a sip of water from the bottle held by his corner man. When we come out for the third round, he engages me again, pressing the action, bobbing and weaving, sliding a lot of my punches, letting others glance off his wide shoulders. I sense that he decides to pick it up with me, even though I haven't yet broken a sweat and I'm practically dancing around him, unhindered.

Finally, I back away and I can't stop myself smiling, then laughing. It's all so terrific, better than I ever imagined. I press in on him, side to side. Slowly, though, he starts to step in, moving to the side, cutting the ring off on me. He positions his back to the ropes and then, sliding over to the left, hits me a sharp left hook to the ribs. As he strikes, I make a giant error, dropping my right elbow ever so slightly down my side to protect the ribs. Immediately, he hits me with another left hook to my arm just to reinforce what he wants. Before I can make a decent move, he takes half a step back with his knees bent and throws a right uppercut. I can feel my chin snap up like a jack-in-the-box as my head tilts backward. Without wasting a second, he bobs over to his

68

left and comes up with a left hook to the side of my jaw. I can hear the crisp sound of leather hitting my face.

With every piece of strength I can muster to stay up, I struggle but I know it's useless: I'm going down. I spit out my mouthpiece, feel the blood trickle from the corner of my mouth as my eyes roll back in my head. When I start to fall to my left, the bastard drills me with one last right hand as I go down. Somehow the referee jumps in and grabs me before I hit the mat – that's about the only benefit of all the money I've paid out to this fucking gym that I can feel at this moment. Through the fog in my brain, I hear the referee yell, 'Was that last punch really necessary?' No reply.

Joey's dressed back in his own clothes, a little red around the cheekbones, sitting on the bench in front of my locker when I walk unsteadily into the changing room. 'What the fuck is the matter with you?' I scream, though I'm feeling pretty shaky. 'You'll pay for that big time, that much I can promise you!'

He stands up and faces me. I take a look at the mirror behind him and see that already my right eye is turning all shades of purple. There are spots of blood at the sides of my mouth, my lower lip is puffy and I wouldn't be at all surprized if I've lost a tooth or two.

'And this is what I can promise you,' he says, his voice infuriatingly softer and calmer than mine. 'If you're going after Jim Bulger, you'd better not underestimate him the way you just did me 'cause he won't just knock you down, he'll put a bullet in your head.'

For a long moment, I stare at him and then weaving like a drunken sailor, I head for the showers.

'Tell the front desk to call us a taxi for Logan Airport in fifteen minutes,' I yell back at him. 'I don't want us to miss the flight to San Diego.'

'Sure,' he says.

I turn around to face him.

'Thanks,' I say.

'No problem,' he tells me as he grabs his bag and follows orders.

I'm feeling not one jot of pleasure over this match that I planned so carefully and for such a long time. There's no denying Joey just won the first round of a match we'll be fighting for a while but that doesn't change the fact that right now he has no control of his life and there'll be another chance for me to wipe his ass all over the floor. Next time, he'll be the one going down and I'll be holding the weapon to be sure he doesn't get up.

Chapter 13
Joey, San Diego

As soon as we get settled in our seats, I close my eyes and don't open them until the plane reaches Cincinnati. We have a forty-minute layover, barely enough time to get to a different terminal and make our connection on to San Diego. Murphy seems especially slow and so I grab his bag and get to the plane a few minutes ahead of him. They're closing the gate but I convince the attractive ticket agent to hold the door for my friend and me.

'He had a bit of an accident and he's having a hard time making it over to the terminal,' I tell her and she smiles sweetly.

'Well, *you* don't look like you had any sort of an accident ...' she says flirtatiously.

'No, I'm fine,' I insist. 'I'm feeling pretty good, as a matter of fact.'

She's still smiling and holding the door open when Murphy comes limping over. He looks awful: the swelling under his right eye is worse than before, his lower lip three times its normal size. He gives the two of us a dirty look, grabs his bag from me and walks through the door to the waiting aircraft.

'Wow, you weren't kidding!' she whispers in my ear, but I shrug and follow my new buddy. Once again after we've sat down, I close my eyes and don't wake until the plane lands in San Diego.

After we've settled in our hotel, a mid-sized Marriott not too far from the San Diego Zoo, Murphy's in no mood to go out for dinner or even to leave the room. I could laugh in his face when he tells me it's the jet lag that's making him feel so lousy. Besides, I'm fine with ordering a light dinner from room service and watching the ball game on TV. Murphy eats his food, an omelette and some fruit, without saying much. I suspect he's having a problem with a back tooth, but I don't ask him about it. He barely glances at the TV and spends his time poring over a briefcase full of notes. Meanwhile, I eat a hamburger and some fries and then

I'm happy watching the game. By 10pm California time, I'm ready to call it a day, especially since it's really after 1am EST, but Murphy's still going strong. Even after all that snoozing on the plane, I still fall right off to sleep. I've no idea what time he goes to bed, but the snoring is a bit of a nuisance, though not enough to keep me awake. I heard enough snoring inside my jail cell to learn how to sleep in the middle of a construction site.

Next morning, Murphy seems to feel a little better but he sure doesn't look any better. We both head out for a jog and I force myself to let him pass me after a mile, figuring it's the least I can do. He stops after three miles, covered in sweat, and I follow suit, though I've barely broken a sweat.

Once we get to the boat show, right at the marina connected to the Marriott, however, he's all business. 'You take the first two rows of boat dealers and I'll take the next,' he orders me. 'Just show them the photos and ask if they've seen anybody like Whitey or Cathy in the past few shows. If you see a spark of recognition, but the guy claims not to have seen Whitey, let me know and I'll take over. Chances are, Whitey paid him handsomely to sell him a boat and keep his mouth shut.'

'You know no one ever called him Whitey, except for the press and the law,' I tell him.

'Excuse *me*?' he says.

'Just thought you should know that if you come across him today.'

'Are you being a smart ass?' he asks.

'I just wanted to be sure you knew that fact,' I answer.

'Sure, I knew,' he says. 'Now get to work already and see if you can find your old friend Jimmy. In case you forgot, that's what you're here for.'

I nod and start to head towards the first dealer when I'm practically knocked over by a group of four girls, probably in their early twenties. 'We know who you are!' one of them, a hot blonde in skintight jeans and bright pink halter-neck, announces, reaching for my hand but I'm way too cautious to let any stranger, even a pretty girl, grab me like that. 'You're Joey Donahue,' she continues, undaunted. 'That mobster's associate!'

'We saw you on *America's Most Wanted* three weeks ago!' squeals a tall, shapely brunette. She turns to Murphy, who's just standing there, his swollen mouth open in astonishment. It can't be easy, but he shapes that sore mouth into a smile and extends his right hand towards hers.

'Ooh, would you please, *please* take a picture of the four of us with this *amazing* man?' she asks. The smile and extended hand fade so fast I'm not sure I ever saw them. He shakes his head in disgust and walks off. Ten seconds later, some other guy – pleased to be even a small part of our little group – snaps away. It takes me a few minutes but I disentangle myself from the ladies after lying and promising to meet them for drinks later that night and get to work. I glance over at Murphy and can see that he's still seething with resentment. Now I catch his eye, glance back at the girls who are still staring at me and shrug. Man, does it feel good to bust his chops.

For the rest of the day, we each talk to ten different boat vendors with no luck. Late the next afternoon, however, I strike gold: I can tell from the moment my guy – a boat dealer no more than thirty years old – glances at the photo of Jimmy that he recognizes him. Better yet, he sees no reason to hide the fact from me.

'Yeah, I'm pretty sure I saw that guy,' he tells me. 'He was at one of our shows last year. I'm not sure which one, maybe the one in the fall. Is he in trouble with the law or something?'

Before I can answer, Murphy's at my side ... actually, in front of my whole body.

'I'm John Murphy of the FBI,' he says, waving his badge in front of the kid. 'I'm going to need you to remember every word of any conversation you had with the suspect.'

Immediately, the kid clams up. 'Actually, I don't think I can remember a thing,' he says nervously. 'Thought the guy in the picture looked familiar, but on second glance, he isn't.'

Murphy pushes even closer to the poor kid. 'If you're lying, you're committing a criminal offence,' he tells him. 'This man is a violent criminal and you're in serious legal trouble if you impede our investigation.'

The kid just shakes his head. 'Sorry,' he says. 'I can't help you.'

'No problem,' I say, moving to the other side of the hulk blockading me. 'It's hard to tell from a small photo but listen, if you have any memories whatsoever, you can contact us at a later date. We'll be grateful for any help you can provide.'

I can tell my simple words have relaxed him a bit, but they've infuriated the 'boss'. After a few minutes during which Murphy is mercifully silent, the kid speaks up.

'Actually, I *do* think that's the guy I met,' he says, glancing uncertainly at Murphy. 'I just got worried when you came at me like that.'

Before Murphy can utter another word and make him even more nervous, I say: 'I can understand that. You haven't had much experience with law enforcement before, right?'

The kid nods.

'We're not here to get *you* in trouble: we just want to know if and when you saw this man and what he might have said to you. Did you sell him a boat?'

'No,' says the kid, more confidently now. 'He wanted to buy a trimaran – a beauty, about $600,000 – but I couldn't do it the way he wanted me to: no name, cash on the table, just sign the title over. That's not how I do business: I want everything on the up and up, always have.'

I nod and gently poke Murphy, who nods too.

'He was polite and he said he understood. I'm pretty sure he went to a few other dealers, too. He liked a boat that my friend George over there – the guy with the red sweatshirt – had for sale. Didn't end up buying that one, either.'

'Thanks,' says Murphy, handing one of his cards to the kid. 'If you ever see him again, please give me a call.'

He reaches over and takes one of the cards displayed on the table in the booth and walks away, heading, I'm sure, for George's booth.

'What's the guy wanted for?' the kid asks me in a soft voice when Murphy is out of earshot.

'Oh, nothing too bad,' I say and he relaxes. 'Just nineteen murders ...'

The look on his face is pure terror but I could hardly resist. I'm feeling pretty pleased with my success with the kid – maybe all my years on the other side of the law helped me get through to him.

George, it turns out, had a similar experience with Jimmy. This time Murphy lets me do most of the talking. Again, it was a trimaran and for a cash and sign-over-the-title sale. Once more, he was refused. George remembers the pretty blonde older lady with him and he identifies her as Cathy when Murphy shows him her photo.

'Thanks so much for your help,' I say, when Murphy turns to leave the booth. 'Do you think he might have gone to anyone else at the boat show?'

George nods. 'Yeah,' he says and Murphy's back by his side in a flash. 'I'm not positive but he might have struck a deal with this other guy, a few booths away from me. I had a few conversations with him: he was from Miami, had a marina down there. He didn't have much stuff here but he showed me a photo of a beautiful trimaran that he was trying to unload: it was real sleek, fully loaded, had everything. And his booth was closed up, tight as a drum, the next day. Wouldn't surprize me one bit if he made a very quick cash deal for a boat that wasn't even here.'

He looks at me and sighs: 'Sure wish it had been *my* palm that had been so well greased. Sometimes it doesn't pay to be so honest.'

I give Murphy a look that I know he understands. He reaches into his pocket and pulls out two fifties, which he hands to George, along with his card.

'Sometimes it does,' he says. 'Are you absolutely sure you can't remember anything else about this guy?'

For a few moments, George looks at the money and the card and then shakes his head. Suddenly he breaks into laughter.

'Wow,' he says, when he stops laughing. 'You're not going to believe this ...'

'Try us,' I say.

'Okay,' he continues, looking back at the card and then at Murphy. 'You're going to think I'm nuts, but I can almost swear this guy's name was the same as yours: John Murphy. Now tell me that's not incredible?'

Murphy shakes his head. 'Not at all,' he says. 'It's a common name. Just look in any phone book, you'll see plenty of them. But you're sure of this?'

'Absolutely,' George nods confidently.

'And he was from Miami?' Murphy persists. He nods again. 'Thanks,' says Murphy and takes out four more fifties. 'Keep two more for yourself and give two to your buddy over there.' he says.

George nods appreciatively. So do I.

I'm beginning to think Murphy and I have crossed some sort of an invisible bridge when I notice three young women staring at me from across the room. They recognize me too, so I try to get out of the way and disappear before they reach me, but those three are fast.

'Ooh, I know you!' one cries out and Murphy's bruised face darkens once more.

'Don't blame me,' I tell him as the girls swarm around me.

This time, Murphy reaches for the camera that one of the girls is holding and snaps the photo.

'Jesus Christ!' he mutters as we leave the Convention Center. 'What the hell is wrong with women today? All they want is to be with a thug!'

'Makes no sense to me,' I say. 'We're not nice people.'

Murphy doesn't answer, just shakes his head. The guy still looks as if he walked into a brick wall and it's good to know I have some of the old power left but as we walk out into the street, my sense of control is quickly replaced by a feeling of dread. We're on our way now, heading down a path I have no desire to follow. I'd give anything to be swallowed up by the crowd of strangers around me but that's not about to happen. Instead, I'm to follow my 'boss', heading for a destination I never want to reach.

Chapter 14
Joey, Miami

Murphy moves quickly and by nine the next morning, we're on a flight heading to Miami. He's full of excitement and throughout the whole flight, he babbles on about how easy this job is going to be.

'For someone supposedly as brilliant as Jim Bulger, he's making himself very easy to follow,' he tells me, even though my eyes are closed and for all he knows, I could be sleeping. 'Of course, up till now the FBI hasn't been doing a particularly intense job of searching for him. I don't know why, but that's the truth.'

I let him ramble on while I do my best to fade out of consciousness. I've always prided myself on being able to sleep during any flight I've ever been on, even the ones where I was shackled and handcuffed, but today my mind is too rattled to allow me to nod off. All I can think of is Jimmy, that strange look on his face the last time we were together. But that's all about to change – or is it? Could he really have slipped up and left such a trail? And how will I feel if we meet again this way? How could I capture or even kill this guy? I can't imagine it. No matter what Murphy splutters, I need to remember no one's a more brilliant strategist than our prey.

By the time we arrive at Miami International Airport, my head's a pounding mess, but John Murphy is practically dancing off the plane. He's got the addresses of two possibilities, both boat dealers in the Miami area, the information provided by the Boston FBI office.

I'd rather head for our hotel and call it a day, but within a half-hour of our arrival, we're in a rented car, driving towards the first address. Lacey's Marine Service is a dump and this particular John Murphy has to be eighty. It doesn't seem as if he's had a trimaran to sell in at least fifty years and he only has a couple of crappy-looking used power boats in his yard.

It's evening by now but that doesn't bother Murphy. We're out of Lacey's in no time and headed down Dixie Avenue to the second address. Murphy Marina turns out to be much bigger than the first place: there are all different styles of yacht in dry dock, anything from 35- to 60-footers, all kinds of motor yacht and motor/sailers. Right away, I spot a Nauticat 38' and a Midget Yacht 26'. When we turn the corner of the building, he's probably got another thirty boats in the water. It's a good-sized operation.

We're about to leave when we see a gorgeous, spanking new, silver SLK 280 Mercedes Roadster pull up. A lanky guy, in his late thirties with long, light brown hair and beard, dressed in designer jeans and an expensive-looking pale blue silk shirt, gets out of the car; he does a double take when he sees us. Right away, I recognize the look on his face: he figures he's got two suckers looking to buy a boat.

'Are you John Murphy?' John Murphy the FBI agent asks.

'John was my father,' he answers. 'He passed away some years ago. I'm Sean Murphy. Can I help you with a boat?'

'You can help us with something more important,' Murphy says in his typically offensive style as he flashes his FBI badge and produces a photo of Jimmy and Cathy, all in one quick movement. 'Have you ever seen these two?' he asks.

The look on Sean Murphy's face is pure disappointment. When he sees the picture, he seems more nervous than disappointed.

'Am I in trouble?' he says.

'Did you sell these two a boat while you were at the San Diego Boat Show?' Murphy asks.

'Yeah,' he replies, 'but what's wrong with that? I buy and sell repos. I got a year to pay my taxes on that sale, don't I?'

John Murphy nods. 'Yes, you do,' he says. 'We just want to ask you some questions about the boat you sold them. Let's go inside and sit down for a few minutes.'

Sean leads us inside, sits down behind a sleek glass desk and gazes out curiously at the two of us. There's something shady about him – I ought to know.

But Murphy doesn't bother to sit down. 'What kind of boat did you sell this man?' he asks. 'I want every little detail you can give us.'

Sean opens a small filing cabinet and pulls out a photo and description of the boat, a white trimaran with a blue bottom named *Belle*. It's a 64' trimaran with a hard-top flybridge, a 2000 Blue Dragon, 170 HP Yanmar, four-cycle diesel, straight shaft. There are electrical bilge pumps in all the compartments, a 220-gallon water tank, an electrical head in the main cabin and a manual head in the guest cabin. It's a real beauty, this *Belle*, and advertized for $625,000.

'I'd like the serial number of the boat and a copy of the Bill of Sale,' continues Murphy.

'No problem,' Sean says, still looking nervous. 'I'll get it for you tomorrow.'

'I need it now,' says Murphy.

For the first time, Sean glances at me and I shrug my shoulders sympathetically. He turns and opens another drawer in the cabinet, leafs through a neat pile of papers and pulls out one which he gives, for some unfathomable reason, to me. Murphy grabs it out of my hand, studies it carefully and tucks it away in his pocket. Sean offers a nervous laugh.

'Glad to be of service,' he says. 'What did this dude do, anyhow?' he asks, turning to me.

But before I can answer, Murphy says: 'His name is James Whitey Bulger and he's on the FBI Most Wanted list for nineteen murders.' He walks towards the door, then stops and turns around. 'Don't forget to pay your taxes,' he says, and walks out of the shop.

I smile at Sean and then mutter in a low voice, 'He's an asshole!'

Chapter 15
Joey, Coral Gables

It's nearly ten that night before Murphy and I settle down at Ruth's Chris Steak House in Coral Gables.

'Well, we've got them on the high seas,' he says, after downing his second vodka and tonic (I'm surprised someone as tightly wound as this guy drinks at all). 'I'm thinking they probably headed for the Virgin Islands.'

I nod and let him talk on. Earlier, I'd heard him report our day's findings to Berman and Rogers. You'd have thought we had Jimmy and Cathy handcuffed to a pole in our hotel room. Obviously these guys have enough faith in our first measure of success to advance us whatever funds we need to move forward – and to encourage us to enjoy a lavish dinner. I can tell by the way he's digging into his filet mignon that Murphy's no longer experiencing any problems in chewing his food. I keep him company, mimicking his order and happily sharing the side orders of twice-baked potatoes and sautéed mushrooms. I'd been equally congenial when it came to the bacon-wrapped scallops and crispy coconut shrimp he selected for our appetizers. It's the best meal I've had since Chopper treated me to a steak dinner the day I got home from prison.

'So, what do you think?' he asks after finishing both the last bite of his chocolate mousse and his illogical explanation of how Cathy and Jimmy are holed up in a small bay off the coast of Virgin Gorda. Which happens to be the same place he and his now-divorced wife went on their honeymoon.

'I was sailing the boat, a 50' beauty – the boat, not the wife,' he says, in an attempt to be funny. 'Anyhow, at the marina I ended up slamming into another sailboat operated, if you can believe it, by Dick Van Dyke. So, what do you think of my scenario?' he asks, putting down a fork after he's scraped away the last speck of mousse.

What I think is that I'm not surprised he's divorced. Nor that his marriage lasted less than a year and twenty years later, he's still single. Also, I don't think Jimmy and Cathy are in Virgin Gorda. I can't remember him mentioning, never mind visiting, that particular island but I'm thinking I'll allow this jerk to go on about Virgin Gorda and his honeymoon and let him plan our visit to the Virgin Islands. It's no skin off my back if the FBI drops some serious dough into our laps and we take off on a fruitless search – I'm in no big rush to find my old associate. For all I care, we could spend the next two years cruising from island to island, searching in places Jimmy would never be.

'Could be right,' I say and I'm about to add more when my cell phone rings. Only two people have the number: Rosie and Chopper. I see by the number it's Chopper.

'Hey buddy,' says Chopper. 'Hate to bother you, but I figured you'd want to know: I haven't been able to reach Rosie all day today or yesterday. I stopped off at her house a bunch of times but she didn't answer and her car was always gone. She didn't answer her cell either. I hate to do this to you, pal, but I wasn't sure what to do now.'

'Thanks,' I tell him. 'I appreciate it.'

Murphy's staring at me, but I avoid his eyes. I look at my watch: it's nearly midnight. Where the hell would Rosie be at this hour?

'I'll make a few calls and get right back to you. Keep trying to get her at home, okay?'

In fact, it only takes one call, to Boston City Hospital Emergency Room, to find my sister and niece. Lucy had an especially scary asthmatic attack and has been hospitalized for twenty-four hours. Rosie tries to sound fine but I can hear the fear and exhaustion in her voice – and I'm about to head out to the Virgin Islands for a six-month vacation.

'He's not in Virgin Gorda,' I tell Murphy after I relay the information to Chopper and make sure he's on his way to keep Rosie company, 'if he's any place, it's in St Barts.'

'St Barts?' Murphy repeats, the smile fading from his face. 'What the hell are you talking about?'

'Look, he and Stevie went to St Barts a few times,' I say, 'with different women. He used to tell me he liked the fact that island was 95 per cent white. That was a carry-over from his time in prison – you know, stick to his own. He stored plenty of dough in offshore banking accounts in the Grand Caymans and in other islands, including St Barts. I'd put all my money on his being in St Barts right now.'

The annoyance fades slightly and Murphy leans his face closer to mine. He's all-professional now.

'You're sure of this?' he asks.

And I'm ready to tell him anything to get this show on the road.

'Remember the passports we found in the piles of information we went through?'

Murphy nods excitedly. 'Of course!' he says, so loudly that he attracts the attention of two women at the next table. 'I have them back in our hotel room. I went over them again last night – St Maarten was stamped at least three times.'

'Yeah,' I say, and he asks for the bill.

'We'll take off for St Maarten and St Barts first thing in the morning,' he tells me as he gets out his credit card. 'I'll call Rogers and Berman as soon as we get back to the hotel.'

But I don't say anything: I'm feeling sick to the core, uncertain if it was the steak or the phone call from Chopper, even the thought that I might be facing Jimmy in a matter of days. All I know for sure is that I'd rather be anywhere else, doing anything other than what I'm about to do. But then I remember my jail cell and somehow I don't feel so sick.

Chapter 16
Whitey, St Barts

Cathy and I've been in St Barts a week when I hit the first bank. It's in Mondovia, a short ride from the villa I've rented for the two of us. Since I've been on the run, I've hit banks dozens of times, but I'm never all that comfortable when I do: I always wait till a day when I've slept well, so I'll be in my best mental state. This morning, I increase the number of minutes I spend on my daily calisthenics from forty-five to sixty so I'll be fit and well-rested when I leave the villa. The whole time I'm doing my exercizes, my mind is far from St Barts, lost in the memories of a time when 'hitting a bank' meant something far different to what I've planned for today.

It doesn't take long till I push my mind all the way back to 1966. I'm back in South Boston, thirty-seven, and out of jail thirteen months after serving nine years from my twenty-year sentence for robbing banks. I've promised myself that I won't do anything for the first year. After nine years in Atlanta, Alcatraz and Leavenworth, I've spent the past year getting my feet back under me, adjusting to being out of prison.

But it's time to start making some money. I know what I need to do, so I contact one of my old friends from prison. Out in Dedham, I meet up with Walter and the two of us sit down for lunch in a small restaurant, not too far from the Norfolk Correctional Facility, a medium security jail. I order a turkey club sandwich, he has pastrami with mustard. 'That stuff's gonna kill you, clog your arteries,' I tell Walter, knowing it's the least of his problems. He looks at me like I'm nuts and continues to eat his sandwich.

While we eat, I tell him about a bank I'd looked at. 'It should get us anywhere between $100,000 to $150,000 apiece,' I say. Then I go over all the particulars except for the location, carefully explaining the escape route where we won't run into any traffic signals. When he orders his third beer, I tell him if we're to do this score, there will be no drinking. 'You've got to stop now,' I say. 'I don't intend to go back to prison because someone's not 100 per cent up to the job.'

But he pushes his drink away and tells me, 'I'm in.'

We spend the next couple of days doing dry runs, casing the bank and driving the escape route. I've got it planned for the following Thursday at nine in the morning, right after the bank opens. There won't be many people there and the guard will still be sluggish from his night job as a security guard at an electrical plant. Wednesday night, we steal three cars and put two of them in position. Thursday morning, we're on the road to Rhode Island at seven. At quarter to nine, we get into position in Pawtucket, about a block away from the First National Bank, walking distance to the entrance, so we can watch how much traffic is going in and out of the bank when it opens. We haven't committed a crime till we walk inside so we can turn away at any time if things don't look too good.

In a few minutes we see everything is a go. As we head in, we pull the black stocking masks over our heads. I have two 45s tucked into the waistband of my pants and Walter has a sawn-off shotgun under his coat. I quickly grab the guard, disarm him and put him on the floor. Walter takes out his shotgun and orders everyone else down on the floor. The only people in the bank are the bank president, four tellers and one old guy making a deposit. Once all seven are down and we have control, Walter jumps the counter, empties all the drawers and the vault, then tosses the money into a black gym bag.

'Take your money with you,' I tell the old guy on the floor. 'I just want the bank's money, not yours.'

Five minutes and thirty seconds after we enter the bank, Walter and I are off. A block from there, we hop into the car and pull away. Two blocks later, in an empty parking lot near an abandoned building, we stop the car, get out, douse it with gasoline and set it alight. Then we walk through the hole in the fence at the parking lot that I cut the night before and hop into the second stolen car, knowing no one can drive through the fence to follow us.

We drive the backstreets of the outskirts of town, punctuated with rundown houses and sad-looking stores, ditch the car a mile away at the parking lot of a mall far from filled with shoppers, jump into the third stolen car parked in the same aisle and drive out of the city limits. Exhausted, Walter closes his eyes but I'm driving and filled with energy. I'd love to go over the details of the robbery, especially the terrified look on the face of one teller, a good-looking woman in her twenties, but I can see Walter's worn out from the whole deal. I figure it must be his lousy eating habits but I don't say anything and let him grab a few minutes' rest. I wake him up when we turn off old Route One and we pull over, park the car, walk normally one hundred yards to a legitimate car around the corner and then we're gone. Back in Boston forty-five minutes later, Walter looks pretty alive as we chop up the money, and it's better than we thought: we end up with over $270,000 apiece. Not a bad day's work.

What a great morning it had been. The adrenaline was flowing, the old excitement returned. After that, I did sixteen equally successful bank hits around New England, most of them with Walter, the rest with a few other guys I knew before prison: quick, simple and efficient jobs, in and out. But when I got into the gang wars and organized crime, everything changed. Today, it's pleasant to remember the simple days when it was all so easy, when there were no dye packs, surveillance cameras or customers with cell phones and police response time was slower. Forty years later, working out in my villa in St Barts, I can't help but wish to be back in 1966: those were the good years.

Not that they stayed so good for poor Walter. He never stopped drinking or smoking, but the funny thing is he didn't die of cancer or liver disease: he died in a car accident. Guess he could have carried on drinking and smoked and eaten all the pastrami sandwiches he wanted and it wouldn't have hurt him. Anyway, all that matters is I'm here now and he's not. Life goes on.

An hour later, showered and feeling relatively confident, I walk into the bank at St Barts, not to steal its money but to remove some of mine. I'm wearing the beige round floppy hat that's popular on the islands, along with white cotton pants, a long-sleeved white shirt with the cuffs rolled up and a pair of boat shoes. I've got on my regular prescription glasses with the tinted lenses so there's no need for sunglasses. I seem no different to the usual American retiree, a tourist looking to spend a nice chunk of the winter in the islands. Except I'm using my Canadian alias, John St. Clair, with a whole new set of identification papers arranged before I took off.

I know exactly where the security cameras are located and I'm able to partially avoid them, though not completely. There's no reason for me to feel concerned as my papers are in order and the bank is quiet on this particular morning. I move calmly and slowly, requesting a guard to open the security gate for me so I can get to my box. A pretty, dark-haired female teller, no more than twenty-five, smiles warmly and lets me into the vault herself. It takes me less than ten minutes to remove my safety deposit box (easily one of the largest they have here) from the locked slot, carry it into a private cubicle and take out $250,000 in hundred-dollar bills, leaving at least four times that amount in there.

I set up this account around twenty years ago during a visit to the tropics with Stevie. Over the years, I transferred money from Grand Cayman to St Barts – it's one of several accounts I have in the islands. I remember the fun Stevie and I had on that trip with a couple of our girlfriends we'd brought with us: visits to classy expensive restaurants, shopping in top designer stores, buying jewellery and leather belts and shoes, anything we or the girls wanted. I'd been after Stevie to do the same thing, to set up some offshore accounts, but he never listened to me. Business-savvy as he was, Stevie never had a contingency plan in case he had to go on the run. So, now I'm in St Barts easily retrieving my money and he's facing the bars of a cell, where he'll spend the rest of his life.

There's no excuse for not planning things well: from the smallest heist to the biggest score, attention to detail is crucial. Settling my money in positions where I could easily retrieve it has always been crucial. Stevie used to joke I could write a book on hiding money; that could be true but there's nothing funny about it. What's the purpose of being free if you haven't got the cash to live well on the run?

In the early eighties, I seriously began to stash my money away in banks. Today, I've more than $12 million in off-shore banking accounts in St Barts and the Grand Cayman Islands along with another $12 million in Switzerland plus $6 million stashed at various locations throughout the US.

The hardest part of setting up the offshore accounts was getting the money down to the Grand Cayman Islands. With close to 700 licenced banks in an area twenty-two miles long, money can stay forever hidden in offshore accounts. To get it there, I used my connections in the drug-smuggling business. At least two dozen times, when the boats left New Bedford and Gloucester to pick up drugs in Colombia, they'd make a detour to the Grand Cayman Islands with a million or so of my own cash. Usually, I'd have Joe Murray, one of the heads of the drug-smuggling operation out of Boston who had an account down there himself, take care of things. He'd just give the cash to the president of the bank, who'd deposit it in my numbered account for a 5 per cent fee.

In Switzerland, I established a numbered account myself, using a letter of introduction from the South Boston Savings Bank, which explained that James Bulger maintained a savings account and was a person of good standing at their bank. After that, I could wire transfer the money to wherever I wanted by writing down the number in my account and typing in a numbered password – which was what I'd do with my accounts in the Grand Cayman Islands and in St Barts.

In the US, things were less sophisticated. It took just a little planning to stash away the dough. I'd rent storage facilities in different states and fill them with old furniture. With an electric jackhammer, I could drill through the concrete floor of the storage rooms and put round cylindrical safes into the floor. After I'd cemented in the holes in the floor, I still had access to the doors of the safes, which I'd cover with old furniture. That way, if anyone looked into the storage units, they'd just see some useless furniture. I'd pay five years in advance for each of the units, which I'd rent under various identifications, and in each unit I'd store up to $2 million in crisp new hundred-dollar bills.

I also keep a good amount of Krugerrand gold bullion coins, along with the bills, each coin containing one troy ounce of pure gold. Krugerrands being the most highly recognizable form of gold bullion, they offer me instant liquidity worldwide whenever I want to sell one. American Gold Eagles, which I could easily cash in at any numismatic store, are also stashed along with the cash.

In Europe, I've got safety deposit boxes in different banks, where I'd take out $12,000 or $50,000 for pocket money. But thanks to Terry, who gave up my bank accounts along with one of my IDs, they've since been compromised but that's not such a big deal: there's only $25,000 in one account and $47,000 in the other. I've got keys to lots of other safety deposit boxes tucked away in a safe place in Boston that only Cathy knows in case anything happens to me, as well as a careful record of all my numbered accounts on a small piece of paper I've memorized and could easily get rid of, if apprehended. I never carry less than $10,000 in new hundred-dollar bills, most often in a leather money belt with the zipper on the inside. And I never use a credit card – it's the easiest way for the IRS (or anyone else) to track you down. You just sleep better knowing all these details are taken care of.

While I place the safety deposit box in its locked drawer in the bank in St Barts, I calculate how much money I have left in all my different accounts. It's gotta be at least $40 million, more than Cathy and I could possibly use in the years left to me, but I want to be sure there's more than enough for her when I'm gone. After all, she's twenty years younger and I expect her to live those years not having to worry about money. And if she decides to go back to the US and face the law after I'm gone, there'll be plenty of money for her legal defence. I myself have no intention of going back. If I end up confronted by the law, I'll go out firing. I'd never go home and subject the family to the ugliness of my trial.

It doesn't take me long to get back to the villa I've rented. It's rather remote but sunny and within walking distance of Lorient Beach, one of the prettiest and least-known stretches of sand on the island. Small, but very private, our villa has lush landscaping, tasteful furnishings and a jacuzzi with an ocean view. Cathy loves the name 'Villa Bon Coin', along with the bathroom with its huge skylight and large glass-enveloped shower. The kitchen's got everything she needs, including a convection oven and a brand new outdoor barbecue grill. I like the air-conditioned bedroom: most people say you don't need air conditioning on this windy, low-humidity island but I sleep better if the bedroom's sixty degrees or lower. It's in a pretty hilly area so I bought a used four-wheel drive, which Cathy's comfortable driving.

Back home, I make her pay attention to where I hide the money and go over the details of how she'll leave the place in a hurry if she needs to, with or without me. She hates this conversation but watches attentively as I wrap up four bundles of hundred-dollar bills in tin foil and place them in the freezer, where they look like packages of steak. In the living room, I move the TV and its stand, loosen two of the floorboards and place the rest of the cash, stored in Zip Lock bags to keep out the musty smell, in a little spot underneath the floorboards. Once I'm convinced she's able to remove the money herself, I'm satisfied. Afterwards, we take a long leisurely stroll along the beach before Cathy makes dinner. Life just couldn't get any better.

Chapter 17
Joey & Murphy, Miami

Murphy can hardly contain himself. Before we even walk into the hotel room, he's dialling Rogers. Midway through the call, he hands me the phone and the look on his face makes it clear he'd rather smash me with it.

'I just wanted to tell you that we couldn't be more pleased with your help,' Rogers tells me.

I glance over at Murphy, who's gazing down at his feet.

'No big deal,' I say. Even with his head down, I can see Murphy grimacing.

'It *is* a big deal,' Rogers insists. 'Now let me make a few calls and get right back to you.'

'Sure,' I say, ending the call and handing the phone back to Murphy, who flips it back into his pocket without glancing at me.

Less than fifteen minutes later, Rogers calls back. Murphy grabs the phone like he thinks I'm going to try and pull it out of his pocket. What's this guy's problem?

'We're all set on an 8am US Air flight to St Maarten tomorrow morning,' he tells me when he gets off the phone. 'The bureau has a solid connection with the local gendarme there. His name is David Larson. He'll meet us at the airport and make sure we get plenty of back-up for St Barts. Rogers will call back in the morning with more information. Let's get some sleep now.'

I nod, hoping I can fall asleep before Murphy starts his nightly snoring serenade. I'm just about gone when I hear him but he's not snoring, he's talking. Which is worse.

'I can imagine this must be a tough day coming up for you,' he says from his bed. I try to pretend I'm sleeping but there's no stopping this guy. 'I mean, the last time you saw him, you couldn't ever have imagined you'd be coming after him like this, right?'

I decide it's hopeless and roll over onto my back, put my hands behind my head and stare up at the ceiling.

'No, I couldn't,' I admit.

And that's enough for him to come crashing in. 'So when did you last see him, anyhow?' he persists. I don't say anything for a while, hoping maybe I'll get lucky and the next sound I hear from his mouth will be a snore.

'Weren't you in New York?' he continues and I know it's hopeless. If I have any intention of getting some sleep tonight, I'll have to placate him now.

'Yeah,' I say, my gaze still fixed on the ceiling, 'in late November. I took the train in to work on Jimmy's new licence. We spent the day walking around, eating an early dinner in a fish restaurant he liked. Cathy was her usual upbeat self, but Jimmy wasn't.'

'Like he knew this was the last time you'd be together?' Murphy interrupts.

For a brief second I'd forgotten where I was, who I was talking to: 'Yeah,' I answer, determined to give him the whole fucking story now and finally get some sleep. 'Like he knew something was coming down, that Stevie would let it out that they were FBI informants, that we would never meet again. At one point, when we were just talking about things back in Boston, he said, "Remember, when they come for you, give me up." Then he didn't say anything for a long while.

'And when we were at Penn Station waiting for my train back to Boston, there was no ignoring the fact that something was different. The three of us sat there for over an hour, just talking, but Jimmy was more serious. When the train finally came, we all stood up. Jimmy and I shook hands and he said he'd be in touch. Even though I knew something was different, I still figured he'd call but he never did.'

'And how will it be when you see him tomorrow?' he asks.

I want to say, 'How the hell do I know? Maybe I'll shake his hand, maybe I'll shoot him in the heart … how could I possibly know how I'll feel?'

'I have no idea,' I say. And this time, I'm through. I roll over, close my eyes and sink into a deep sleep.

Chapter 18
Murphy, St Maarten

Early the next afternoon we're on St Maarten where we're met at the airport by David Larson, head of the island's police force and an excessively polite, large, dark-skinned man with a bald head that he leaves unprotected from the sun.

While we're waiting for Chief Larson to make the arrangements to get to St Barts, I take a walk around St Maarten, comparing it to Virgin Gorda in the British Virgin Islands. It's been nearly twenty years since Mia and I went there on our honeymoon. The island was exquisite, like nothing I'd seen before, with these underground baths that went on for miles and a sunset at Gorda Peak that defied description. Pinks and blues and violet all mixed together, streaming across the sky like vivid splashes of colourful kites. And those boulders at the baths were like mini mountains. I'd like to say it was an idyllic week, as perfect as our surroundings, but I knew even then that Mia and I weren't so beautifully suited to one another as I'd hoped.

How could I forget that scene at the baths? Mia was lying on her back on the beach in her red-and-white polka dot bikini when I jokingly said it was perfect we came to this island since it was named after her. And she innocently asked me what I was talking about. 'Didn't you know Christopher Columbus called it the "Fat Virgin" since its silhouette resembles a rotund island lying on her back?' I asked her. I thought it was such a cute story and she'd be impressed I knew some folklore about the island but she threw me a filthy look, sat up fast, and grabbed her towel. That was it for me for the day: there was no hot sex that night. In fact, I didn't get lucky that night, nor the rest of the week. That night there wasn't even dinner. She ordered room service and ate at a table in our room watching television. I guess it was a pretty stupid thing to say.

I'd only known Mia a few months when we got married so maybe we should have waited a little longer and we might have

93

realized we were mismatched and that she wasn't anywhere near ready for this marriage. She was a secretary in a legal office near the Bureau and we used to have lunch at the same coffee shop every day. She was gorgeous and I practically stood on my head to get her attention. I quickly found out that she had just broken off a longstanding engagement and was not interested in a serious relationship but I foolishly pursued her, buying her expensive jewellery and always convincing her to go out to dinner to some fancy restaurant. I'd never had a girl that hot interested in me.

Before either of us knew what happened, I'd given her an engagement ring. She even wore the gown she'd bought for the wedding she'd called off to ours. I remember our wedding was a lot smaller than the one she'd originally planned and I don't think she was too happy about that. The reason we went to Virgin Gorda was because she was the one who paid for the honeymoon there and she couldn't get back. It was a dumb idea and I should never have agreed, but I guess I was pleased not to have to shell out any money for the trip since I'd sunk a small fortune into the ring.

When we got home from the honeymoon, Mia was sulky and depressed and I couldn't say anything right. It took me a few months to discover she was seeing her old fiancé again. I actually tailed her one night when she 'went out with the girls'. It's the only stakeout I'd ever gone on and I'm an FBI agent. I flipped out when I realized what was going on but when I confronted her about it, I was calm. I wanted us to see a marriage counsellor to try and work things out but she wouldn't hear of it. She married the guy on our one-year anniversary, a week after the divorce became final. That marriage lasted five years longer than ours.

When I finish the walk, I'm feeling pretty crappy when I see Joey sitting on the step in front of our hotel talking to that idiot David again. It irks me no end to see the way the jerk respects him, like he can't tell the difference between a criminal and the law. And I don't feel any better knowing Joey has all this freedom to walk around and do whatever the hell he wants. I'd like nothing more than to smack him around but then I remind myself that in a matter of hours my whole life might change and Mia will be more than a little sorry over what she so stupidly tossed aside. I must be crazy, but I can't deny the fact that I'd give just about anything to get back together with her.

Chapter 19
Joey, St Maarten

I'm given a brief respite when Murphy decides to take a little walk while David makes plans for our flight to St Barts. But all too soon he's back, barking orders and giving me a headache (actually the whole island gives me a headache). Everything seems overly bright here: white buildings with bright blue trim, flashy pink, yellow and green clothes, though scanty amounts of them, on the tourists I see milling around the airport; even my dark sunglasses do little to block out this luminosity. For a moment, I miss the darkness of Boston, which so often and so importantly kept me covered from view. I am, as I've always suspected, not made for this type of island resort life but for now I'm grateful for the cooling breeze rippling through the tall coconut trees, which seems to mitigate the warm sun beating down on us.

Despite his dark skin, David is equally vivid in his white uniform with its short jacket and short pants. As soon as he gets back from his walk, Murphy acts insanely pumped up and shakes David's hand way too heartily. For some crazy reason, however, David seems to think I'm in charge and directs all his questions to me. When I pull out a photo of Whitey and Cathy with their two dogs, a photo Murphy apparently doesn't have with him, he's had it. He moves briskly in front of me and shows David his own group of photos and asks him to immediately go over the plans he's made with the St Barts police. 'We're losing precious time,' he tells him, talking way too fast. 'Let's cut the formalities and get going.' I feel like asking why he made us lose a half hour with his dumb walk, but I keep my mouth closed. Besides, what do I care if we give Jimmy and Cathy some time to get away?

David flashes him yet another of his obviously never-ending supply of wide grins and acts as if Murphy's made a big joke: 'Everything is ready for you now,' he says in a languid, sing-song tone, smiling widely to reveal two gold teeth in his lower jaw, grinning at Murphy while somehow still talking to me. I can see

Murphy's face redden in the ever-rising afternoon heat. 'We were sent pictures early this morning and I have already hand-carried them to my good friend and associate in St Barts. He's waiting for you now.'

At this, Murphy's annoyance vanishes and he smiles back at David now. I feel an odd shot of adrenaline whip through my body.

'He has seen someone who looks like James Whitey Bulger there?' I ask.

David's smile is as bright as ever: 'He's a man of few words but he's a smart man, you will see. I have a plane ready for you. I'll accompany you there even though I have no jurisdiction in St Barts but rest assured, my good friend will take good care of you after I leave.'

'I can't thank you enough,' says Murphy, putting one hand inside his pocket and pulling out five $100 bills. David nods politely at me rather than at Murphy and takes the money. We walk to the waiting plane, David chatting away to me as if I were the FBI agent and Murphy my lackey. If I didn't feel so strange inside, I'd be laughing my face off.

Chapter 20
Whitey, Alcatraz, 1960

My buddy Juan from the Eden Rock Hotel calls me late in the afternoon and says he needs to talk to me. I've filled this guy's pockets with enough cash in the past year to ensure he'll be my eyes and ears around the island. I knew his type the first night I met him. Cathy and I were eating at a small outdoor restaurant on the grounds of the Eden Rock, where he was the manager. Just from the way the three of us chatted, I could tell he was used to providing all kinds of services for his guests. Call it intuition or a sixth sense, but I soon understood that guy was on the take, that he made it a practice to shield wealthy guests who needed protection, and that amount of money from the authorities would convince him to sully his reputation or disturb a successful business.

Today, I can tell from the sound of his voice it's important. He asks me to come to his office, but I'm in no condition to go anywhere, still in the throes of a vile headache that followed one of the worst nights I've had in a long time. I drank way too much wine last night at dinner and I'm furious with myself for allowing it to happen. Cathy's gone on errands and I have a vague recollection of mistreating her when we got home last night but there's no way I can trust myself to drive the winding road into town to the Eden Rock. Unwilling to risk talking to Juan on the phone about something so important, for the first time I give him directions to the villa and do all I can to relieve the pain in my head before he arrives.

I'm sitting outside on the veranda when he drives up. My head's still throbbing but I feel a bit steadier.

'Something's going on,' Juan tells me as soon as he sits down on my deck. 'I'm picking up vibes from a friend in St Maarten that someone is looking for an American wanted for many murders and I know the Chief Constable of St Maarten is due to arrive in St Barts. I'll do what I can to convince him there's nothing happening here, but I wanted you to be aware, my friend.'

'And I very much appreciate it,' I say, reaching into my pocket for the wad of $100 bills that I placed there as soon as I hung up from him. He shakes his head as if to say it isn't necessary, but I force the bills into his hand. Of course, this time he doesn't refuse.

'Can you try and find Cathy for me?' I ask, as he smoothly slips the money into a pocket of his pants. 'I think she's in Corossol picking up a handbag. She needs to come home right away.'

'Of course,' he says. 'And you two will stay here until the danger is passed, I presume?'

'We won't move until you tell us it's safe to do so,' I tell him.

'He's not so smart, the constable from St Maarten,' muses Juan. 'I'm sure he'll have pictures, but I doubt they'll give you away. You and your wife look too much like everyone else here. Still, we must be careful.'

'I know exactly what to do,' I insist.

'Good,' he says, rising. Taking his keys from the spot on the table where he placed them, he stands in front of me, absently dangling them. It's a large group of keys, at least ten, and they rest on a heavy circular key ring. The sound is almost more than I can bear and it's all I can do not to rip them from his hand. Ever since my days in Alcatraz, the sound of jangling keys triggers a terrible response in me: all I can see are the jailors standing in front of my cell (often for hours at a time), loudly swinging their keys. They would disturb my sleep, torturing me with the harsh sound, reminding me that they could come for me any moment, for any reason. Now, with my head still aching from the effects of last night's wine, the sound of those keys is starting to drive me mad.

Juan looks at me strangely but wisely says nothing. He merely turns, the keys now silent in one hand, and heads back to his car. I'm as grateful for the silence as for his warning.

For a moment, after he leaves, my vision is a bit blurred and I close my eyes to calm the ringing in my ears. His keys have transported me back to Alcatraz, depositing me back in the prison weight room. I don't fight the memory – it's a good one and like an old friend, it returns whenever it feels the need to remind me of what once was. And so I'm standing in the prison weight room at Atlanta, no more than thirty, just beginning my workout when I see the redheaded fag saunter across the room. He doesn't come near me, but he moves close to the guy doing push-ups on the floor and stands there, admiring the other prisoner. The redhead is big, probably six inches taller than me and at least fifty pounds heavier, and he's breathing heavy now, lost in his fascination with the body below him, moving back and forth in perfect symmetry on the floor.

And I don't hesitate: I pick up the thirty-pound dumbbell and bring it down over the redhead. His skull explodes like a ripe cantaloupe, only one filled with thick red juice and seeds of fine matter. The guy doing push-ups stops and stares dumbfounded as the body crashes to the ground in front of him. I hold the dumbbell above it and smash it down two more times to make sure his skull is completely shattered, then I walk out of the room.

They put me in the hole for three months but no one can prove I did a thing. No one saw anything, not even the guy doing push-ups. So they send me to Leavenworth but that's okay with me. The world is minus one fag and I'm delighted to be the person who performed the good deed.

When I open my eyes, I glance at my watch and see no more than ten minutes have gone by since Juan left, but I'm feeling perfectly rested now, the effects of last night's drinking episode completely vanished. It's amazing how good a beautiful dream can make you feel.

Chapter 21
Joey, St Barts

Things are moving fast. Yesterday we met with a bunch of officials in St Barts, most of whom were initially reserved but warmed up when David's friend Louie made it clear there's money, good money, involved here. At the marina, we saw three trimarans, two of which fit the description of what I assume could be Jimmy's boat. One of the boats, the one I suspect is Jimmy's, is stripped clean and yields no usable fingerprints. I can't say exactly what it is, maybe the smell of the boat or some strange sensation I picked up there, but I'd bet the bank it's his boat. It didn't surprize me, although it frustrated Murphy in a big way when the owner of the marina was nowhere to be found. And it wouldn't surprize me any more if the missing owner received a lot of cash to take a nice vacation or even a permanent undesired trip to a place he never wanted to see.

Today, however, things seem to be going better for our little team. Fifty thousand dollars later, Murphy has a strong lead. There's a guy named Juan, who works in a hotel on the island, who's been known to help foreigners in trouble. Louie's gotten nowhere speaking to him but when he agrees to bring Murphy and me to meet with the guy, I recognize his type immediately. Intelligent and well spoken, Juan remains loyal to those he helps and won't easily switch his allegiance. We exchange pleasantries, shoot the shit and Murphy jumps right in to how dangerous Whitey Bulger happens to be. Right away, I know this won't sway the guy one iota: he's made his decision and undoubtedly has been well paid for it. It'll take a lot more than money and logic to convince Juan to give him up.

More than ever, I want this mess over: I want to find Jimmy and get my life, whatever it is, back again. But another part of me is eager for Juan to hold onto his information to give Jimmy a chance to escape.

'What do you think?' Murphy asks me after Juan excuses himself to take care of a distraught guest whose dinner reservation has been screwed up. 'Does he know where Whitey is?' It's a sure sign that Murphy is losing it when he asks my opinion. He's done everything possible to keep me out of the picture, but he's now too worked up to think rationally.

'Possibly,' I say.

'What do you mean, *possibly*?' he asks, his face reddening. 'Is he hiding something? Should I offer him more money?'

'Yeah,' I say, not surprised at the way Murphy is hyperventilating. I glance over at Louie, who's completely relaxed, sitting in a chair by the open window and smiling at the two of us as if we're all enjoying a pleasant chat about what beach to go to this afternoon. But we're not going to any beach: we're close, very close, to Jimmy but my 'partner' isn't up to this at all.

'Offer him some more money,' I say. 'But the truth is, if he's gotten to know Jimmy well, there's only a slim chance that he'll cut ties with him and help you.' I know I won't be able to stand being with Murphy much longer – he makes me sick. 'Tell him we have photos of him aiding and abetting a known criminal, of money crossing hands.'

At this, the light goes on in Murphy's eyes and he pulls it together. The minute Juan reappears, all smiles and probably not only because he's settled the reservation situation but also made a call to his 'friend', Murphy's ready for him.

'Let's just get a few things straight,' he tells Juan, his voice no longer genial. 'We have photos of you aiding and abetting a dangerous criminal, of money crossing hands. You need to know that we understand the laws of your island well and can have you extradited to the United States for this crime. Don't misunderstand me, I'll stop at nothing to bring this vicious murderer to justice.'

Juan's eyes flicker for a moment but the smile remains firm. He doesn't scare easily, but it's possible that Murphy made a small dent. 'I wish I could help you,' he tells me, his voice respectful and soft, 'but I have no idea what you're talking about.'

'I'm sorry that you won't cooperate,' Murphy tells him, his voice equally soft and respectful. 'I've got no choice but to ask that you be detained by your local constable.' He turns to Louie, saying, 'You have those papers prepared, do you not?'

Louie is smart – or perhaps just well paid. The thousands of dollars that Murphy has given him have made him all the wiser. He nods to Murphy and me then looks sympathetically towards Juan, shrugging his shoulders in the universal expression of 'Sorry buddy, my hands are tied'.

I keep my eyes on Juan, who might be wavering or else he's playing the game very well. Either way, Murphy goes in for the kill: 'We could avoid all this legal mess and pay you well for your troubles – very, *very* well.' Yet again, he pulls out a wad of bills, the elastic bands still firmly in place, and hands Juan four packages of $5,000 each. Of course, Whitey has paid him well, too, but perhaps not this well. I see immediately that I'm right. His right hand moves imperceptibly from his side. 'No one will ever know of your involvement besides Louie and me,' Murphy continues. 'Your secret is safe – and my government will never forget your help in this critical matter.'

When Juan reaches out for the money, I know the game's over. So does Murphy, who's visibly shaking with excitement. I'm shaking, too, but I'd have a hard time explaining why.

Louie works like a demon for his machine has been well oiled with our money. We all understand that since no crime has been committed in St Barts, there's little the local police can officially do to help us but calls have been made and rules set aside. Within seconds, a caravan of three cars arrives. Juan writes down an address and retreats to his hotel, accompanied by a local policeman … just in case. A quick glance at his face before he goes tells me Juan is not happy with his decision. It occurs to me that he likes the man he was protecting and I can understand why, but he's been well paid for his unhappiness.

I sit in the back seat of our car with Louie and Murphy. The head of the St Barts police department drives, with a sergeant beside him. Four uniformed officers ride in each of the other two cars. I'm strangely calm now as I sit there discussing our plans with the other four men.

When we pull up to the villa, a few minutes past three in the afternoon, I see shades drawn and immediately sense that something is very wrong. Though the villa is built into the hillside, partially hidden from view by leafy palms and giant flowering bushes filled with blue and pink blossoms, the white front of the house is exposed. Somehow, its shaded windows look deserted, the villa itself empty. As planned, the eight officers exit the other cars and surround the villa while the Sergeant, the Chief of Police, Louie, Murphy and I stand on both sides of the front door. I don't know if I want my hunch to be right or wrong. Louie knocks, but there's no answer. Not a sound comes from inside. My hunch, I'm now certain, is correct. The Chief of Police bangs louder and announces his presence in a firm, authoritative voice. Still no sound ... Removing the pistol from his holster, he kicks at the front door twice, breaking it open.

As we enter, I see the villa is quite lovely, though just four rooms: a kitchen, dining room, living room and bedroom with its own sitting room. It's simply furnished, comfortable and not at all ostentatious,. In the bedroom, I see the drawers to the dresser are open, along with the closet door, but no contents are visible. There's no sign that anyone has ever lived here. In the refrigerator, the vegetables look organically grown, the contents on the bottles of juice and condiments listing no preservatives. No surprize, since I know Jimmy eats nothing but the healthiest of foods.

We head outside, my steps slow and heavy, into the lush landscape and I notice the barbecue pit. I walk over to it and observe charred pieces of paper, more telltale signs of Jim Bulger having been here. Nothing in this barbecue is recognizable yet it all fits his modus operandi: leave not a scrap of paper that might indicate you were there. He's gone, completely vanished, but I know he was there. The look on Murphy's face is pure desolation. It makes me want to smile. I turn away and stare out beyond the yard, knowing only too well that I'm on the wrong team: the losing side. But, for this moment anyhow, that's okay.

Chapter 22
Whitey, Ocho Rios

By the time we get to Ocho Rios, Cathy's exhausted but I'm still going strong. Yet I've got to give her credit: she's a trooper. From the second she returned home with Juan and realized it was time for us to leave, she sprang into action like a whirling dervish, forgetting our problem the night before and moving forward, no glances back. She liked St Barts but understood what was happening. At any sign of danger, we're out of there in a half hour or less. And this time it was less.

Weeks earlier I'd made plans and when the time came, I knew where we'd go and how: a privately-owned puddle jumper on an equally private air strip to St Maartens, leaving the boat behind, having moved it to a smaller marina days earlier and stripped it clean. An hour later, we're on a flight to Cancun. There's a three-hour layover before we're heading for Montego Bay. One more hour and we're in a rented jeep, off to Ocho Rios.

It's nearly twenty hours since we left St Barts but I've never felt more energized. I've always liked Jamaica and figured some day, Cathy and I would be settling in there. She perks up a bit when I come back from the first place we try with a set of keys to what I promise will be an even bigger and more beautiful villa than the one we had in St Barts. This one has skylights in each room, opening up the building to perpetual sunshine and bright light. I could do with less light, but I know how much Cathy craves it. There are ceiling fans in each room, as well as a mini gym in a small guesthouse on the edge of the property.

The pool is kidney-shaped, surrounded on all sides by tall, manicured shrubbery, so no reason to ever don a bathing suit here. Our furniture is fancier than in St Barts, sleeker and more modern. I knew my contact here, a realtor named Hélaîne who I'd met on previous visits here, would come through with something special. She was only too eager, as in the past, to take my money.

I've been thinking about Juan and hope he got plenty of money for giving me up. If I were still in the business, I wouldn't hesitate to work with that guy: he's smart, crooked and daring; also as loyal as he was able to be. Who knows, maybe someday our paths will cross again? I'm sure he understood there was no way I'd be sticking around the second I heard someone was looking for me but I can't help wondering who that someone is. I don't think it's a bounty hunter since I can't imagine he'd get involved with the local police. Of course it could be the FBI, who can print and spend as much money as they want. Up until now, they've been noticeably quiet about looking for me. Before I made the Most Wanted list, I doubt they actually were, but they might have stepped up their campaign now.

All in all, it makes me a little edgy, a little more cautious. Since I'm not in contact with anyone back home, I'm not concerned with anyone there giving me up. Of course it could be someone who wants revenge and is willing to pay big bucks for it: someone with means, like one particular victim who was a businessman and whose family is worth hundreds of millions. Or even one of my former associates who figures he knows more than he does. All I know for sure is that someone's looking hard for me and it'll make life extremely interesting from here on.

For now, though, I need to concentrate on looking carefully over my shoulder and making sure Cathy is happy. Whoever the person is who tracked me to St Barts ought to be careful looking over his own shoulder. When I find out who he is, and I will, I'll be sure to take care of him well before he takes care of me. It'll be the perfect opportunity to prove just how good I can be at what I do best. After all, murder – well planned, slow and excruciating – is my specialty. As I walk through the rooms of our new Jamaican residence, I'm feeling pretty good, better than I have in months. Nothing like a little challenge to wake me up and get the old adrenaline going, nothing at all.

Chapter 23
Cathy, Ocho Rios

Jimmy was absolutely right when he said Ocho Rios is the prettiest resort town in all of Jamaica and I'm loving its natural beauty, especially the stunning waterfalls and exquisite beaches. Everywhere I drive or even walk, I run into another dazzling waterfall: azure-blue water races wildly over walls of stones, leading to another sandy-white beach that stretches endlessly across the horizon. At his suggestion, I've been quite active since we got here and I go horseback riding a couple of times a week. I take long walks, too, and I love to head over to the Dunn's River Falls and watch the tourists disembark from the huge cruise ships and walk up and down the Falls. Some use a guide, holding hands as they climb, and others simply head up by themselves. All ages, all types ... I can't stop staring at them all.

Mostly, I just want to look at these normal people, of different nationalities, and try and imagine what their lives must be like. Do they have families at home who are missing them? Maybe they have children ... Do they have dogs, illnesses, jobs or diseases? Are they newly-weds or old-time married folk? Have they ever committed a crime? Are they happy with their lot? What do they dream about? And what do they think when they look at me? I could stare at them for hours. Occasionally, I talk to some of them, but never for long. It's fun to have a normal conversation with a stranger who has no idea that my face is on an FBI 'Most Wanted' poster.

One day I thought about following a couple back to their bus and just walking onto the cruise ship and seeing how far I could get. I'm sure they have lots of security, but maybe I could have gotten onto the ship and leaned against the railing and watched the shore fade into the background as I headed out to sea. What a feeling that would be. Of course it's insane to imagine I could ever do such a thing but the thought of it makes me light-headed. It's best, I know, not to think about it at all: I made my choices, just the way they all did. Besides I'm living in a gorgeous villa with everything I could possibly want at my fingertips. Not bad for a little girl from South Boston.

Even though he's not sleeping well, Jimmy's loving it here, like he's lived here all his life. A couple of times he's taken me over to Montego Bay and Negril. I'm not so sure it's safe to be riding around this island, but he says we're okay on the routes he picks out for us. He's also rented a boat and done some deep-sea fishing with a guy he met down at the marina. I'd like to make a friend myself but after the scare at St Barts, I don't know how comfortable I'd feel starting a new friendship. Jimmy has no problem striking up a conversation with a stranger and spending time with men he meets, but it's probably better that I keep busy by myself and just enjoy his company.

Anyhow, there's plenty for me to do here. Our villa's not too far from Pagee Beach and just a few miles from Ocho Rios. The best part is the seaside gazebo overlooking the ocean and a small but beautiful pool surrounded by all sorts of lush plants. Jimmy bought a book and we tried to identify them – neither of us had ever heard of some of them before. And I love the gorgeous outdoor dining veranda, with its huge barbecue pit attached to the villa. Our furniture's modern and brand new, too. I can't help but feel like a princess when I'm sitting by the pool, sipping an iced tea or a pina colada.

Still, despite the pool and horseback riding and walking to the Falls – I'm happiest at the beach – I can lie for hours, sunbathing and reading. Jimmy hates it when I tell him that I fall asleep, alone there, and makes a point of calling me on my cell phone every thirty minutes to be sure I'm awake.

And though he won't talk about it much with me, of course I understand someone's actively on our trail now. All he says is that lots of people have been there before and this latest one's just keeping him on his toes. Since the day I took off with him, I've trusted Jimmy with my life and I'm not about to start doubting him now. No matter what army was after him, Jimmy'd win every battle. As for me, I don't think I'd ever walk onto that ship even if it were, by some miracle, possible. But nearly every time I fall asleep on the beach, I dream about what it would be like to say goodbye to this life and head back home. When I open my eyes and see where I am, often I find tears running down my cheeks, but they don't last for long and that's a good thing.

Chapter 24
Whitey, Pagee Beach, Ocho Rios

It's a gorgeous day in Ocho Rios. Not that every day we've been here these past six months has been anything but gorgeous: blue skies, low humidity, gentle winds, long stretches of white sand beaches, who wouldn't enjoy this exquisite island? Cathy loves it. She's never happier than when she's lying on her stomach on a beach towel, engrossed in one of her novels. I swear she could stay in the one spot from the moment the sun rises until the last of the sunset disappears from the sky; she wouldn't even need to eat or drink a bottle of water.

It's different with me – I can't sit still like that, I have to get up and take a walk or a swim, or find someone to talk to. And there's always someone to talk to: some old-timer dying to share his stories with a stranger or a young mother watching her kid play nearby, who has no problem discussing her marital or financial woes with somebody she's never met before and most likely, will never meet again.

Cathy says I have the face that makes people want to talk and it's true all kinds of folk warm right up to me and rattle off details of their life they'd never share with anyone else. It could be because I enjoy listening to what people have to say. In another life, maybe I might have been a psychiatrist. Not that it would have been easy for me to sit in one chair all day while unhappy characters unload their pain. Still, who knows? Perhaps I could've saved some folk from taking their own lives rather than having my face plastered on a poster for taking at least eighteen lives.

Anyhow, it's a perfect day on Pagee Beach. Cathy's lost in her book and I'm walking on the edge of the shore when I see three native guys stop in front of her towel. We're in a pretty isolated part of the beach and there's no one else around.

'Hey,' the tallest of the three calls out to her. He's pretty jacked, like his two buddies, walking around like he owns the fucking beach.

Cathy moves her head to one side and says, 'Excuse me?'

'Hey,' he says again, while his two sidekicks offer stupid smirks. 'You looking for a native, honey?'

She turns over and stares at them, pushing herself up on one elbow, slowly tying her bikini top behind her neck and tugging at the bottom of the suit to make sure it's in place. She might be pushing fifty, but she's got the body of a twenty-five-year-old and the face that goes with it. 'You talking to me?' she asks, the annoyance in her voice evident to anybody with half a brain. This guy speaks good enough English, with just the right soft island lilt, to convince me he has that half. His skin is so black that it shines, his hair in dreadlocks and halfway down his back.

'Yeah, honey,' he answers, hungrily leaning down towards her. 'You down here to go native, baby?'

'Excuse me?' she asks again, looking and sounding disgusted.

Fuckface sits down on her towel, real close to her: 'I was just asking if you want …' But he doesn't get to finish his sentence because now I'm standing in front of him, separating him from his two friends. He stands back, initially surprized, but then he looks me over and says, 'Hey, old man, I'm not talking to you.' I don't move and he stands up real tall and says, 'Old man, I don't want to hurt you.'

'Let's take a little walk,' I tell him and he's all ready to do just that. His buddies think this is funny, especially when I tell them, 'Just me and this big guy here, okay?'

They shrug and take off, sure their boy can handle himself against the old fart. As we start to walk away, my new-found buddy turns back and yells to his two friends, 'I'll meet you back at the club after I take care of the old man. I might even let him watch me take care of his woman.'

Cathy shoots me a look that says, 'Be careful,' and I smile down at her. She turns back over onto her stomach and resumes her reading. Like I've said a thousand times before, this lady is smart.

Native boy and I walk around fifty yards when he stops to face me, getting ready to level a punch at my abdomen. There's no one else around so I take care of him real quick: I've got the ice pick out of the pocket of my swimming trunks and into his throat before his fist reaches my chest. He's down in flash, making a tiny gurgling sound at the back of his throat, knees curled into the foetal position before he fades off into oblivion. It's so easy, it's almost pathetic. I stare at him, crumpled up, his big, shiny-black body leaking only the smallest trickle of blood onto the white sand. When I look around there's no one nearby, just miles and miles of beautiful sand and turquoise ocean. Grabbing him by the arms, I can easily push the body into a nearby clump of trees and cover the small slivers of blood with fresh sand.

When I get back to Cathy, she's standing up, her long T-shirt flowing to her knees, our towels neatly folded over one arm, her books, suntan lotion and water packed in an over-the-shoulder beach bag. Five minutes later, we're off the beach, driving towards our little villa in the jeep. She knows the routine as well as I do: Jamaica's been nice but it's time to move on.

An hour later, we're leaving the villa with our suitcases in the trunk of the jeep.

'What do you think about Rio de Janeiro?' I ask and she smiles. 'We might just be able to get there in time for Carnival.'

'Sounds perfect to me, old man,' she says, snuggling up close as I drive slowly and carefully to the airport.

Chapter 25
Cathy, Rio de Janeiro

I'm amazed how well I've adjusted to this new city. For a girl who never left Boston, I've become an incredible traveller. Then again, look who I'm travelling with: his plans are brilliantly thought-out, he knows before our plane landed at Antonio Carlos Tobin International Airport that we'll stay in a small but lovely hotel in Rio de Janeiro for a week while he finds us the perfect apartment. He wants to make sure we're settled well before Carnival begins, which he assures me I'll love. And that's exactly what he does.

Seven days after we enter Brazil (as Mr and Mrs John Berkley), we have a darling little apartment in Largo do Boticario, an old residential area populated with other Americans who speak as little Spanish as us, yet we're still among the carefree Cariocas who inhabit this city. It's a noisy little enclave, with street vendors out early in the morning, selling fresh produce and trinkets. The noise continues through the day and gets even louder at night when small bands of musicians dressed in splendid colours and accompanied by scantily dressed singers (many of these large-breasted beauties topless) liven up the dark skies as they practise routines for the upcoming Carnival.

It's as if each merry group is trying desperately to outdo the one it follows in a parade of vibrant oranges, reds and golds. Exquisite curly-haired kids in multi-layered, bright coloured skirts, dancing freely beside the adults, faces painted to match their outfits, many of them wearing huge headdresses sprouting feathers, flowers and even wild animal shapes. Often we use ear plugs to try and sleep, or even when we're standing outside and watching the endless parade of breathtaking costumes.

After the gentle silence of St Barts and Ocho Rios, Jimmy seems to crave the noise and energy of this dynamic city. His sleep is still far from perfect but at least when he's unable to sleep or wakened by incessant nightmares, he'll find dazzling distractions in the street below our windows. So often I wake to see him standing on our enclosed balcony, swaying rhythmically to the music beneath him, delightedly clapping his hands.

Jimmy appears to have shed a good twenty years since we arrived here. Thanks to his daily exercize regime of calisthenics, including deep knee bends, crunches, push-ups, isometric exercizes and lifting weights for forty-five minutes, along with his excellent eating habits and our daily walking schedule, he's always managed to look a good twenty years younger than seventy. Yet now, here in Rio, I swear he could pass for a man of forty-five – and it's beginning to worry me a bit.

Women have always been attracted to Jimmy; they can't help it. Handsome and intelligent, he has a natural way of making every one of them – even those who are not attractive – feel special. But there's one particular woman, a waitress at the little restaurant near our apartment where we've been going every day for lunch, who might become a problem. Her name is Serafina and she's no more than twenty, a natural beauty and the worst kind. The type that has no awareness of her beauty so she never flaunts it, just wears it so unaffectedly that all those around her are drawn to it. And wouldn't you know it, the first day we arrived she appeared at our table, her shiny, thick black hair pulled back simply with a red ribbon at her long milky-white neck, her huge black eyes meeting Jimmy's blue ones as if they were already lovers. It sent shivers down my spine but I gave her my order and smiled. Young and innocent, she was totally unaware of the spell she was casting … on my man. On the man I love more than anyone else in the world. It wasn't going to be easy but I knew the best thing was to sit back and trust him, hoping I was wrong … and right.

And so I make sure every day, around three in the afternoon when Jimmy heads over for his egg sandwich and orange juice, I've left the gorgeous beach along the Copacabana stretch and returned to our apartment, sun-tanned, relaxed and ready to accompany him to the restaurant. He knows what I'm doing, but is too smart to mention it. I suspect he's visiting the restaurant other times as well, but I can't overdo my checking up on him.

What really bothers me is that I got a quick look at a list detailing his daily schedule that Jimmy recently made and read 'fix shoes', 'buy book on Truman', 'look for new wallet' and 'get flowers' on the small sheet of white paper. He's usually pretty secretive about the list, though he writes one religiously every day but for some reason he'd left this particular list in his pants pocket and I found it when I was doing the laundry. It had been written two days earlier and I'm certain that I didn't receive any flowers that day.

So, I make sure as often as possible that we greet Serafina together and exchange pleasantries through her broken English and our broken Spanish. I meet her eyes, my hand gently on Jimmy's, letting her know who I am to this man. It's not easy, but despite the language barrier, I get the message across – subtly and firmly, woman to woman – that I'm capable of far more than merely gently touching a hand, if necessary.

Chapter 26
Whitey, Rio de Janeiro

I've wanted to come to Rio for many years and I'm pleased to have finally made it. From the second we arrived, I realized, just as I'd long suspected, there's something magical about this city that energizes me like no other place. It is, among other things, a city of masks and the perfect place for someone like me to hide. We were here in time for Carnival, which pretty much overwhelmed me with the relentless energy and partying that was going on. And they didn't just dance through the streets, they surged through with superhuman energy – just watching them was a dizzying experience. Many nights I stood there, gazing at the endless parade, too mesmerized by the beauty and energy around me to do anything other than stand still, breathe and stare. About the only other parade I've ever seen is the South Boston annual St Patrick's Day parade. No way could you compare the two: Carnival is a blast of beauty, rhythm and energy I'd never imagined. Cathy's been pretty blown away by it all, too – I'm just glad I could give her such an experience. She deserves it.

And now that it's over, I have the feeling that we could stay here forever. Then again, one never knows what tomorrow will bring. I'm more than aware there's someone on my trail and I've spent a lot of hours trying to figure out what he might know about me and my time on the run. Last night, I was thinking about all those travel books I left behind in my Quincy house. Some of them certainly mentioned Rio, but there were plenty of others about places I never had any intention of visiting. Still, it's something I should keep in mind so I make no plans for the distant future. Instead, I keep my eyes wide open and my senses acutely aware of any possible danger. None of this bothers me.

If anything, the sense that someone with half a brain could be looking for me makes my adrenaline flow and every day more exciting.

And there's been another reason for my excitement: the attraction of a beautiful young girl, a waitress at the restaurant where I eat every day. She's a good fifty years younger than me but I can see in her eyes that this age difference means as little to her as it does to me. It hasn't taken me long to win her interest. A $100 tip for our $10 lunch, a lingering touch as I hand her the money; questions about her family and despite my poor Spanish and her lousy English, she manages to understand and answer – she's there for the asking. She's from a very poor family and believes I'm a retired doctor: she's asked me a few health questions about her mother's asthma and thanks to medical journals like the *American Journal of Respiratory Diseases*, I have no trouble answering.

Of course, Cathy's too smart not to know what's going on. She's made it her business to be at my side every time I walk into the restaurant. Today, she's looking carefree and exceptionally pretty, wearing a bright yellow sundress that emphasizes her bronze suntan.

'How is your poor mother today?' she asks sympathetically as our beautiful little waitress fills the water glasses.

'Better,' says Serafina, her stunning black eyes fixed on Cathy as she struggles for the right words. 'Mucho better.'

'Is she using the nebulizer I gave you for her?' I ask, and she nods, her smile so enchanting and full of gratitude that I can't help but return it. It was no big deal for me to buy the nebulizer. Here, you can buy any kind of prescription drug or hospital supply over the counter. Sure has helped me get my blood pressure meds.

'Will she be well enough to go to Venezuela to see your uncle now?' Cathy asks and Serafina nods again, but her eyes remain on my face. I know this isn't good but there's nothing I can do about it. And the sweet feeling I'm getting just knowing I can have her feels too damned good. 'I hope the visit goes well,' Cathy concludes as we both notice the looks sent our way by impatient diners at nearby tables. We're monopolizing our lovely waitress, the favourite of all who come here to eat and stare. Cathy holds my hand tightly as Serafina, smiling forlornly at me now, clutches her pitcher of water tightly to her magnificently full chest and walks slowly away from our table.

Now it's late at night and Cathy's sound asleep while I lie beside her, unable to nod off. Already I've spent a few hours watching the wild dancers in the street, but things are eerily quiet now and I know if I fall asleep, it will not be good. The throbbing pain in my head grows stronger with each passing minute.

So I lie still in the bed, trying not to think of her, but of course that's impossible. There's nothing like the touch of young skin and I want it so badly that I can practically feel it at this moment. Serafina's beauty overwhelms me every time I see her, as does my desire to fuck her. Even though Cathy believes she's always with me when I see the girl, I've managed to get to the restaurant alone on more than a few occasions. And on each of these visits, I can see how willing the girl is – and how vulnerable.

Still, her vulnerability is not what's preventing me from having my way with her. It's Cathy who holds me back. Her loyalty, her devotion, how could I discard that for a fling with a young girl? It would crush her to know that I did that: she's no dummy and she's seen the way I act around this girl. No man still breathing wouldn't want to fuck the little beauty. The smart thing would be to stop going to the restaurant, but I'm not that smart. I'll continue to see her and enjoy her beauty, I just won't bite into the forbidden fruit. This time, anyhow. Finally, as images of Serafina fill my head, I'm able to drift off into a dreamless sleep.

Chapter 27
Cathy & Serafina, Rio de Janeiro

I know what's going on, I'm not stupid, and it's getting worse. He thinks I have no idea he's seeing the little waitress when I'm not around, but of course I know. Does he really think I'm *that* stupid? I see the way she looks at him and the way he touches her hand longer than necessary. What I don't know is if he's already slept with her. If he hasn't, he will – and very soon.

Not that it's the first time this has happened. For heaven's sake, I shared him with Terry for all those years and she never even knew until I told her. What a scene it was when I practically dragged the woman to our condo and showed her exactly where Jimmy spent the nights when he wasn't with her. I thought Jimmy would kill me when he walked in and saw the two of us together in the living room, but he didn't. He didn't give either one of us up either. And I can't forget she was the one, not me, who he first took off with. Then there were all those young girls in Southie, no more than eighteen or nineteen, he fooled around with them but I could handle all that when we were home. Away like this, I can't stand the thought of him cheating on me. I keep asking myself why I gave up everything I had to follow a man who'll treat me like this and it's beginning to drive me out of my mind, a little more each day.

Last night, he was up with his nightmares all night long, shivering in the warm night air as if his temperature was 104. There was nothing I could do but lie there and watch him suffer. To be honest, I didn't feel badly for him. All I kept thinking was, if she could only see you now – that would rip the lust out of her beautiful big black eyes for good. It was terrible and I'm ashamed of myself today, but there's no way I can stop thinking about him holding this exquisite young girl, touching her body and wanting her so much more than he wants me. I want to run away, I want to kill her, I want to kill *him*, I want to be home with my mother and sisters. I don't know what I want ...

Chapter 28
Joey & Murphy, Boston

I don't care what anyone says: I'm convinced Joey managed to get a message to Jimmy that we were on his tail, both in St Barts and then in Costa Rica, where I was certain he'd fled. Just the way he told Whitey that he was about to be indicted back in Boston, the day Whitey took off and never turned back. I only wish I could have murdered that asshole in the hotel room in the Papagayao area of Costa Rica, to where I'm convinced Cathy and Jimmy headed from St Barts. You can't tell me the crumpled-up brochure for the hotel that I found in a trashcan at a beach near their villa meant nothing.

'Jimmy would never leave behind such a clue,' Joey insisted, but of course I ignored him. And when we finally got to Costa Rica, once again his pal Jimmy was long gone. Is it just coincidence that he manages to disappear? I stayed there for two weeks and gave it my all: covering every inch of beach in Papagayao, showing Whitey's photo to anyone we could find. When Joey complained about the heat, I suggested he go back to prison and the piece of shit says, 'Could I, please?' – like it's a joke, like I wouldn't give anything to grant his request.

When the call finally came from Boston, he told Rogers he'd seriously considered escaping to the border of Nicaragua and begging the Sandanistas to let him join their forces. I could hear Rogers laughing his fat head off at that – glad they're having such a good time at my expense. While we packed for our trip, I told Joey that I was vacillating between wanting to send him back to jail and trying to get him to fight me in another ring. He practically begged me to put on the gloves again, but every time I decided we'd do it, something came up.

The first thing I do when we get back to Boston is to set up a meeting with Rogers and Berman. They're both sitting in the conference room when I get there, looking no happier than I feel.

It wasn't easy to convince them that Joey shouldn't be a part of this meeting.

'Where's Joey?' is the first thing that Berman asks me.

'I left him back at my apartment,' I say, and he rolls his eyes.

'Hope he doesn't pick up some strange disease there,' is his reply and it doesn't sound as if he's making a joke. 'The one time I was there, I was sure you'd had a robbery but you told me that was the way it always looked. It's about the last place you should bring a guest to.'

'In case you forgot, Joey Donahue is not a guest,' I tell him. 'He's a criminal who should be behind bars – and if I have my way, he'll be there soon enough.'

'We figured you might try and blame the St Barts fiasco on him,' my good friend Rogers says, 'not to mention your two-week happy holiday in Costa Rica, paid for with taxpayers' bucks. Don't waste your breath: Costa Rica was your idea and a goddamn dumb one, too. But every tip Joey's given you has worked out so far. Whitey's only one step ahead of you, he's just smarter.'

'Ever wonder why he's one step ahead?' I ask. 'You don't have to be a rocket scientist to realize Joey's feeding him information, just the way he always did. I've had it with that bum! It's time to lock him up. I'll have a much better chance of getting to Whitey without that criminal working behind my back.'

'Forget it,' Berman tells me. 'Accept the fact that he's the only road we have that leads to Bulger. Just stop complaining and get to work and find him! Spend a few weeks here going over everything you can find and then we want you two back on the road again – and this time, you're not coming back until you find him. Take these with you,' he adds, as I start to leave, handing me a folder with some newspaper clippings inside. 'Just so you know all the nice things our little friend from the *Herald* is saying about us these days.'

After I walk out of the office and see Joey lounging in a chair, pretending he's all involved in a magazine, I know he's managed to hear every word of that conversation.

'Get your ass out of here!' I tell him and head for the elevator. When he takes his sweet time getting there, I close the door in his face and ride down to the lobby. Naturally, he's standing there when the door opens, leaning casually against it, acting like he hasn't just raced down twelve flights of stairs to beat me. It's just the thought of walking him back to a cell once this whole scene is over that helps me swallow my fury.

That night, after Joey's gone to sleep, I open the folder that Berman gave me and find three pathetic newspaper columns.

WHERE'S WHITEY? BY CARL HOWARD
SPECIAL TO THE BOSTON HERALD

Now, that's a shocker. Our local little hood, Whitey Bulger, on the FBI Most Wanted list. Who would have ever thought? With all the real bad guys they have to catch, they're now adding our homegrown gangster to the big list. Right next to Osama bin Laden and Robert Rudolph. Yup, he ranks up there with the guys who blew up the World Trade Center and abortion clinics. It's been a whole four years since he took off and now, finally, they've been able to complete the paperwork and get him on the big list, making him the 459th fugitive to have earned such a distinction. It has to make all of us proud just imagining all those blue jackets with their bright yellow FBI letters out there checking under the rocks and in the closets and on top of the roofs for our very own special Southie hero. Working night and day, leaving no stone unturned in their vigilant manhunt.

Nineteen murders, huh? You really think so, guys? I guess I was pretty dumb thinking all he did was sell a little pot and squeeze a few pockets here and there. You know, take care of the riff raff around town; keep Southie safe for the Southies. But if that's what the blue jackets say, that's what it is. I don't know about you, but I'm sleeping so

122

much better at night knowing we're safe from the likes of Whitey Bulger, knowing it will be just a matter of days till his smiling face is removed from the poster in my post office and all the federal buildings and placed securely behind bars. And I will sleep even sounder when his faithful little sidekick, Cute Cathy, is off the streets too.

Actually, I've got a pretty good idea where he is and I'll share it with you. Personally, I don't need the million dollars since I make so much right here at the *Herald*. Good luck to the first of you who packs up your trusty Swiss army knife and goes after him. So here's the real scoop: Whitey's holed up in the plush bedroom in the home of the FBI director, lying in his bed, waiting patiently for his best friend to come home after a real hard day's work.

I grit my teeth while reading the article: it's the kind of crap being spoon-fed to the people of Boston. They all think the FBI agents here are completely incompetent. Well, we'll see about that. I turn to the next piece.

WHERE'S WHITEY? BY CARL HOWARD
SPECIAL TO THE BOSTON HERALD

What a surprize. The FBI posts a sighting near Hilton Head. Oh yeah, that's our guy, hanging around some shrimp boats, getting himself all soiled with nets and bait. With Cutie Pie Cathy right beside him, pulling in the shrimp, her blonde hair blowing in the humid breeze. Almost as good a sighting as the one a few months ago in L.A., where Cathy was spotted heading out of a beauty parlor, the formula for those springy little blonde curls tightly clenched in her delicate little palm. No doubt our Boston FBI is working its tail off chasing this Dynamic Duo. They want them so bad it hurts.

After all, Whitey doublecrossed them. They had a deal. He gave up the Italian mafia and they let him kill anyone he wanted, players, women, whatever struck his fancy. But then what does the ungrateful little gangster do? Thanks to the big mouth of their former favorite son, Zip Connolly, he takes off without even saying goodbye. And leaves Stevie and Joey, the two members of his terrific trio behind too, both behind bars while he's skipping around free as a bird. Kind of makes you think a little, doesn't it? The intrepid blue jackets with the bright yellow letters on their backs catch these two with no problem, but the big kahuna, the one with all the brains and the most blood on his pants and the most stories to tell, the one that just might tell some tales our men of the law might not want repeated, takes to the wind like a jolly old kite.

Smell something rotten in Southie? Oh yeah, you'd have to be brain dead not to see the message: If Whitey walks, he won't talk. Makes perfect sense. No surprize at all.

I never realized what a hard-on Howard had for the Feds – I always read the *Globe*, or *The New York Times*, even *USA Today*, but not this tabloid rag. I'm beginning to get the picture that there's a lot of heat on the Boston office and it isn't all coming from DC. I flip to the final piece.

WHERE'S WHITEY? BY CARL HOWARD
SPECIAL TO THE BOSTON HERALD

This morning, I just happened to stop by the office of our local FBI, otherwise known as the FIB office, where a word of truth hasn't been spoken in so long they wouldn't have the slightest idea how to deal with it. I was hoping to just check in with them, you know, see how their massive search for our local bad boy Whitey was going. After all, a million dollars is resting on this guy's white head. Figured they'd probably be too busy to see me, but thought it was worth a try.

Sure enuf, they were busy all right. Busy sipping coffee, eating donuts and throwing darts at the likeness of Osama bin Laden. Guess they figured since he was taller than Whitey, they'd have a better chance of picking up the guy on the number one spot easier than they could grab the number two guy. I've got to give them credit, though. They did look up when I came in. And offered me a Krispy Kreme, which they must have imported from the D.C. Bureau.

"How's it going on the Whitey search?" I asked as I sat down and began to munch on my donut.

"Whitey?" one of them asked, looking real confused. Would love to tell you his name but his name tag was hidden by his expensive blue jacket. It was a hot summer day but those guys just never take off those blue jackets. Kind of like firemen ready to jump into their boots, the second the alarm rings. These guys are even more prepared than the men in red.

"You know," I said, "the guy on your poster, right next to Osama over there."

"Oh yeah," he said, shaking his head confidently now. "Thought we had him yesterday." The other jackets all nodded, one even put down his donut and coffee so he could nod even better than the rest of the crew. "Got a hot tip that he was in Newport, on a sailboat in the middle of the Halifax Race. We got out there within fifteen minutes of the call, but the wind died and we couldn't move. He must have had a power/sail because he was out of there before we made it to the first buoy."

"Wow," I said, helping myself to another Krispy Kreme. "That sucks! What was the name of your boat, anyhow?"

"*Kryptonite,*" he answered.

I nodded. "That explains it," I said. "Not much you can do when you're dealing with Superman."

125

When I'm through, I tear up the miserable pieces of shit and hurl them in my bedroom wastepaper basket. That little motherfucker Howard really wants to bust our balls, just the ammunition Berman needs to make sure it's *my* balls being busted.

For the next three weeks Joey and I are stuck in my apartment, which I admit is in a crappy area of Roxbury, in a six-floor building that needs a paint job, an elevator that works, furniture in the lobby, clean carpeting in the halls and a complete change of resident.

'When I moved in here ten years ago,' I tell him, the first time we walk in, 'I figured I'd stay a year and then find a nicer place but I'm so busy I'm never here, so why bother?'

''Cause it's a fleabag,' he says. 'Shouldn't such a respected member of the FBI live in a decent joint?'

'Why should anyone care where I live?' I ask. 'Besides, none of my associates ever come over.'

'You mean you don't all hang out together every weekend?' he asks.

I give him a dirty look. 'You can sleep on the couch,' I tell him, tossing yellowed newspapers and books off the ratty-looking, brown wool couch. 'I imagine it's better than a jail cell.'

'Not much,' he says, glancing at a framed photograph amid the mess on the table next to the couch. I've got my arm around Mia, she's a stunning brunette and I look a whole lot better and younger. We're wearing bright island clothes and standing on a beach in Virgin Gorda – that was the first day of our honeymoon, the only day we took any pictures together.

I grab it before he can study it any further. 'That's Mia, ex-wife,' I say, slipping the photo into a drawer in the table. 'Any time you're ready to stop sightseeing and get to work, let me know.'

During the next three weeks we're at the FBI building each day, working with Rogers and Berman to pore over any minute detail of Jimmy's life that might offer some hint of his whereabouts. At night, the two of us return to my apartment, where Joey infuriates me by trying to clean up the joint. One night, he asks why my marriage fell apart. 'She didn't like my snoring,'

I tell him and he nods. He looks at me like I'm going to say more but I just turn off the light and tell him I've had enough for one day.

What was I going to tell him? That she never loved me, that she went back to the guy she was going to marry in the first place, that I was just a mistake in her life, that I have no idea why I loved her for such a long time after the divorce. I know a good-looking guy like Joey would never understand what I went through but his love life will be ending soon and the only connections he's going to have to his Jeannie will be in a prison visiting room.

Chapter 29
Joey, Jeannie's Place, Boston

On one of the few weekend nights when Murphy gives me a temporary reprieve and allows me to sleep at my own place, I mention the photo to Jeannie (I hadn't told Rosie anything about my situation, except that I had a job which would require me to do some extensive travelling). I'm grateful to Miller and Berman for giving me enough money to pay my rent and Rosie's, but Jeannie knows everything.

'He must still love her,' she tells me. 'Why else would he keep her photo there?'

'Hard to believe,' I say. 'He never makes or gets any personal calls – the guy's like a monk.'

'Not Mr Social Life, like you, huh?' she smiles and I've no choice but to fuck her so completely she'll remember why I'm worth all the shit I bring along with me.

It's later that night when we're lying in Jeannie's bed, watching some dumb movie on television, that she hands me the answer I've been looking for. 'I bet he's in Brazil,' she says, as we watch a Carnival scene. The heroine's darting through a crowd of wildly dancing, exotically costumed party-goers, desperately trying to avoid her pursuer, who's dressed like a ten-foot chicken with a terrifying red beak and throngs of bright orange feathers on his back. 'Remember how he kept talking about Carnival that night you and I went out for dinner with him and Cathy? And Carnival is always the week after Fat Tuesday – that's next week. I wouldn't be at all surprised if that's where he was.'

I nearly fall off the bed. This woman's incredible and she's right; Jimmy had gone on and on about this Carnival thing all night long, he was talking about it for days afterwards. He made plans to go but we ended up doing a big score the week he planned, so there was no way that he could drop it and head out of town. But now that he's free to go wherever he wants, it just makes sense that Buenos Aires would be a strong possibility. That night, I sleep beautifully in Jeannie's bed.

The next morning, when I tell Murphy what I'm thinking, he's surprizingly agreeable.

'I found Brazil marked on three separate travel books,' he tells me, already acting like it's his idea to go there. 'On the Fromers, the pages are all turned down on Rio. It seems to be a special favourite, even though Brazil's not on his passport. So you agree this could be the place, huh?'

'I know he likes quiet places,' I say, still surprized we're having this rare, normal conversation. 'But he had plenty of that in St Barts, so he's probably ready for some excitement. I even remember some VHS tapes he bought about Rio. It's a shot in the dark but not a bad one, the more I think about it.'

'It wouldn't hurt to focus on Rio in case he goes there in the future,' he continues. 'We'll head out there the end of this week. I'll have all our arrangements made today.'

I'm not anxious to leave Boston, with Rosie and Lucy and Jeannie, and head off on this mission but I figure it's time to try and wrap the whole thing up, one way or the other. Nothing's worse than spending any more time in Murphy's crappy pad except, of course, a lifetime in a jail cell. 'Great,' I say.

'I'm thinking maybe we could spend some money to get his photo and the reward information in newspapers in Rio,' he says as he picks up the phone to call the Bureau, starting to fill with the same manic energy he had in St Barts. 'I'll set up an 800 Boston phone number which we'll use in the ad. It wouldn't be so bad for him to know someone's after him, don't you think?'

I can't help but agree. 'He loves the idea of the chase,' I admit, still finding it hard to believe that this time it will be me on the other side of the fence, looking to do him in instead of joining forces to grab whatever bastard he's after, 'and the newspaper ad can't hurt.'

But he's not listening to me: already he's the bloodhound, picking up the scent of the hunted animal. Rio de Janeiro, here we come, ready or not!

Chapter 30
Whitey & Serafina, Rio de Janeiro

It's a little after noon and I've just finished reading the *International New York Times* when I pick up the local newspaper, *Gazeta do Rio*, that I've been using to practise my Spanish and there it is, right on the front page: a good-sized photo of Cathy and me walking the beach in South Boston. It's not the photo of me on the Most Wanted poster; this one puts the two of us together and makes Cathy pretty recognizable. I take a long minute to make sure I'm thinking clearly. No doubt the person who orchestrated the St Barts scene has somehow tracked me to Rio. Good for him. Maybe it was the travel brochures back in Southie that sent him here or perhaps he placed this same advertisement in other newspapers around the world. But I've got to hand it to him: it's a good photo, with an interesting write-up on the two of us and our habits. Someone smart enough might make the connection. But none of that matters: what matters is I need to get out of Rio fast.

Not that it's such a bad idea anyhow. Things have been getting out of hand with Serafina. So far I've held myself back, but I know it's only going to get harder as the weeks roll on. Cathy's been acting as if I've already fucked the girl, which pisses me off since it's only out of respect for her that I haven't. Even if I hadn't seen the photo, the two of us need to leave Rio.

I'm certain the only trail I could possibly leave after six months here is my connection to Serafina and the restaurant. She's talked to me about her family and how poor they are, about her uncle in Caracas, who wants her mother to come visit before he dies. I'd thought for a while that I'd like to see Venezuela, but I wouldn't risk that trip now. Other than Serafina, Cathy and I have kept pretty much to ourselves and left no other sources here who might provide hints of our travelling habits.

It's no big deal to take off today. Cathy's due back from the beach in an hour, determined as always to accompany me to the restaurant. But we won't be going there today: we'll be heading for the airport and a flight to Rome. Anyhow I've had enough of South America, it's time to lose ourselves in the Eternal City. Cathy will love the art and the churches, never mind the leather. And I'm ready for some excellent pasta. Good luck, whoever you are out there. I've got to give it to you, Mr Sleuth, you've flushed me out of two holes but that's about it for you. Now it's time for me to get serious and turn things around. Stalking you should be a whole lot more fun than having you stalk me – and I can't think of a better place to ensnare you than the labyrinths of Rome.

But first I'm thinking I'll throw down some crumbs to liven up the chase and make things a lot more interesting for both of us. Just enough to give Sherlock Holmes some idea where I am, to build up his confidence and let him think I'm slipping, getting careless. After all, I've always been the hunter and this idea of someone hunting me is intriguing. It's time to make the trail a little more visible so I can begin to build a serious trap for my wannabe secret agent.

After I pack my few belongings into an over-the-shoulder carry bag, I take a piece of paper and scribble the word 'Alitalia' on it, along with a telephone number. Then I light a match and burn away most of the paper to leave the letters 'Alit' on the sheet. Just before I throw the scorched paper down the toilet, I give him an extra bonus: the letters ROM. How lucky can he get?

I take another look at the newspaper before I burn it and toss the charred remains in the toilet, too. 'Nice try, whoever you are out there,' I say, as I see the letters bobbing along, unscathed by fire or water. 'It's good you're getting some idea of what I look like … because the next time you see that face is gonna be the last time you see anything at all!'

Chapter 31
Joey, Rio de Janeiro

It's remarkably easy to convince the Bureau we should head to Rio. I think if we told them we should go to Alaska, they'd just ask when ... and make all the arrangements. One could get used to this kind of VIP treatment. Within four hours of our phone call, they have Murphy and me on a series of planes heading out to Brazil. It's amazing when you think how little they accomplished during the years that Jimmy's been on the run. When I mention to Murphy on the plane that they seem to shine as a travel agency, he takes offence.

'Everything involves a ton of paperwork,' he tells me and I have to hold myself back from saying, 'You should know since that's all you've ever done there.'

'Believe me, they don't take spending taxpayers' money that easy,' he insists. 'You're lucky I convinced them to let you come with me this time.'

'Oh, really,' I say, 'like, you were ready to do this part by yourself? 'Cause you could go with my blessings. I'd be perfectly happy to stay in Boston and let you go after Jimmy, all by yourself.'

He gives me a withering look. 'You're lucky we're in the air,' he mutters. Lucky me just closes my eyes and doesn't say another word until we land in Rio.

By the time we get to Rio, Carnival is over, and probably a good thing. The city seems exhausted from the energy spent in the last week but it's still filled with a feverish spirit that makes you feel as if you have to let down your defences and have a good time. Even Murphy smiles a few times as we roam the streets and are greeted by revellers who don't seem to have noticed Carnival is over.

Four days later, like clockwork we have our first lead and an excellent one, too. Someone calls the Boston number to report that he thinks he saw a man and a woman who might look like the couple in the newspaper in a small restaurant in Rio. Within two hours of receiving the lead, Murphy and I meet with the caller in a park near the restaurant. As always, Murphy comes out swinging, practically accusing the poor guy of harbouring a criminal within five minutes of our meeting. Luckily Jorge, who speaks excellent English, is not easily intimidated and states his point simply and without hesitation. A student at the Coppead Graduate School of Business at the Federal University of Rio de Janeiro, he's a nice-looking kid in his late twenties who frequents this restaurant nearly every day before classes.

'So the man you've seen in the restaurant looks exactly like the one in this photo?' Murphy asks, practically shoving the picture of Jimmy in Jorge's face.

Jorge looks at the picture and shakes his head approvingly. 'He looks a lot like the man I see at the restaurant,' he tells us. 'Except the man I see looks a little younger and he has a goatee and always wears a wide-brimmed straw hat.'

For the first time Murphy looks at me and I nod: 'Makes sense to me,' I say. 'Jimmy could easily have a goatee and wear a straw hat and look younger than the photo.'

'And what about the woman?' Murphy continues, showing Jorge a different photo of Cathy.

He studies it carefully. 'The woman I see with this man also looks younger than this woman,' he says. 'And her hair is red, not blonde. She looks prettier than in this picture: she is always smiling and says hello. She sits very close to the man and sometimes holds his hand.'

'So what exactly have you heard the man say?' Murphy asks.

'He seemed very friendly too,' Jorge says, 'but mostly he talked to the very pretty waitress, Serafina. Everyone flirts with her, but I could see that this man was quite smitten. And so was Serafina, I've never known her to act so brazen. The strange thing was that the woman with the man always acted so nice to Serafina. I guess that's why I noticed them so much.'

I'm beginning to get the same hazy feeling that I got when I spoke to Juan in St Barts: I want it to be Jimmy, I don't want it to

133

be Jimmy but I'm sure I want it to be over. 'And when did you last see the man?' I ask, not allowing my voice to betray any nervousness at his answer, when Murphy takes a break from his inane questioning.

'Five days ago,' says Jorge, far more relaxed with me than with the Grand Inquisitor, 'last Monday. He was still there when I left around five.'

'And you haven't seen him since?' I ask, silently cursing our luck. Why hadn't I thought of this earlier? Will the insane race ever end?

'Afraid not, but with the Carnival it was hard to see anyone,' Jorge admits and I can tell by the look on his face that he's smart enough to know this sad fact may keep the reward money out of his hands. Still, there's the matter of the waitress: all may not be over. Without losing another moment, we follow Jorge to the restaurant.

It's a little after five in the afternoon when the three of us walk in and I see at once that the main attraction in the half-filled room is the pretty Serafina. Jorge, Murphy and I sit down at the table closest to her. I can't speak a word of Spanish, but Murphy has a surprizingly excellent command of the language and gets right to the point. 'I'm looking for a man who has come here before,' he begins to tell her when she comes to take our order.

'I can understand English,' she tells me and I nod appreciatively. I hand her the photo before she hands me the menu. Right away, I know when she looks at the photo that she has seen this couple and from the pained look on her face, I can tell she is most unhappy to learn that her friends could be bad people.

'Yes, that is the kind doctor Tom and his wife Mary,' she tells me. 'What have they done that is so wrong?'

'He's not a doctor,' I tell her as she slides wearily into the chair beside me. Murphy doesn't look happy that she's sitting next to me, but I don't give him a chance to say anything that might silence her. 'In America, he's a killer but he was my friend so I know he can seem like a nice man. The police need to find him before he hurts anyone else.' I point to Murphy. 'This man is a policeman, who wants to bring him back to America to stand trial and so do I.'

I've barely finished telling her my message when she begins to cry softly and I regret that I've upset her so quickly. There's no doubt this girl is a true beauty, as well as a gentle, warm person.

The man who looks like the owner of the restaurant glances over at us, obviously annoyed that Serafina has sat down. Probably anxious to earn what he hopes will be some of the reward money, Jorge gets up to talk to him while I continue to talk with the waitress. Murphy, for some reason, seems content to let me run on and I want to encourage this poor woman to calm down and give me some more information.

'I must find him fast,' I tell her, as she stares at me with huge black eyes brimming with tears. 'I know he can be very kind and I'm sure you did nothing wrong in talking to him, but I need to know anything you might have learned about him.'

No big surprize: Murphy can't stay silent for another second. Moving his chair closer to Serafina, he leans so close that the poor girl looks frightened. I reach out to lightly touch her arm and try to offer her a reassuring look, but he has her full attention.

'Now, we need some answers very quickly,' he says, as I remove my useless hand. 'Where he is staying in Rio? Where does he go during the day? Who has he talked to besides you? When was the last time you saw him? What did he tell you about his plans for when he leaves here? What was he wearing the last time you saw him? We promise to pay for whatever information you can offer.'

But Serafina is the first person I've met in the search for Whitey who's not affected by the promise of money. She takes her eyes off Murphy and stares miserably at her hands, shaking slightly in her lap. Before she utters one word, her boss – an ultra-skinny bald man with a gold cane and a flashy pin-striped suit – comes over to our table and whispers something in her ear. Even more sadly, she nods and stands up as he smiles at me. This man, I know right away, is not averse to receiving any cash that I might be handing out.

'I no seen him in six days,' she tells us miserably, in her broken but comprehensible English. 'I not know where he stays.'

Jorge returns to sit down at the table. Serafina's boss whispers something in his ear now and he nods.

'Did the man talk to you about your family in Venezuela?' Jorge asks her gently. 'Your uncle in Caracas?'

She offers him the sweetest of smiles and glances up at me with a look of resignation. 'Yes,' she states simply. 'We talk about that.'

'Do you think he's left Rio?' asks Murphy and she nods, her eyes focused again on her hands. 'Do you think he might have gone to Venezuela? Does he know where your uncle lives?'

'I not know where he went,' she repeats, staring at me now, and I can see she's telling the truth. 'He say he never been to Venezuela and we talk about Uncle and his small business in Caracas. I not tell him where Uncle live, he not ask. I not think I see him again.'

At this, she starts to sob quietly again and Murphy takes out some money and places it on the table. She does not touch it, but her boss and Jorge quickly pocket the cash that Murphy then offers them.

For a few more minutes, Murphy talks with her boss but gains no further information. Afterwards, we leave the restaurant with Serafina's final words ringing in my ears. I refuse to believe they are true for me, too: this is just another bump in the road, nothing more.

Murphy and I spend a few more days checking out all the apartments within five miles of the restaurant, or at least as many as we can, considering the vast number of high rises that fill the crowded space. After Serafina fails to turn up for work, Carlos (the owner of the restaurant) takes us to her house, saying it's unlike her not to show up and not to call him. The house is very small, no more than a shack. Her younger sister, who's probably about twelve, tells us that Serafina and her mother went to Caracas

136

the day before to visit the uncle. Obviously, she must have finally taken the money we left on the table and used that, along with what she managed to save from Jimmy's heavy tips, to take off with her mother.

The kid was very nervous around us, but I think she was telling the truth. There were two smaller ones there, two little boys, and the sister seemed to be in charge of them. It looked like a sad situation so I convinced Murphy to give her some money for no reason, really.

When Serafina's sister gives us the address of her uncle, Murphy and I discuss going to Caracas ourselves. 'Do you think he would leave Cathy and take off with that girl?' Murphy asks, as we arrive at yet another neighbourhood to show our photos to the managers of every building we enter.

'My gut feeling is no,' I tell him. 'He's too cautious to do that, and too loyal to Cathy. I can't imagine him ditching her just because of a young beauty: Cathy has proved her worth to Jimmy. You can't underestimate how clever the guy is – he's made no mistakes so far, I don't think he'd make one for Serafina. He might have planted the whole Caracas thing just to throw off anyone who comes looking for him.'

As always, whenever I offer an opinion about Jimmy, Murphy has to study my face as if he can tell by its expression if I'm telling the truth.

'Yeah,' he finally admits begrudgingly, 'you could be right.'

Later that day, when he checks in with the Boston office, I'm not surprized by what he tells them. 'From what we heard in St Barts, Jimmy's loyal to Cathy and treats her well,' he says. 'He wouldn't ditch her to run off with this little beauty. I'm beginning to think the whole Caracas thing is a smokescreen in case someone comes looking. You can't underestimate how smart this guy is.'

I shake my head, staring right at him while he talks. 'What clever ideas you come up with,' I tell him as he gets off the phone. 'It's easy to see why you've risen so far in the Bureau.'

He doesn't say a word, just heads into the bathroom. I'd love to see him emerge with two sets of boxing gloves, but of course I've no such luck.

I'm beginning to feel as if we'll never find another clue that Jimmy might still be in Rome when suddenly it's payday. At the Largo do Boticario, one of the places that Jorge suggests we check out, the manager is pretty sure he rented an apartment to a couple who look like the people in the newspaper photo that I show him. They were there for six months but he hasn't seen them in a week. Nor has he been in the apartment. He's not sure if they'll be returning but they paid – in cash, of course – for the rest of the month. I can feel my heart beating wildly again, just as it did in St Barts, but I hold myself together as Murphy asks to see the apartment. It takes a bit of cash but five minutes later, we're alone in the three-room apartment where Whitey Bulger and Cathy Green, I'm 100 per cent positive, lived up until one week ago.

No doubt they won't be coming back as there's not a piece of clothing or one personal possession remaining. The refrigerator holds a bottle of organic orange juice, several bottles of water and some cheeses, but that's it. It's when I walk into the bathroom that I nearly scream. There, floating in the toilet, are a few burned papers, one of which has the letters 'Alit' still visible. It doesn't take me long to construe these letters are part of Alitalia Airlines. And then I see it: tiny but legible, the letters ROM. How unlike Jimmy to be so careless, like he was when he left the marked-up travel brochures in his Southie condo. Obviously, I was wrong: the great escape artist is not perfect.

But somehow it's happened. Something has caused him to let down his guard on the run just long enough to leave a clue. Practically hopping around the bathroom with excitement, Murphy's so pleased with himself that he can't stand still. While he pats himself on the back for his incredible investigative skills, I ignore him and carefully remove the paper from the toilet, silently thanking Jimmy for using waterproof pen, and let it dry on the top of the sink. Meanwhile, Murphy's on the phone to the Bureau, telling them to check out the Alitalia schedules to Rome, as I calmly place the drying pieces of paper in my jacket pocket and follow him back to our hotel room to pack up. It's only when we're checking out that he frantically begins his search for the piece of paper. For a few minutes, I let him jump around in front of the confused desk clerk before I take the paper from my jacket pocket and hand it to him.

We're close, real close and if I had my way I'd grab a plane back to Boston and on my hands and knees, beg Berman to send someone else in for the final chase. But there's no such choice: I'm on my way to what I strongly believe will be the last chapter of my thirty-year story with Jimmy.

Chapter 32
Murphy, Rome

I know I'm drinking too much, but I can't help it – the delays have driven me crazy. No matter where we are – in the terminal, the lounge or on the plane – Joey just sits in his seat, closes his eyes and falls asleep; nothing bothers this guy. When the plane finally takes off for Rome, I'm so wired there's no way I can sleep and so I talk, like I've never talked before. I know I'm driving Joey crazy, but there's nothing he can do about it: the plane is full. He couldn't change his seat, even if I let him.

'I'm in the wrong line of work,' I tell him. We both know it's the booze talking, but he's listening: seems interested, and that keeps the words flowing. 'I've never shot a gun except on a range. I'm good enough to pass my annual test – that'll come in handy if I'm attacked by a paper target. You're good with a gun, aren't you?' I ask him. He nods. 'I read that about you in one of your records,' I continue and he nods again. I can tell he's still listening. 'Where the hell did you learn to shoot?' But he just shrugs and says, 'I practised a lot.'

'You know, you've had more freedom to live your life than I ever did, don't you?' I say to him, but he doesn't respond so I continue. 'Sure, you were away for more than six years and you may go away for more now, but that doesn't change the fact that your life has been a thousand times fuller than mine. You've done things I could never imagine. Yeah, crimes, but that's what you always wanted to do. I've got to hand it to you, you did it well – I'd say you scored a perfect hundred on that course. Well, a ninety-nine, anyway – you did get caught. All I've ever done is push papers around a desk. No one ever showed me a fraction of the respect you got everywhere you went.

'I went into the FBI all gung ho: to do the right thing for my country, to protect the people. I was going to be a success, to do important things with my life. But you know what? The chance to succeed never came – I didn't kiss the right asses, didn't have enough seniority, didn't follow the letter of the bureaucracy. I know my problem is my big mouth. I keep sticking my foot in it – telling the bosses off, turning off the other Boston agents. Ah shit, half of them were crooked anyway! But I made some stupid mistakes and it cost me. And that's all I'd have to show for my twenty years with the Bureau if this opportunity hadn't come my way. Joey, just between us, this is it for me: if this doesn't work out, buddy, I'm through.' He nods again, seems sympathetic. I notice he's emptying his glass and motioning the stewardess for another drink.

'Tell me what it was like,' I ask him and he looks at me like I'm a crazy drunk. *Am* I? Maybe I am. Even though my name's Murphy, I could never hold my liquor. He nods and takes the drink from the stewardess, downs it way too fast and then he talks. And I grasp every word like it's a rare jewel.

'It was just business,' he says, looking straight ahead, talking in a soft voice that I have to strain to hear, 'always just business.'

'What do you mean?' I ask.

'The extortions, the drug deals, the beatings, the murders,' he says, sounding different to how I've ever heard him, like he's not talking to the world's biggest pain in the ass, 'it was never personal. And I did it because ... because it was simple. I enjoyed the money. It was the only way I saw that I could get ahead and escape my surroundings. Let's face it, nobody wants to spend his life in the Projects.'

'So you made a pile of money and committed a lot of extortions?' I say, anxious to keep him going.

He stares into his empty glass. 'The funny thing is, sometimes it's your own friends who fuck you,' he says, his voice getting a little sloppy now.

'What do you mean?' I ask.

'It doesn't matter now, Murph, because I already pleaded out to it, but here's a good one for you ...' He leans back in his chair, the empty glass now on the tray. 'It had to do with this drug dealer we extorted – he had a big marijuana business, down the islands.'

'The Caribbean?'

'Nah, Nantucket and Martha's Vineyard – the guy was worth millions, was making millions.'

'*Nantucket*? I find that hard to believe in Martha's Vineyard.'

'Do you want to hear the fucking story or not?'

'Go ahead, go ahead … I'm sorry.'

'Anyway, we found out from a lawyer who had this guy as a client that the guy, let's call him Mike, was a big-time drug dealer: he moved a lot of marijuana. So we started finding out everything we could about him and in our research, we discover that he owned a business in downtown Boston. And it just so happens that a guy we know who bets through one of our bookmakers is a friend of Mike's so we devize a plan to set him up with our bookmaker 'cause he likes to bet on sports.

'We just bide our time and the first three weeks, Mike's losing. He's losing, and he keeps on sending over the money with the guy who introduced him to our bookmaker. And finally, he has a big week and he hits for almost $50,000. Now he decides it's time for him to go collect his money and meet this bookmaker. So, on a Thursday, Mike's friend brings him over to meet the bookmaker and when Mike walks into this social club in Roxbury, he strolls through the main door, all happy. And when he walks in through a second set of doors, Jimmy, Stevie and myself are waiting for him. Jimmy aims a pistol at his chest, a .22 with a silencer. I grab him and we bring him upstairs. It's like a big function hall, with this one chair in the middle of the bare floor; we sit him in the chair and Jimmy introduces the three of us to him.'

'What did this guy Mike do?' I ask, when he stops (the last thing I want is for him to stop talking).

But he goes right on: 'What everybody usually does. He starts shaking. This guy was out of his element – he's just a yuppie, wearing khaki pants, loafers, a polo shirt, with a pale blue sweater draped round his shoulders and tied in front of him – basic asshole yuppie. He says right off, "Forget about the bets, keep the money! I don't want the money."'

'Jimmy looks at him and says, "We're not interested in your bets, we're interested in your business." The guy says, "I've got a small travel business and I sell antiques on the side." But Jimmy says: "No, your marijuana business, your drug business." And the guy says, "I don't know what you're talking about, I'm not involved in drugs."

'With that, Jimmy fires the .22 into the ceiling, looks at him and says, "Do we look like assholes to you? You've been moving 1,600 pounds a week down Martha's Vineyard; you've been moving between 700 and 800 pounds every two weeks down Nantucket, so we know more than you think we do. You have two choices: one is pay us, and be with us while the other one is not to."

'And this fool actually looks back at Jimmy and says, "Well, I'd prefer to be on my own," like he has a choice in the matter – he thinks he's negotiating with one of his clients. Then Stevie steps in, and pulls him up and makes him stand on the chair; he starts to frisk him to see if he's wired. The whole time this is going on, I'm laughing – I just can't believe this guy's reaction, that he thinks he can tell us he's gonna be on his own and walk out of there. And then I start to get aggravated, and I walk up to him and I hit him as hard as I can in the solar plexis with my right hand. I can actually feel his ribs wrap round my fist; you can hear the air go out of him and he just tumbles to the floor. For a couple of minutes he's lying there and unable to breathe.

'Then Jimmy looks at me and says, "Hey, we don't want to kill him yet." Stevie picks him up off the floor and places him back on the chair. He walks over to the bar, gets a glass of water and hands it to him.'

I can tell by the way he's laughing that Joey actually enjoys remembering the whole scene all over again; it's like he's right back in that big empty room on the second floor of the social hall in Roxbury. Still laughing, he goes on.

'Then Bulger says, "Maybe you didn't understand me. Either you're gonna pay us and be with us, or I'm gonna kill you."'

His smile fades a little and I ask, 'So, what happened?'

'To make a long story short,' he says (and he's not laughing any longer), 'he ends up agreeing to pay us a million six. About a week later, I meet Jimmy and Stevie. We're walking along the beach and Jimmy tells me the score fell through, that the DEA got wind of it, so we just have to let it go. And he warns me, "If this guy ever comes round, you don't know him – you never met him before. He could be wired."'

'That doesn't sound like much of an extortion,' I tell him, disappointed by the ending.

'Here's the best part, Murph,' he continues, a small smile returning to his face. 'When I get indicted, I'm charged with that extortion and I find out they did get the money off him at the time. Stevie and Whitey decided they shouldn't give me all that cash at once – they wanted to keep me hungry to make more.'

'So, your friends fucked you over?'

'Yeah, but I didn't find out till years later. I wonder how many other things I got fucked out of.'

The thought of Joey being screwed by his partners fascinates me: even this guy, this master criminal, can be fucked over, it seems. There's still a long flight ahead of us and I'm dying to hear more.

'There must have been times when things went perfectly,' I persist.

'That's enough for now,' he tells me firmly as he calls the stewardess over once more. 'I need another drink.'

Chapter 33
Murphy, Il Piccolo

The minute we enter Il Piccolo, the small hotel not too far from the Spanish steps that the Bureau has chosen for us, I'm told to call my office, *direttamente*. Rogers answers the phone in Boston and for the first time since I've known the guy, he sounds happy to hear my voice.

'We've been trying to reach you since your flight left Boston,' he tells me. 'Why isn't your cell working now that you're off the plane?'

I glance at my phone and sure enough, I forgot to turn it on when we landed in Rome, so I click it on now.

'It's been giving me some trouble,' I lie. The last thing I need is for Rogers to have another reason to dis me to the Bureau. 'So, what's up?'

'The Rome police have arrested a couple that they believe to be Whitey and Cathy ...'

I can't believe what I'm hearing. 'I'll be right over there,' I tell him, flinging my suitcase onto the marble floor with a loud thud, probably smashing the new bottle of the Givenchy cologne that I picked up in Rio. I hang up the phone and turn to Joey. Once again, he's staring at me like I've lost my mind. 'Drop your stuff here,' I order him. 'They've got Whitey and Cathy – they're at the police station! Go grab us a taxi.'

'Whoa!' he says in that irritatingly slow, calm voice that makes me want to rip the words from his throat. 'There have to be dozens of police stations in this city. Any idea which one you want us to go to?'

At that moment my cell rings. 'Curious as to where the hell you're going?' Rogers asks. 'Or you planning to jog to every police station in Rome?' At this I say nothing, refusing to look at Joey, who I know has a disgusting smirk on his face. 'Get a pen and write this down. Ready? Got to Polizia del Stato – that's the

Rome cops – the station at Piazza de Collegio Romano, 3, near Piazza Venezia. Maybe that will help.'

I hang up and shove Joey back out the front entrance of the hotel. The concierge is taking his sweet time getting us a cab until I pull out my FBI badge. I'm feeling pretty good about that one successful feat until I see the guy smile at Joey, who nods and puts his hand back in his pocket. Yeah, I should have thought of it: money, the universal lubricant.

'I can't wait to put my cuffs on Whitey,' I tell Joey, as we settle into the back of the taxi, but he barely glances at me. I'm sure he's wishing this hadn't happened – he never wanted to find his old buddy in the first place. Hell, this isn't the way I'd hoped it would end up either, but at least I'll be the one to accompany the mobster back to the US and I'll be the first American to cuff him. 'I can't wait to put my cuffs on him,' I repeat, probably more times than I should, but I can't help myself.

At the door we're met by an overly polite guy with a red moustache that's the size and shape of a giant paintbrush; a weird looking guy, for sure, sort of like Super Mario's demented cousin. Right away, I can tell he's a *carabiniere*, the national police force that I noticed all over the airport, submachine guns slung across their chests. He's wearing their flashy black uniform with the trademark white diagonal leather sash and a huge gold motif on his hat. I read somewhere that Armani designed the uniform: if he's trying to impress or frighten me, he's getting nowhere.

But he speaks perfect English and after we do all the introductions and the handshakes, Second Class Warrant Officer Luciano Molinieri of the Carabinieri Special Operations Unit dealing with organized crime tells me, with the respect he knows I deserve as his American counterpart: 'We've been interrogating the man and woman for four hours. Up until now they've refused to admit who they are, but in the past hour they're beginning to cave in. We've had much difficulty getting their fingerprints to check against the database with Interpol and with your Federal Investigation Bureau.' Joey sniggers at this because the screwed-up acronym spells FIB, not FBI. 'With your permission, sir, we'd

146

like to continue to interrogate them until we get their full confessions. We're also expecting the results of the fingerprint match momentarily.'

But I practically knock the guy down in my attempt to push past him; like I'm really going to let him continue with his dumbass interrogation. I just hope he hasn't compromised their rights.

'Absolutely not,' I tell him. 'Just bring me to them immediately. And how the hell could it take you four hours to fingerprint two people? What'd you do, run out of ink?'

The smile vanishes from his face, as do his good manners. His right hand tightens around the Beretta M12 submachine gun. I slow my step: the last thing I want at this point is a problem with this red-moustachioed clown and his gun. These guys used to be part of the Italian army and they've gone through the same kind of training as our SWAT teams.

'We have rules and laws here, too, sir,' he tells me, 'and we will handle the matter as we have handled all international crimes in the past.'

'Can we take a quick look at them, sir?' Joey asks, just as polite and calm as he can be.

Before I can tell him to shut up and let me handle things, Super Mario nods. 'Of course,' he says, 'you can have a look in our viewing room. You should feel free to suggest questions for our interrogators to ask.'

We follow the asshole up two flights of stairs, which Joey walks like he's strolling along on flat grass while I'm lagging behind like an old mutt. It must be the jet lag or the momentary disappearance of the adrenaline that had me all fired up, but I'm suddenly so exhausted I have to hold onto the banister to make it up the stairs. I don't even need to see his ugly mug to know that Joey's laughing his ass off over this one.

With his headstart on the stairs, Joey manages to beat me to the viewing-room window. He nudges his way to the front, past a gaggle of Rome Policia di Stato – the city cops. I haven't even had a chance to look at the couple before he breaks out into raucous laughter: 'Go ahead and cuff them, Murphy,' he tells me. 'That ain't Jimmy and Cathy.'

I look through the window and see a couple, probably in their late sixties, sitting in two folding metal chairs, all alone in a big room except for a Rome cop in the corner by the door. The man's wearing a Philadelphia Phillies baseball cap, a tan, zipper-up-the-front jacket and loose jeans. He looks like any generic old bald guy, no more Whitey Bulger than millions of other old men, but being old and bald don't make him Whitey. As for the woman, who's wearing a short black skirt and a red sweater over a pink blouse, she's blond, I'll give her that and pretty in a made-up way, but she's way too short. It's hard to get much of a feel for her since heavy make-up is streaked all over her face. Obviously, she's been crying.

The *carabiniere* looks like Joey shot him with his own machine gun: I swear his moustache is like it went flat, like all the air went out of the balloon that was once his body. 'What are you saying?' he asks Joey. 'Are you being the jokester?'

Joey shakes his head. 'It ain't them,' he repeats. 'Sorry, but it ain't Jimmy and Cathy.'

'*Jimmy*?' one of the Rome policemen asks.

'He calls Whitey "Jimmy,"' I tell our *carabiniere* friend. 'Maybe we should speak to the couple before you release them,' I add.

'I'm not so sure we're going to release them just this quick,' he says, snapping his fingers. 'Perhaps you should look over the testimony we have – you know they could have put on big disguises.'

I glance over at Joey but he just shrugs. What the hell? I might as well have something to give the Bureau. 'Let's go,' I tell Luciano, who's all smiles now. He lets us into the interrogation room.

Introductions are made all around. Their names turn out to be Jimmy and Sarah Ellerin, which is about the only connection they have with the infamous mobster and his girlfriend. 'We're from Livingston, New Jersey,' Jimmy tells me in an accent that sounds like Tony Soprano – one more connection, I guess. 'We never heard of this Whitey character. If he's such a big-deal murderer in Boston, how come we never heard of him in New Jersey? Listen, we came to Rome to celebrate our fortieth wedding anniversary. We've been here two days.'

'We were having such a good time, too,' Sarah tells me. 'Having a nice lunch in a little coffee shop when this gavone grabbed us.' She shoots a nasty look towards Luciano, who smiles back at her pleasantly.

'They confessed they were Mafia on the run,' he tells us, shoving a pile of papers into my hands. I quickly look down at the transcript.

'I said no such thing,' Sarah says hotly. 'I said my feet were killing me and that I had a run in my stockings.'

Luciano ignores this and puts his finger on another sentence. 'See here,' he says, much less pleasantly now. 'When we left them alone, the man say to his wife, "I'm tired of running. Let's find that damn jewellery store already and grab what you want." Now, how can they explain that?'

'Simple,' says Jimmy to me. Well, more to Joey than me. 'I said we were tired of running around the city, looking for a jeweller. I promised Sarah a ring for our anniversary. I don't know what these idiots want from us: they ask us a million questions and ignore our answers. I'd like to speak to someone from the American consulate. Could you guys arrange that?'

'Hmm, you have to admit those words do sound a bit suspicious,' I say, but Joey's right on me.

'You better let them go before there's an international problem,' he tells Luciano, *sotto voce*, so I won't overhear him, like he's got the authority to make such a decision. I'm wondering why they didn't just run their drivers' licences with the NJ DMV. Shit, that would have cleared this up pretty quickly.

'I'll decide when and if these people are to be let go,' I say and Sarah begins to cry. Not softly or sweetly, but with a loud howl like I've never heard before.

Suddenly there's a knock at the door and another *carabiniere* appears, asking our guy Luciano to come out for a moment. Seconds later, the two men return, followed by a tall, white-haired man who looks quite dignified – far more so than poor Jimmy and Sarah. The minute Sarah sees him she's out of the chair and into his arms. He holds her tightly.

'Don't worry, honey,' he says soothingly. 'It's just a case of mistaken identity – you'll be out of here in a few minutes. I'm Sarah's brother,' he tells Joey and me, extending his hand and acting far more dignified than the suited-up policemen. 'I'm Paul Sherman. My wife Jane and I are here with Jimmy and Sarah. We'd taken a different tour today and just found out what's going on. I'm a lawyer in the Manhattan District Attorney's office and I can assure you I'll do whatever needs to be done to get my sister and brother-in-law out of here now. I have their passports and all the necessary documentation to prove to you that a mistake has been made.'

But Joey just stands there, shaking his head. 'Perhaps we'll leave you here with your sister and brother-in-law and go outside for a minute to discuss the matter,' I suggest, and lead the way out. 'Are you absolutely positive? That's not Whitey?' I say, as soon as the door is closed.

Joey looks at me like it's a big effort to answer. 'I don't know if you ever met the man,' he finally says, 'but I spent twenty-five years with him, every single day.'

How the hell can I answer that? 'Okay,' I tell Luciano. 'I think you're going to have to let them go before we create a bigger problem.' By now, I'm feeling as dejected as he looked a few minutes ago – I can't believe what a mess these policemen have made. It'll be a miracle if the *Globe* doesn't get hold of the story and have a ball with it. 'Let's get the hell out of here,' I tell Joey.

Suddenly, a door flings open and a Rome cop runs down the hallway with a sheaf of pages that must've just come off the fax machine. He huddles with the *carabiniere* for a moment. Now I don't understand Italian, but I do know body language and I can tell from getting a glimpse of these pages that they came from the

Interpol fingerprint database and they don't match Jimmy and Sarah from New Jersey. The *carabiniere* then barks some orders, obviously to have the prisoners released.

'We'll take care of the matter,' Luciano assures me. 'And if it turns out the way it appears, that we have indeed made a mistake, why then we will make restitution. I will personally drive the peoples to a lovely trattoria that my brother-in-law owns and give them a coupon for …' he pauses, thinking it over, 'twenty per cent off their entire meal, wine included.'

'You're quite a sport,' Joey says, and our man Lucy rewards him with a giant smile, not realizing the sarcastic cut he's just received for being a cheap bastard.

As we walk out of the building, Joey and I are besieged by a mob of paparazzi swarming the steps to the police station. 'Is it true they just arrested Whitey Bulger and his girlfriend?' one guy asks in perfect English, shoving a camera at me. Obviously, someone in the station tipped off the press. I've got my jacket over my face almost as fast as Joey; there's no question he's had a bit more experience with this type of situation before. Even without our photo, I can already see tomorrow's front page in the Boston papers – I just hope they don't put anything in about the Bureau.

Joey's having a great time, chuckling away to himself during the taxi ride back to our hotel; this has really gotten his motor running. 'I guess they don't give an eye exam as part of the physical to become a policeman in Italy,' he sniggers. However, I just turn away, too tired to tell him to shove it as he continues to enjoy the moment.

Chapter 34
Cathy, Rome

I just love Rome. I've never loved any place I've ever been as much as I love this city – and I've never loved Jimmy more. Finally, I have him back, kind and loving and generous. What happened in Rio is over. We haven't talked about it, but I know he and Serafina were lovers. But there's no sense in worrying about something in the past: probably it was my fault – maybe I wasn't as loving as I should have been. There will always be women prettier and younger than me who will be attracted to Jimmy: he can't help it, it's just who he is. He's got this magnetism about him – I don't know how else to explain it – but he loves me in a way he could never love any of them. I just need never to forget that fact.

Jimmy always said I'd feel completely at home in Rome and I do. I don't know why since my family is Scottish, I'm not even a Catholic, but there's something about this city that won my heart from the moment our Alitalia flight landed here. Part of it's the age of the city, its history, the thousands of years it's been standing there. America's such a baby country, so new and sterile in comparison to the richness of this place. I'm so happy just to wander the narrow lanes, gazing at the cobblestone streets, imagining how much history each stone has witnessed.

And the churches are so solemn and radiant. I've never seen churches like these: they're physically imposing yet strangely soothing. I've lit enough candles in this city to cover a birthday cake for a one-hundred-year-old woman! Some days I just sit in a pew and stare at the altar, at the magnificent paintings and etchings of the Lord and Saints, then I'm filled with a sense of peace that I've never felt anywhere else before.

It's funny, but years ago when I was a teenager, I believed I would be a nun. Peggy thought I was nuts. I kept trying to convince her to join a convent with me. 'How many identical twin nuns could there be?' I'd say. She'd tell me to stop watching *The*

Flying Nun, that there was nothing fun about being a nun. But now, I can understand why I had such a desire. In another life, that's what I would want to be. I have to smile when I think that a woman on the run with one of the world's most notorious criminals is sitting in a church, wishing she were a nun. I'd love to go to confession, just once, but I don't dare do that. Heaven knows what I might say if I were to sit down in front of that curtain, but I could trust a priest. Maybe one day I'll do that, just once before we leave. But I have to keep these thoughts to myself. If Jimmy found out …

For now, I'm content to sit in the church and to enjoy this sacred city. There's so much to see, so much to learn, and people smiling and trying to make conversation even though I can't understand a word they're saying. I can hardly wait to wake up every morning and walk out of the charming little flat on the Piazza della Minerva that Jimmy rented for us, with its narrow hallways, long straight windows covered with blue-and-white checked curtains and the antique bed with its matching blue-and-white bedspread. I stroll over to a little bakery on the corner of our street to pick up fresh bread: I have to buy two loaves because I finish one just walking home. And what fun it is to go to the tiny market beside the bakery to buy fresh cheese and eggs for our breakfast from the short, wide woman in black, who smiles when she sees me and bows slightly at the waist when I leave, clucking after me in Italian. Of course, I have no idea what she's saying, but I know her words are as kind as her smile and I want to put my arms round her and hug her. If only she were my mother and I'd lived with her all my life, how different I would be: how much better, how much safer.

Jimmy loves the crowds here: he's most relaxed when he can fade into a crowd. He comes to some of the churches with me and reads everything he can find about each ruin we visit, never mind the Coliseum, where he could give the tour himself now. During our tour of the Vatican, he was so attentive that anyone looking at him would have thought him a passionate Catholic.

I was watching him yesterday when we were touring the Aurelian Walls and he looked so perfectly and beautifully ordinary. He'd taken his reading glasses, along with his favourite Cross pen, out of his fanny pack and was making notes on the brochure we'd been given when we entered. I felt no different to any of the other tourists at the Walls. And this morning, after he threw a bunch of coins in the Trevi Fountain, he insisted I do the same. I knew exactly what to wish for: that Jimmy and I would be together for as long as I lived.

'What did you wish for?' I asked.

But he just smiled and said, 'The same thing you did.'

I kissed his unshaven face and he kissed me back. Along with his unexpected sweetness, he's more energized and full of purpose than he's been anywhere else we've stayed.

I never want to leave this city: I have everything I could possibly want from life right here, in this place, with this man.

Chapter 35
Joey & Murphy, Rome

Back in the room, it's obvious I'm not going to be able to get right to sleep. Murphy's way too worked up, more pissed off than anything else. I can tell he's working his pathetic little mind trying to figure out a way to blame this latest fiasco on me.

'You didn't show those guys enough respect,' he tells me. 'If we need them again, we're going to have a tough time getting them to work with us.'

I'm just not in the mood to listen to his shit – I've had enough of it on the plane and in the police station. Now I'm too worked up to get to sleep, even if he did shut up: I've had enough of this asshole to last me a lifetime. 'I'm getting out of here,' I tell him in the middle of his latest rant.

This time he's muttering about why we didn't give a press conference, why we didn't 'use the press to our advantage': 'If you hadn't been in such a rush to get out of there, we might have been able to send a message to Whitey and that could've netted us some info.'

'See you later,' I say as I grab my jacket and head for the door.

'Hey, where the hell do you think you're going?' he yells back at me, his arm reaching out towards me. If he touched me, I wouldn't hesitate – he'd be on the floor in less than a second. But he holds back just in time.

'For a walk,' I say, opening the door to the room. 'You want to try and stop me?' Nothing would feel better than washing the floor with this moron – I can't believe I'm stuck in yet another room with him, getting nowhere, just chasing a shadow no one can find. Anything would be better than this. Taking off is looking better and better. I know that I could never join, never mind find, Jimmy and Cathy; that I haven't any resources to stay out there alone, but when I think of hanging around with Murphy for another year or so, going nowhere, taking his shit, it's more than I can bear. Prison was better than this life.

'Oh, I don't have to stop you,' he tells me. 'All I need to do is make a call back to Boston and your family and friends are gonna have a real hard time – we'll bust their balls every chance we get!'

My hands are twitching, moving back and forth to form the fist I know is headed towards his jaw but I fling my hands into my pockets and head out the door. I've no idea where I'm going but if I stay here, I won't stop punching till he's dead. And while I know that wouldn't be the right move, there's nothing I'd enjoy more.

I wait for him to follow, but I don't hear any steps behind me: all I notice is the slamming of the door.

I check my watch and see that it's 7pm in Boston. I'm sure Rogers is still in the office – where the hell else would he be? He's got no other life. And then I smile, despite myself: like *I* have? Sure enough, he answers on the first ring. 'It wasn't them,' I tell him. 'Joey tried to make a big deal out of them, but I knew the second I saw them – just some elderly couple from New Jersey celebrating their fortieth wedding anniversary. Joey has no finesse when it comes to this stuff and couldn't have been ruder to them. I did whatever I could to calm both them and the police down and deflate any inflammatory news stories. The way Joey was working the paparazzi, though, I can't promise anything.'

'Too bad,' says Rogers.

'Yeah, well that's not the biggest problem I have,' I say. 'I tried to talk to you in Boston, but you wouldn't listen.'

'If you're gonna give me that shit about Joey feeding Whitey the info, save it! Just get some sleep and get back on the job tomorrow.'

'No problem, I'd love some sleep,' I say, 'but the fact that Joey Donahue left the room a few minutes ago without my permission and is most probably meeting up with Whitey at this very moment makes it a little difficult for me to sleep.'

'For Christ's sake,' he groans, 'who could blame the poor bastard? I can just imagine how well you took the whole scene at the police station – he deserves a medal for being with you this long! We're lucky if he ever comes back.'

I know he's waiting for me to explode, but there's no way I'll give him that satisfaction. 'I'm keeping notes on this whole thing,' I tell him calmly, ignoring his last words, 'and when it's over and I come up with nothing, someone's going to see exactly what happened – and it's going to be very obvious you were warned and ignored my warnings. I hope you're prepared for that.'

'You're a piece of work,' Rogers says. 'You just can't get over the fact that he beat you in the ring, can you?'

I'm stunned with his remark – the sonofabitch!

'What the fuck are you talking about?'

'Do you think you're the only agent who goes to that gym?' he stays, relishing every word. 'Is that what you honestly believe?'

I slam down the phone and immediately regret it – I shouldn't have let him get to me like that. He's always playing me off and I fall right into his traps. I've probably been the butt of his jokes at the office for years.

I'm tempted to head out the room myself to find Joey and cuff him right then and there, but I'm too tired to move. Instead I sit down on the bed, head in my hands, and wonder if any of this is worth it. What the hell am I doing anyhow? I'm looking for a needle in a haystack with a fucking criminal. Why? Am I a total fool? For a long time I just sit there, asking myself the same question, over and over.

And then I realize the answer and I know just what I'm gonna do. I don't even have to look up her number – it's number two on my cell phone. I just hope this time I can find the right words to make it all work out – I've rehearsed them so many times before – but this time I have a feeling it's going to go the way I want. Finally she'll hear me and understand we belong together, I'll make her understand.

When a man's voice answers, I say nothing. All I can hear is Mia's voice, asking so sweetly, 'Who is it, honey?' And then I hang up.

Chapter 36
Whitey, Rome

I'm feeling especially invigorated at the thought of my pursuer luxuriating in the knowledge that he's unhinged me and made me careless. Nothing could make me happier than thinking this detective, or whoever the hell he is, is going to follow the crumbs I've spread out right into my trap. It's like the good old days when Joey and I'd plan a score for weeks, obsessing over every detail until we had it just right. It was never a success until we'd committed the crime and gotten away with it. The money was our reward but even more than that was the feeling of having accomplished a brilliant coup. Some crimes netted us hundreds of thousands, even millions, but it was the incredible high, that heady rush of adrenaline when you knew you were about to succeed, to get away with it, that made it all worthwhile.

But now I'm on my own and in a foreign country, on the run. I'll succeed exactly the way I have in the past only this time my success won't net me thousands of dollars, rather just one death – a murder I'm going to enjoy more than any other I've committed. It's going to take a little while – and I'm going to get to know my victim a bit more – but when I off him, I'll make sure he finally understands how ludicrous it's been for him ever to have thought that he'd be the one to capture me.

One thing I do need to do, however, is to get a new passport. I'm concerned my old one might be a problem, so I've been looking around for the right opportunity to score a new one. Right now, sitting at the Bar Della Rotonda on the Piazza Della Rotonda, I've a feeling that opportunity has just come around. I've been bullshitting with a guy named Franz from Austria all night, listening to interesting stories about his travels. He heads a company that makes some kind of pesticide-free fertilizer and he travels all over the world, selling his product and instructing farmers and landscapers on its applications. He speaks perfect English and he's quite a charming guy. He thinks I'm a retired history professor and is just as comfortable talking about ancient Rome and the Vietnam War as he is about fertilizers.

I'm enjoying his stories, but what I want is the passport I spotted earlier in the evening in his briefcase when he opened it up to show me a brochure about his company. Finally, when he re-opens the briefcase – this time to show me a newspaper write-up about his fertilizer – I see my golden opportunity. I can make out the edge of the green European passport still nestled beneath some papers to the right side of the briefcase beside the newspaper he's extracting.

'Hey, does that guy know you?' I suddenly ask, pointing to a group of men behind us. 'The guy in the red shirt keeps staring at you.'

In the brief minute that it takes Franz to turn around and look at the red-shirted guy, I've removed the passport from his briefcase. When he turns back again, shaking his head and saying he has no idea who the man could be, that green passport is in my jacket pocket, right beside my blue American one. I know he plans to leave Rome tomorrow but to stay in Italy for at least two weeks and so it could be that long before he notices his passport is missing.

An hour later as I head back to our apartment, I have a good laugh over what I've been reduced to. In the past, I've shaken down guys for millions of dollars but now I'm a common thief, ripping off some poor jerk's passport. Still, I need this little booklet as much as I needed those millions. But there's work to be done: with Cathy's hairdryer, I heat up the lamination on the passport. Next, I use a razor to slice right in on the edge, peel back the softened lamination and with tweezers, remove Franz's photograph. Carefully, I insert my own photo, replace the lamination and hey presto, I'm Franz Richter, a sixty-two-year-old Austrian. Now I'm free as a bird, ready to travel all over Europe, to hunt down my hunter.

When I go to bed that night, I'm not surprised that I can't close my eyes – and I know exactly why I'm roaming around the flat, unable to sleep for even ten minutes. I felt the jolt when an

American with sleek black hair at the next table to my good buddy Franz and me ordered his drink earlier on. 'Do you have Glenlivet for my scotch on the rocks?' he asked loudly. Just the word 'Glenlivet' triggered the memory that's now pushing itself into my consciousness, demanding attention. So, a little after two, I sit down in the comfortable dark-green upholstered armchair, pour myself a glass of orange juice and surrender to the wonderfully pleasant memory.

It's 1980 and I've driven down to P'town one summer night to see a friend. Stanley's two weeks behind on payments for the $100,000 he borrowed from me, but he's got a nice bar down there named the Half Hitch and I know he'll be good for it. I plan to meet him there at 11.30 but arrive a little early and drive down Commercial Street slowly, just taking in all the sights in this very gay town. As I pass City Hall, I look at the park with its small rod-iron fence extending the length of the area. Along the fence, which the locals refer to as the 'Meat Rack', all the young boys are lined up, just looking to get picked up. As I watch them, I get a knot in my stomach and the bile starts to rise up in my throat – I can actually taste it, along with the adrenaline. All I can think is, how can I kill all these fags and get away with it? As I drive by, I laugh to myself, knowing not even I could manage that feat.

After I park my car in a lot off Commercial Street, I head into the Half Hitch and right away, find Stanley in a small room off the main bar. We shake hands and he passes me an envelope. I look inside and see $30,000, which includes $5,000, the vig on the $100,000 for two weeks at two and a half points, plus $25,000 off the principal: he now owes me $75,000. I nod and stick the envelope in my pants pocket.

'So, how's business?' I ask him.

'As you can see, it's great, Jimmy,' he tells me. 'There's really not a lot of problems at the bar except for the occasional catfight – these people love to spend money.'

'Doesn't it bother you, being around this type of people?' I ask.

'I don't care who I'm with, so long as they're paying my bills,' he says. 'Let's go out and have a few drinks.'

I take him up on his offer and settle in at the bar. Stanley orders us each a beer and when the waiter brings the drinks and a couple of glasses, Stanley waves his glass away and drinks right from the bottle, probably afraid of getting some disease. While we're talking about business and the money he owes me, I notice a guy around forty years of age, about 5'10" and in pretty good shape. He's well groomed, in neatly pressed khakis and a light blue Oxford cloth shirt, the sleeves evenly rolled up to his elbows. His black hair is neatly slicked back and he's wearing round, wire-rimmed glasses. I notice the way he walks around, talking to some of the younger guys in the bar, putting an arm around them, rubbing their shoulders – I can see the other guys are uncomfortable with this, but he doesn't seem to care.

About a half hour later, Stanley tells me he's got a late dinner date and has to take off. 'No problem,' I tell him. 'I'm just going to have another beer and take off myself.'

After he leaves, I go over to the end of the bar where Mr Cool is standing and order myself a beer. 'It's beautiful down here, isn't it?' I say to the guy. 'Wish I could get here more often.'

He jumps right in, friendly as can be. 'Oh, it's your first time?' he asks, and I nod. 'I come here all the time,' he continues. 'It's quiet and a great getaway – no one knows your business down here.'

'Yeah,' I say. 'I know all about folk trying to know your business.'

The guy moves in closer to me. 'Jesus,' he says, 'maybe you come down sometime and I can show you the sights.'

'I'd like that – I really don't know anyone down here. So, what are you drinking?' I ask, as I call the bartender over.

'Do you carry Glenlivet?' he asks the bartender, who nods. I order another beer.

'Actually, I've got to be going,' I tell him as he sips his scotch on the rocks.

'Where you going?' he asks, putting down his glass.

161

'I haven't eaten all day,' I tell him. 'I gotta get a quick bite before I head back to Boston.'

'Hey, I know a nice little place that stays open to two,' he tells me, 'serves pretty decent food.'

'Is it far from here?' I ask. 'I don't know my way around this place.'

'It's not far,' he says. 'My car's parked right across the street. Why don't I drive you there? I could use something to eat, too.'

'Okay,' I say. 'What kind of car are you driving?'

'I drive a four-door silver Lincoln,' he says, polishing off his drink.

'Okay,' I say. 'I'll meet you outside in five minutes – I've got to use the men's room and wash up.'

I walk into the bathroom and see a couple of guys in there doing lines of coke and giggling with each other. Ignoring them, I walk over to one of the stalls, kick the door open easily with my foot and relieve myself. When I come out, the two guys are gone so I wash my hands, comb my hair, smile at my reflection in the mirror and head outside. Sure enough, the guy's parked across the street, just as he said. I walk over, get into the passenger side and he drives away. He makes small talk in pretty much a one-way conversation, describing his life and how tough it is living this lifestyle, hiding it back home.

Finally, I say, 'Yeah,' but all I'm really thinking is, 'you motherfucker, you're not going to have to hide much longer!'

Then he reaches over and touches my forearm.

'You know, I'm really not that hungry,' I say. 'What if we go somewhere?'

'I love the dunes at night when the moon is full and shining down over them,' he tells me, smiling broadly.

'Yeah, that sounds like a good idea,' I say.

He parks the car in a parking lot down by the dunes. It's after midnight and there's no one there – I figure most people are still in the bars. We get out and climb onto the wild grass surrounding the dunes: we're barely onto the dunes before the guy starts to unbutton his shirt.

162

I take off my white cotton long-sleeved shirt and throw it on the sand, keeping on my T-shirt. Then I reach down, like I'm gonna open my belt. What the poor faggot doesn't know is that my belt buckle has a 5" dagger attached to it – it fits inside a leather sheath built right into the belt. As I unbuckle my belt, the guy's getting more excited by the second, ripping off his shirt in one frenetic motion. So, I wrap my fingers around the belt buckle and just as his shirt hits the sand, plunge the dagger into his abdomen. I go in deep, with full force, like I'm punching him in the stomach and stab him three or four more times, ripping upward with each thrust. He falls to his knees, holding onto his stomach, but there are too many holes and his intestines are sticking out. Unable to utter a sound, he falls over onto one side. I lean over him, yanking his head back by his hair and exposing his throat, which I cut from one side to the other.

For a second I stand there, looking down at him and feeling wonderfully content with what I've just done. But I don't allow myself too much time to admire my handiwork: there's work to be done. I quickly look around the area to make sure I didn't drop anything, then reach into the guy's pocket and remove his car keys. After I wipe off the knife on my white T-shirt, I slide the dagger back into the sheath of my belt and then I use the T-shirt to remove any traces of blood on my arms. I put the white cotton shirt back on, covering any remaining blood. A few drops of blood are still on my dungarees, but they're barely noticeable against the dark fabric.

Then I drive out of the parking lot, park the car on a quiet side street and walk two blocks to a little convenience store, where I buy a pack of cigarettes, a Zippo lighter and a can of lighter fluid. The clerk is busy watching a movie on the TV above the counter and pays no attention to me. With my purchases, I walk back to the car, drive it to an area where there are no houses around, a half-mile from where my own car is parked, get out, squirt lighter fluid all over the dashboard and front seats, put the two front windows down so the fire can get oxygen and won't burn itself out quickly, light the Zippo and throw it into the open window.

Immediately the car goes up in flames, removing any fingerprints it might have held, along with my bloodstained T-shirt.

Walking back to my car through the outskirts of town, I mingle with the crowd. The bars are still hopping and everyone's having a great time. I stroll down Commercial Street to the lot where I parked and head back to Boston, a little hungry but completely relaxed. I get into my car, put on a nice oldies station and listen to some Dean Martin and Nat King Cole as I drive home, never going above the speed limit.

It's been a perfect night and I couldn't feel any more satisfied: one less faggot, one more notch in the belt for the kid.

Chapter 37
Joey, Rome

When I get back to the room two hours later with the expensive
Italian stiletto I just purchased stored safely in my pant leg,
Murphy's still awake. He's sitting in a chair, holding his cell
phone and looking out the window. I feel a stab of sympathy for
the pathetic dope. No doubt he called Boston about my taking off.

'We've been awake way too many hours,' I say. 'Think it's
time to call it a day.' But he keeps staring out the window. 'Look,
buddy,' I say, my short-lived sympathy beginning to disappear.
'You better snap out of this by tomorrow. If we're to have a
chance of catching Jimmy, you better have your head on straight.'

He looks at me and I can see his eyes are red. Probably
exhaustion, but who knows? He puts his phone back in his pocket.
'I called Mia,' he says dully. 'Big mistake – some guy answered.'

'For Christ's sake,' I say, 'what's wrong with you? You think
she's sitting around waiting for you all these years? I saw her
photo, she's a good-looking woman – of course she found another
sucker. And as for you, there's a million other women out there –
hell, there are more women than men in the world! If you hit on
one woman out of every ten, one's bound to say yeah. It's up to
you to step up to the plate.'

'Yeah,' he sighs. 'Yeah, one will say yeah.' Then he smiles,
just a small minor smile. 'Thanks.'

'You're welcome,' I say, as I head into the bathroom. The next
morning, he's up before me and we're back on the road, acting as
if the plane trip, the police station and the scene in the room never
happened and that's fine with me.

When Rogers faxes us the following newspaper article, I laugh
it off. Howard the Coward's nothing but a big mouth with no guts.
He's safe behind a typewriter at the *Herald*, writing his shit about
anybody he wants but in real life, away from his computer, away
from the newsroom, he's the biggest coward of all. A couple of
times when we had some spare time on our hands, me and Jimmy

wanted to kill him, but we got busy and he got lucky, so he's still alive back in Boston, writing his shit, pissing off anybody he wants. Today he's pointing his pathetic little finger at Murphy, who doesn't take it too well at all. He rips the fax out of my hand and turns so red reading it, I'm afraid he's going to have a stroke.

WHERE'S WHITEY? BY CARL HOWARD
JANUARY 3

You couldn't make this stuff up, not that I ever would. With clowns like FBI agent Jerky John Murphy, a brainless geek who wouldn't know the difference between Osama bin Laden and James Bulger leading the charge, our intrepid Boston Bureau attacked a sweet little couple from New Jersey who were celebrating their wedding anniversary in Rome, handcuffed them, dragged them into the police station and questioned them for more than 8 hours. You see, the guy was around 5'10" and nearly bald and the missus had blonde hair. Well, of course that was the signal Jerky Murphy was waiting for. He charged into the station, guns drawn, ready to put on the chains and drag the dastardly criminals back to Boston. Yes, indeed, Jimmy and Cathy were finally being brought to justice.

Hey listen, we all make mistakes I might even have made one once, Murph's entitled to his. Actually, it seems like he made another little one in St. Barts, and in Costa Rica and in Buenos Aires. So he's having a nice little trip for himself. How nice. What else would you want your tax dollars to go towards? I can't think of a thing.

And by the way, don't worry about the couple from New Jersey. They were well paid for the inconvenience they endured. Thanks to Jerky Murphy, the sweet little couple were personally escorted to a lovely restaurant and given 20% off the ENTIRE meal. Who could ask for anything more?

After two weeks, it's apparent that the two of us are back to square one. Every lead turns out to be a bum one and I'm at my wits' end – once again, I'm not sure how much more I can take of this guy. I can't stand the way he eats or the way he talks, I can't bear his snoring at night. I feel bad for Jeannie who takes the brunt of my frustration, forced to listen to me during our nightly phone calls. Luckily, the FBI has given me an access code so I can call home once a day. When I talk to Rosie, the calls are quick and to the point: how are the kids? Is Tim still in jail? Does she need any more money? Chopper does a great job of stopping over to see her nearly every night, for which I'm grateful. Jeannie stops by often, too and has brought over dinner many nights but I'm equally grateful to her for listening to me complain and her attempts, unsuccessful as they are, to get me to learn to live with this moron with whom I'm sharing an all-too-small hotel room.

But one night, Jeannie stuns me with an incredible piece of information. 'A couple of weeks ago, I was having lunch at Susie Fletcher's house,' she tells me as I stand in a phone booth in the hotel lobby, feeling especially cranky after a particularly miserable dinner with Murphy. 'We were going through some old photos that Susie was putting into a scrapbook and she was showing me this one she has of Jimmy when he was in seventh grade. We were both saying how hard it is to believe this cute little blond kid could grow into a vicious murderer – it's a black-and-white photo and his hair looks pure white, even at age twelve. I read the brief sentence under his picture, which says, "Jimmy enjoys baseball and reading and hanging around with his friends, Brian Kelly, Michael Allen and Tommy Riley". Anyhow, today who do I run into at the post office this morning, but Tommy Riley? We were walking out together when he started to talk about you, asked me how you were; said he'd always wanted to talk to you about Jimmy, had some information he'd always wanted to get off his chest. You had to see him, Joey – he was so rattled. He's in pretty bad physical shape; he was so out of breath, I made him sit down in my car and drove him home.

'When we got to his house, he begged me to come in and talk to him some more. He told me he's retired now, a widower, but he used to work for Public Works in Boston. He's got four daughters, none of whom live around here, and he's still living in the Mary Ellen McCormack Projects, where he and Jimmy grew up together. I asked if anyone ever came to talk to him about Jimmy and he said no; that he would never have said anything anyhow. But he wants to talk now; says he's not sure how much time he has left and he has something to get off his chest. I wish I could have gone in then, but I had to get to work. I promised him I'd come back tomorrow and I intend to. Do you have any idea what he might possibly want to tell me?'

'Not the slightest,' I tell her. 'He could be just some old man who wants to spend an evening in the company of a beautiful redhead. Just don't fool around with him – it could kill him.'

'I'm horny enough that he looks pretty good to me,' she says, and I can't help but smile.

'Have fun with Riley,' I tell her. 'You deserve a good time. I'll call you tomorrow night, okay?'

That night, I have an especially hard time trying to fall asleep. I've no memory of Tommy Riley but I'm all worked up about Jeannie's meeting with him. The next day goes by so slowly – knocking on doors, being turned away by more than twenty hotel managers, listening to Murphy's continuous whining about his upset stomach and sore feet – that I'm completely worn out when I get into the phone booth and call Jeannie but the sound of her voice energizes me more than anything I've heard in a long time.

'I have amazing news,' she tells me. 'I've been pacing the floor till you called.'

'You fucked him, didn't you?' I say, and she giggles.

'By the end of our visit, I was ready to,' she laughs. 'He told me how he and Jimmy and Joe Anderson and Brian Kelly were like the Four Musketeers back then but nothing was ever the same after Brian died in 1943. Apparently Brian and Jimmy were inseparable: the four kids would hang around corners together, play ball, get ice cream, pitch pennies … He stopped for a while, took a few puffs on his inhaler and for a moment I thought I was gonna lose him but he pulled himself together and told me the most amazing story.

'I got the feeling he hasn't talked about it in many years but he was taking a certain pride in telling it right. Apparently, Jimmy was attacked by a pervert who tried to abuse him in the park; Jimmy was no more than twelve, but according to Tommy, he beat the shit out of the creep with a baseball bat. No one could believe a skinny little twelve-year-old kid could fight like that, but he did. Then the same bastard got into the boiler room of the building where Brian lived, and raped and killed him – strangled him with a piece of rope.

'Tommy says the monster went to jail, but that didn't help Jimmy; something changed in him after that murder. He wasn't physically big but he became violent. Kids were fighting with their hands in those days, but Jimmy would tear off his opponent's ear or bite deep into his nose. He did physical damage big time. If you had a problem with him, it wasn't going to be a stand-up fistfight, he would use everything he could to hurt you and nobody wanted to be on that side of his fist.

'Joey and Tommy tried to talk to him, to get through to him, but they couldn't reason with him – he wasn't the same kid they'd known for all those years. Whatever violence he'd had inside of him was let loose now and there was no holding back. Tommy says he knows how violent he became and what he's capable of doing but he swears that before Brian died, he wasn't any different to the rest of the kids.

'He says the last time we saw Jimmy was in 1993. He was down by the liquor store and Tommy went in to get some beer. Tommy says they shook hands and all, but that was about it – Jimmy didn't want to be around him. Tommy always suspected he blamed himself for what happened to Brian; that he must have felt if he'd taken care of that piece of shit, his best friend wouldn't have been murdered.

'He thinks the FBI probably don't want to find him and that he imagines Jimmy is on some remote island, happy to be away from the rest of the world. Honestly Joey, I wonder if Jimmy's spent the past sixty years reliving a murder for which he feels responsible; imagining how his best friend died and hating himself for not preventing it from happening. Just as Tom said, this could well be the trigger that set off his extreme violence.'

I can't say much more to Jeannie – my head's too full of the story she has just told me and I need time to think clearly.

'You're something else,' is about all that I can tell her.

'Just find him and come on home,' she tells me.

'I'm trying,' I say.

'So try harder,' she tells me, 'but be careful. Okay?'

'Okay,' I promise but for the first time, I want to get off the phone from her. I need to think, quietly and carefully. Instead of going back to the hotel, I take a long walk around the hotel's neighbourhood and start to think about all the rumours about Whitey being gay; being seen in so many gay places. And the idea takes hold in my mind like a puzzle piece I've been searching for. I never for one moment thought he was gay and now I'm thinking he's homophobic. Perhaps through all those years of brutal violence, he's been propelled by a hatred of gay men.

I'm halfway down the Via del Venuto when it hits me: the Matheson murder. Matheson was a school teacher, who we heard was handling 200 pounds of pot a week in Farmington, New Hampshire. Jimmy and I paid a little visit to meet this guy and shake him down. You knew the second you saw him that he was gay: the way he dressed and talked and walked, it was flagrant gay behaviour. We were waiting for him in his condo. The guy was shitting in his pants the second he saw us there. We'd barely said ten words when he was ready to give us anything we wanted but Jimmy took off on him, beating him nearly senseless. I never interfere in Jimmy's work, but that day I did, pulling him off the unconscious body before he finished him off. For a second, Jimmy looked like he was going to go after me, but he controlled himself, shook his head in agreement and followed me out of the condo.

He was quiet for the hour-and-a-half car ride back to South Boston, but when he dropped me off, he thanked me for stopping

170

him from killing Matheson. 'That queer deserved to die,' he told me. 'A queer teacher should be killed, but not today.' Six months later, we read about his suicide in the *Globe*. Seems he shot himself. 'Shame, wasn't it?' Jimmy asked me as he read the piece aloud. I knew from the way he looked at me that it hadn't been a suicide – I'll never forget the rage with which he beat that poor guy. I'd seen Jimmy attack and kill multiple times, but never like that, never with such uncontained fury.

Walking through a light rain that's now beginning to get heavier, I can also bring to mind other instances of Jimmy's homophobia: his reaction to gay waiters, gay salesman in Barney's and Mr. Sid's, gay politicians ... His distaste could never be described as mild. I'm no psychologist but I have to try and figure this out. Certainly Jimmy doesn't think all gay men are paedophiles, but homosexuals could easily have become the perfect target for his rage, allowing him to hurt folk who might not have had anything to do with the Brians of the world. Perhaps it's a way of atoning for his guilt over Brian's death – it's not so much about killing homosexuals as killing his guilt with the easiest method but even this method can't work for any length of time.

Somehow, I have to try and figure out how to use this new information, to put it to good use in this search. There's a way to channel it into the search but at the moment, I've no idea what it might be.

By the time I get back to the hotel, it's after midnight and I'm soaking wet and exhausted. I've never been so glad to hear Murphy's snoring as I sink into my bed at the other side of the room. My brain couldn't take one more second of conversation, or thought. But as I fall asleep, I can't push the look on Jimmy's face as he pummelled poor Matheson out of my mind. The devil himself could not have looked angrier or any more ugly.

Chapter 38
Joey & Murphy, Artemide Hotel, Rome

The next morning I'm up before Murphy and showered and shaved by the time he opens his eyes. Once again, as I have so many mornings here in our hotel room, I resist the urge to head out the door, down the steps onto the street and simply disappear into the crowd. But I can't do it today: I need to talk to Murphy and see if we can possibly work together on this latest theory that Jimmy is a homophobic killer and figure out if there's any way that piece of information can help us find him.

I'm sitting on my bed, staring at Murphy when he finally wakes. He looks at me, then at the watch on his left wrist. 'It's 5.30 in the morning,' he tells me, as if I don't already know. 'What the hell are you doing up?'

'I've something to discuss with you,' I tell him and at this, he sits bolt upright in bed.

'Yeah, what?' he asks, and I can see the flicker of worry in his eyes. These past miserable months, he's shown a lot of emotions, like frustration and anger, but worry hasn't been one of them.

'A friend of mine in Boston called me last night with some new information about Jimmy's childhood,' I say, 'and I put it together with some scores I'd been through with him and it made sense. I'll skip the whole story and shorten it down to this: I have good reason to believe, for the first time, that Jimmy had a bad experience with a paedophile when he was a kid, a paedophile who ended up killing his best friend. I think that experience translated into an extreme homophobia – I personally witnessed his overreaction to a gay guy's petty crime against us.

'I'd like to have the Bureau look up any unsolved murders on gay men in Provincetown, Boston's South End, New York, San Francisco and Agunquit. Whitey's not gay – he has another reason to be spending time in gay bars.'

At first, Murphy just stares at me as if I'm crazy, but slowly his expression begins to turn. 'You really believe this shit?' he asks and I nod. 'If this turns out to be a waste of time, I won't be the only one who's gonna make sure you pay for your mistake.'

'I can take that risk,' I tell him.

'We got nothing else,' he shrugs, 'might as well try this crazy theory.' Then he checks his watch again and decides the time is okay to call the States. I listen to him request the files on unsolved gay murders in the places I've mentioned; on any murders that involve strangling or stabbing males around the ages of thirty-five to forty in those areas.

'Let's get some breakfast,' he tells me as he heads for the shower. 'I've got a feeling this will be a very long day.'

Two hours later, we get the call from the Bureau: it didn't take long before they picked a large number of unsolved murders in the gay communities I've mentioned. None of this surprises me.

'Whitey stands accused of nineteen murders but there's always been the common knowledge that he committed at least forty murders, most probably more,' I tell Murphy, afterwards. We're still in the same little place we went to for breakfast, drinking yet another cup of coffee. 'Some of those bodies were imagined to be lying at the bottom of the ocean, but that might not be true at all. Maybe those bodies belonged to gay men – their deaths could have been attributed to hate crime murders or lovers' quarrels or even the gay lifestyle – but I'm more convinced than ever that the murders were committed by Jimmy to avenge the murder of his best friend, to make sure no other kid suffers the same death. Perhaps he's still doing that now.'

'If so, it gives us some new locales to look up your old boss,' says Murphy.

Chapter 39
Cathy, Piazza della Minerva, Rome

We're comfortably settled in our hotel suite, watching the BBC, enjoying a bottle of Chianti and nibbling on a delicious loaf of bread and some fresh chèvre that I picked up this morning. Since we've arrived in Rome, it's become sort of a ritual of Jimmy's to follow this station late every afternoon before we head out for our evening walk and dinner. This afternoon, we're watching *Vigilante Justice in America* and Jimmy's been all worked up since it began. The show talks about how Americans have more access to guns than any other country and how they take the law into their own hands. In England, people can't legally buy guns in the way that they can in America, so they don't have this problem.

The programme features a case in the States where a small boy is molested by a neighbour and the boy's father goes next door and shoots and kills the neighbour. There's a panel of four discussing this particular case and three of the men condemn the father; they each give another case where justice doesn't work because people take the law into their own hands.

I'm having trouble following it because Jimmy keeps interrupting the speakers with his own thoughts. At the beginning, I find what he has to say more intelligent than the words of the panellists but when he starts getting upset about it, I begin to wish we'd never turned it on.

'They're full of shit!' he's telling me, on his feet now, unable to sit down and listen to the rest of the show. 'They have no idea what the fuck they're talking about. Believe me, if more people went after these child molesters and rapists, there would be less crime.'

'But you can't just go out and shoot someone because you think they're abusing kids, can you?' I say. 'I mean, that guy wasn't positive his neighbour did it. Shouldn't he have allowed the police to take care of it?'

'The *police*?' Jimmy practically snorts at me. 'Oh yeah, they'd *really* know how to handle the case! Once the bastard's lawyer showed up at the station, they'd find some technicality that would allow him to go free.'

'I know how you feel about the police and how they never did anything about the heroin dealers in South Boston,' I persist, 'but do you really think people should follow this guy's example and just shoot anyone they suspect to be guilty?'

'Why the hell not?' he answers me. 'It would be whole lot better to have a parent make a mistake than to have some little kid raped and have his life destroyed.'

I'm not sure what I think, but I can't imagine why he's become so enraged, so quickly – he'd been completely relaxed and in such a good mood when we sat down to watch the show.

'I guess so,' I answer tentatively. 'Still, there has to be some sort of evidence …'

At this, Jimmy turns off the television so violently that I'm afraid he broke the remote. 'These shows make me fucking sick!' he erupts, before I can finish my sentence. 'All those assholes sitting around, talking about a situation they know nothing about. I'm no angel – I've committed plenty of violent crimes – but when I see a group of men trying to make excuses for the behaviour of child abusers, I'd like to fucking shoot them!'

When we leave the hotel, he's still furious and he can't stop talking about the show – and he doesn't calm down at dinner. It's a shame because it's such a darling trattoria and the tables are close together. Jimmy's usually so cautious about the way he handles himself in public, but tonight he's too fired up to exercize his typical control. Every time I try and change the subject, he gets back onto that stupid show – it's all I can do to keep myself from telling him to get off it already.

I know as well as anyone else that he's being more than a little hypocritical when he talks about criminals being punished for their crimes. He is, after all, on the FBI's Most Wanted List for nineteen counts of murder – it would be almost funny if it wasn't so serious but to hear him go off on those rapists and murderers, you'd think he's the most upstanding citizen America has to offer. I know he's gone off about child molesters before, told me how they're the most hated group in prison and how he got special pleasure from making their time in jail as difficult as possible but this is far worse than those discussions.

At dinner, he notices me smiling when he's off on yet another rant about child molesters and stops mid-sentence. 'So, you think it's funny, Cathy?' he asks in a furious whisper, leaning across the table so his face is flush against mine, 'a little boy being abused is something to smile about?'

'Of course not ...' I start to say, but before I can get the words out, he stands up and throws three $100 bills on the table and walks out. For a long time, I sit there after he's gone, grateful we're on the run and in a public place: Jimmy would never draw attention to himself, it could have been a lot worse. I see the waiter hovering nervously to the left of the table, uncertain whether or not to approach me, but I can't move. I'm so sorry that Jimmy misunderstood my smile, but more than that, I'm filled with regret that I'll never understand this man I love so much.

Finally, long after the waiter and other diners have lost interest in me, I'm still sitting there, crying silently over all that I'll never know, wishing I could just leave, but accepting the painful knowledge that I never will.

Chapter 40
Whitey, Piazza Navona, Rome

I'm walking on the Piazza Navona when I see him. Actually, it's his reflection that I catch in the window of a shop as I pass by. He's walking behind me, deep in thought, his hands thrust into his tan raincoat – a Burberry, I'm quite sure, since I recently bought one for Cathy at a store here in Rome. He's walking quickly – not as quickly as me but still a step or two quicker than the typical passer-by on this busy street, filled with expensive shops and boutiques. I immediately recognize his face: the broad shape, the thick salt-and-pepper hair that falls onto his forehead, the wide-set eyes and bushy eyebrows, the deep cleft in his chin. Not a bad-looking man yet there's a look of dissatisfaction, perhaps it's some sort of an awkwardness which prevents him from being considered handsome. He's tall, probably close to 6' and not too heavy, maybe 185 pounds. I'd guess he's well into his fifties and for a guy that age, he's not in bad shape.

It takes me a second and then it all falls into place: I saw this guy over by Government Center, about fifteen years ago. He was talking to two Boston detectives. I remember it well because one of the detectives, Jerry Blakely, was on the take and worked for us. When I saw Gerry a few days later, I asked him who he was talking to. 'Oh, that guy in the trench?' he said. 'He's an FBI agent – a nice guy and totally harmless – he never gets out of the office.' He told me his name and I can't remember it just yet, but I never forget a face.

Today, I don't have to lose this guy: he never even saw me. Still, I take a quick left to make sure of that. But he was looking for me, I'm sure of that – after all, I know someone's been on me and it's no coincidence I saw this guy today. What are the chances of a Boston FBI agent being in Rome at the same time as me? He has to be the one tracking me.

I still have no idea of the guy's name when I stop for a moment at an outdoor café to catch my breath. Judging from his age and the fact that he was alone, chances are he's retired and looking for me. Considering his actions in St Barts and the ads in Rio, I'm wondering if someone else is with him. Chances are, it's another FBI agent. Whatever ... But what's important is that I now know what he looks like and where he is. Now I have to figure out my next course of action. I've got time, though – he doesn't know I spotted him.

Murphy ... John Murphy. The name comes to me like a sudden jolt of electricity. How nice. Now I know his name and it's really funny that this guy thinks he can catch me. Hey John Murphy, whatever were you thinking? That you and some other FBI agent could flush me out on the streets of Rome, handcuff and bring me back to the States for trial? Or maybe even kill me in a match up? The FBI has always been a full page behind me, but this is getting ridiculous. You have some guts, John Murphy, I grant you that; brains, too, but you're no match for me.

As I finish my dish of raspberry gelato, I shake my head. It's then that I make the decision it's time to reach out for someone back home. I have to contact him to make certain I have all I need to handle this situation. I'd always known we'd speak again, but now the time is here to make that connection, I feel a genuine delight in the rightness of it all. And for me, things couldn't be working out better.

Chapter 41
Whitey & Bobby, Rome

Bobby answers on the first ring, just the way I knew he would. He was always that kind of guy – nervous and hyper. I can see him – short and stocky, with an open smile and round, good natured face – grabbing the phone quickly, moving swiftly and rather clumsily, but still getting just where he wanted to go. And I remember the way he was on the first day I met him, a good thirty-five years earlier. It was 1965 and I was thirty-six, fresh out of prison and working the job my brother had arranged for me at the court house, where Bobby was a court officer. After nine years in federal prisons, much of my time in solitary or tough conditions at Alcatraz, Atlanta and Leavenworth, I was still suffering culture shock. Pushing a broom around the floor of the court house was fine … for a short time anyhow before I found more lucrative and exciting ways to spend my time.

But I liked Bobby and he was pleasant and helpful for the few months I lasted in that job. I've seen him around town many times since those days at the court house. Sometimes he'd drop by the liquor store to pick something up or just say hello, no big deal. But he's gregarious, and he knows a lot of people and would have a good take on anything going on at home. Since the easiest way to get caught would be to get in touch with Joey or one of my brothers or sisters (or anyone I was close to), I've cut all my contacts back home but since Bobby and I never had any sort of relationship that would put him under a cloud of suspicion, he's the perfect person to keep in contact with. And he likes the new job I've given him: to be my eyes and ears around town.

'You know who this is, Bobby?' I ask him, as I stand in the phone booth, a block away from our Rome hotel (I had no trouble using the phone card I bought at a newspaper stand nor getting his home number from information), but it's starting to rain real hard now and even though the door of the booth is tightly closed, water still drips from the inside.

'I have a pretty good idea,' he says, as if it's the most natural thing in the world that I've called him of all people again. At this, I smile, pleased my hunch has been right: it's been a good six months since we've spoken but Bobby Cooke is still the ideal person to reach out to.

'How you been, Jimmy?'

'Just fine,' I say. 'And you?'

'No complaints,' he tells me. 'It's always good to hear you're okay, too.'

'Just fine,' I repeat. 'But I was hoping you could give me another rundown of what's going on at home. Any news you might have, you know what I mean?'

'Sure, I do,' he says. 'It's funny you should call now 'cause I was just talking about you last week.' At this, I say nothing, just wait for the talkative guy to go on and he doesn't disappoint. 'I was at this wake … Johnny Curtis slipped away after this long bout of cancer. You remember him, don't you?'

'Yeah,' I say. 'Nice guy, hope he didn't suffer too long?'

'Longer than he should have,' he says, 'but anyhow, at the wake I ran into Tommy Riley. You remember him, too, right?'

'Sure do,' I say. 'Tommy and I go way back.'

'Yeah, he told me that,' he continues. 'Tommy's married to my cousin Mary. Anyhow, at the wake he told me Joey Donahue's girlfriend – you know, that pretty redhead, I think her name's Joannie or Janie or something – dropped into his house one night, a few weeks ago. She started asking him questions about you and who you hung around with; he said the two of them talked a bit about Brian Kelly.'

'*Brian Kelly*?' I repeat, surprized to hear that name mentioned. 'Why would Tommy be talking about Brian Kelly?'

'Who knows?' he says. 'You know Tommy Riley – he always had a big mouth, never knew when to close it; he'd talk to anybody about anything.'

'Yeah, he did have a problem running his mouth,' I agree.

'Anyway, he said they talked about how Brian died and all that,' he continues. 'Tommy said it shook him up, that he hadn't thought about it all in a lot of years but now he's going around telling everybody this pretty girl came to talk to him.'

I can't believe what I'm hearing. How the hell did Jeannie or Joey make the connection between Tommy Riley and me? Why would Joey be interested in any of this? Unless … and then it hits me like a lead balloon: Joey's the one tracking me. Joey, for some crazy reason, is working with this FBI agent. Why? Last I heard he's been out of jail for a year or two; it just doesn't sound coincidental that his girlfriend's snooping around about my past and I've an FBI agent tracking me. Could it be the reward money or his anger at finding out that I was an FBI informant? If his girlfriend's talked to Tommy Riley and gotten the whole story about how Kelly died, Joey's one smart guy, about the smartest guy I know. He might have figured out a whole lot more about me than anybody else.

With Tommy shooting his mouth off about the visit, it won't be long before the FBI finds out what they talked about. For almost sixty years I haven't mentioned Brian Kelly. Bobby's talking about some other guys I know, but I can't pay him any attention – my mind's too filled with surprize at what Joey and this Murphy might well have done.

'So, I run into your brother Billy pretty often,' Bobby's saying now and I put everything else out of my mind for a few minutes and concentrate on Bobby. 'He looks good.'

'That's good to know,' I tell him. 'Listen, if you run into any other members of my family, let them know I'm all right; that I'm doing fine. Don't go by the house or anything, but if you see them on the street, just let them know that. I appreciate what you just told me and I'll give you a call soon to check up on things again, if that's okay with you.'

'It sure would be okay with me, Jimmy,' he says. 'I know you cut contact with everyone, just like you had to, and I'm mighty pleased every time you call me. You keep feeling free to call me anytime you want. And if I see your family, I'll just tell them he's doing fine. Okay?'

'And Bobby,' I add, 'if you see Joey Donahue, tell him the same thing, okay?'

'Sure,' he says.

'Just curious,' I continue. 'Did you see him at Johnny's wake?'

'Nah, he wasn't there,' says Bobby. 'I was there all night and I never saw him come in.'

'Well, I gotta go, Bobby,' I tell him. 'You take good care of yourself, okay?'

'Yeah, you too, Jimmy.'

When I walk out the phone booth, it's stopped raining – which is good because I need a long, long walk to try and put all this together. How the hell would Joey ever team up with an FBI agent? But then I have to laugh: how the hell did I ever team up with my FBI handler for all those years? They must've trapped Joey, made him a deal he couldn't resist. Money, prison time, who knows? But if Jeannie's checking out information about my past, there has to be a reason: things like that don't happen for no reason and if Joey's teamed up with Murphy, we're talking a whole different story here. No one knows me like Joey. But then again, no one knows Joey like I do. Hell, I pulled him in when he was an eighteen-year-old bouncer and made him my most trusted associate for the next twenty-five years. He's as smart as they come – and he learned a hell of a lot from me, too. That would be some kind of scene, facing Joey at the other end of a gun. Can't even imagine it. Won't be easy, but I'd kill him in a heartbeat if it was him or me.

I walk for several hours, thinking and thinking, just the way Joey and me would do so out at the Fort, away from transmitters. And I can't help smiling at the thought of Joey, right here in Rome: looking for me, working with Murphy, trying to figure out where I might be. If Joey has the info about Brian and me, he's smart enough to put it all together and use it to track me. It's not going to be quite so much fun to pull Joey down, not like it will when it comes to taking care of Murphy, but who knows how this will turn out?

As I finally head back to my hotel, I'm feeling pretty good: after that phone call, I know a hell of a lot more and I can feel the old adrenaline pour through my blood stream. Hey, maybe it'll turn out that Murphy's the only one to take a hit. All I know for sure is that I'm gonna come out of this scene alive. Whether one of the bodies I take down turns out to be my closest associate remains to be seen.

Chapter 42
Cathy, Trattoria, Rome

Jimmy isn't telling me anything but I know something big is going on. He's been spending hours and hours poring over his maps of Rome and lots of other places in Europe; I see maps of Austria, Germany, France and Holland. Every time I ask him to let me know what's happening, he tells me, 'Nothing,' and goes back to his maps and guidebooks. I haven't really minded because I'm spending just as many hours in one particular beautiful church that I just love: I've gotten to know the priest a little, too. He's quite young, but has a special aura that makes me feel so calm every time I'm near him. I haven't gone to confession and don't intend to do so, but if I were ever to attend, he'd be the priest who I'd want to hear my sins.

'If we're going to leave Rome, I'd like to know before the very last moment,' I tell Jimmy at lunch, but he just shakes his head and orders a bowl of rigatoni and marinara sauce. 'You know, I really like it here …' I continue, but he's ignoring me. It's as if he's sitting here alone. I'd like to get up and leave, but I love this little trattoria and I was looking forward to my capellini with clams.

'Someone's following us,' I say softly, and for a moment I have his full attention. 'Not here,' I add, 'but I've a strong feeling the same person who was following us in St Barts and Rio is here now in Rome – I can just tell from the way you're acting that something's up. Can't you let me know what it is rather than tell me to shut up and stop worrying? I just know the next thing I'm going to hear is, "Pack your suitcase, we're leaving in ten minutes."'

I hate the bitchy way I sound, but I can't help it. I'm so happy here and yet I'm so worried someone's close on our trail. I want Jimmy to talk to me honestly, to let me know what's happening – I hate being kept in the dark like a small child. But our dishes arrive and all he cares about is his pasta and marinara sauce, so there's no sense in trying to get another word out of him.

For the rest of our lunch, he's eating happily and with gusto, but he's not fooling me one bit. I can see the way his head is slightly tilted, so he has an unrestricted view of the tiny restaurant door. His body is tenser than normal, his hands rub against each other more frequently – he's worried, more worried than usual, about whoever's following us. Just yesterday, he made an abrupt stop as we were walking around the piazza and headed in the opposite direction before turning around a second time and walking back to our hotel. He held my hand tightly as we walked, saying nothing, just concentrating on this new path.

Suddenly, I can't eat another bite of my delicious lunch. Relax, I tell myself, this is nothing new but I can't control the fear rising in my stomach, solidly moving its way up my throat, making me nauseated with terror. Before I know what I'm doing, I'm standing up and walking – no, racing – to the bathroom. I get there just in time to empty the small amount of pasta and clam sauce that I was able to swallow. My knees are shaking so badly, there's no way I can stand back up and pull my face away from the icy-cold porcelain bowl. I hate myself for being in this position, I hate being so afraid and so I force myself to suck in short, rapid breaths until the fear begins to loosen its stronghold over my stomach. Jimmy will take care of whoever's chasing us: he's smarter than any other human being on the face of this earth.

Slowly, I stand back up, walk out of the stall and splash cold water on my face. Then I rinse out my mouth with the bottle of mouthwash that I keep in my pocketbook and reapply my make-up. When I emerge from the bathroom and sit back down at the table, Jimmy glances up at me with a quizzical look on his face. His plate is empty. How stupid can I be to have worried about anything? No one's as cool and smart as this man.

'Sorry,' I say, as I stretch the red linen napkin over my black pants. 'I think I just had a bad clam.'

For a moment, he stares at me and then shakes his head in agreement. 'Why don't you order something else?' he asks considerately.

'Actually, I think I'm more in the mood for some tiramisu,' I tell him.

He nods and calls for our waiter. I watch as he orders my dessert: he's so natural, so calm, so in charge. No one, I remind myself as I sit perfectly still, forcing my hands to lie peacefully in my lap and wait for my dessert, can hurt my Jimmy. No one ...

Chapter 43
Whitey, Cathy & the Stray Dog, Rome

It's a beautiful day and I'm sitting in our hotel suite waiting for Cathy to come back from her shopping so we can head out for dinner. She should've been back at least an hour ago, so I'm beginning to get annoyed – it's not like her to be this late, especially since she knew I had a lousy night's sleep and hasn't eaten anything all day. Actually, she's been acting funny all week and spending way too much time in that fucking church that she won't shut up about.

I know she's worried about someone following us, but there's nothing I can say to calm her down. I've been concentrating on every turn we take, every person who crosses our path, looking for Joey or Murphy every minute of the day and night, but there's no way she'd be able to sense that. It's not like her to act this nervous. I try to concentrate on the book I'm reading about Caesar and the Gallic Wars when I realize I can't focus on any of the words. Where the hell is she? I hurl the book down on the floor, grab my jacket and stomp out the door.

I've only walked two blocks when I see the crowd. The minute I spot the group of people, I get this bad feeling. I've no idea why, but I suddenly feel a little weak in my knees. I keep on walking and sure enough, I spot Cathy, kneeling in the middle of the street, the Burberry that I recently bought her covered in blood. It takes me a long moment to see that the blood is coming from the dog she's clutching to her chest. As I get closer, I can tell the dog's about the size of a cocker spaniel and despite the blood all over its fur, I can see that the fur is fawn coloured. It looks like a small deer – only there's no doubt, from the way the dog is holding its head, the way its tongue dangles loosely from the side of its mouth, that the poor thing is dead.

I'm so relieved to see Cathy isn't hurt and the blood belongs to the lifeless dog that all my anger at her being late and the centre of a crowd dissipates. The woman is sobbing, refusing to hand over the dog to the policeman, who is bending over her, trying to convince her in broken English to give him the dead animal. But Cathy's tough, even in her devastating despair, and there's no way that policeman is going to separate her from the dog.

Without a word, I push the policeman away and take up his position beside her. At first he looks startled, then angry, but when he sees how Cathy looks up at me, sobbing even more now and holding the little dog less tightly, he shakes his head in agreement, stands up and backs off a bit, urging the crowd to do the same.

'I was right here when it happened,' she struggles to tell me between gulping sobs. 'I had just patted him and was walking away when he ran into the street and that car hit him. Oh Jimmy, it was so awful!' she stops and looks up at me, even more upset now, and I can understand why. Calling me 'Jimmy' in front of a crowd is a grave error: we never use our real names in public.

But I shake my head and pull her closer to me, so I'm holding her and the lifeless bloodied dog against my own chest. 'It's okay, honey,' I murmur. 'It's okay. He didn't suffer: it was quick, very quick.'

It takes a bit longer but finally she releases her tight hold on the dog and allows the policeman to wrap its body in a gray blanket and carry him away. Slowly, the crowd disperses and I'm able to get Cathy to her feet and carefully, my arms wrapped tightly round her still-shaking body, lead her out of the square and back to our hotel.

Like Cathy's raincoat, my jacket and pants are covered in blood but I don't care – I only care that she's all right. The woman loves dogs so much, as much as any other could love a child, and I'm sad once again that I can't give her a dog or a child to love. As I've told her so many times, criminals shouldn't have families because everything they do affects them. All I can give her is myself. But after I walk her into the bathroom and leave her there to shower and wash off the blood, she comes out wrapped in a towel, changes into a nightgown and gets into bed. And all the while I'm thinking how lucky I am to still have Cathy in my life.

188

Chapter 44
Joey & Carl Howard, Rome

Jimmy's not here any longer, if he ever was. I'm so frustrated, I could smash my fist through a wall and this latest Carl Howard column that Rogers sent me yesterday hasn't improved my spirits one bit. Looks like that cowardly columnist has decided to zone in on me now – would love to see him say this to my face.

WHERE'S WHITEY?
By Carl Howard
Special to the Boston Herald

January 17: Rumor has it our fearless FBI agent Jerky John Murphy has a cohort, somebody who recently punched his ass all over a Boston boxing ring. I can't get any confirmation but it appears to be somebody who has powerful hands and a connection to local hero Whitey Bulger.

Now, who would want to team up with old Jerky to bring home the big rooster and his cute little chicky? You don't think it could be Joey Donahue, do you? Now, that guy does know his way around a ring. And he is, for some strange reason, out of jail and to my knowledge, out of Boston, too. Now I'm not about to make any declarations of fact at this point, I'm just asking all you loyal Whitey followers to take a look in the local bars and the streets of Southie to see if you spot Joey Donahue anywhere around.

Of course the big question is why would this crafty criminal want to be helping Jerky? What does he have to gain, maybe the million-dollar reward? Maybe the satisfaction of paying back the FBI informant/boss he once followed to the ends of the earth? Maybe a free trip to all the top vacation spots in the world? All I can say for sure is that if Jerky has attached his chariot to Joey's,

```
it's about even money with all the bookies
that Whitey's coming down. Hey, it's no
crazier than the Red Sox winning the World
Series twice in four years, is it? Stay tuned
for further developments on the always
fascinating saga of WHERE'S WHITEY?
```

For weeks now, Murphy and I have wandered through this miserable city, checking out all the gay bars, along with hotels and apartment buildings, walking through the churches, piazzas and restaurants until I've worn out the soles on a perfectly good pair of Reeboks – and walking into a gay bar with this asshole is easily the most embarrassing experience of my life. But there's not been the slightest sign of Jimmy anywhere: Murphy's still energized, determined he's here and that we'll find him. I'll give the guy credit – he's like a goddamn cheerleader, pushing me on, refusing to take one night off from our lowsy search. Poor Jeannie's taking a lot of abuse too, as I've told her more than once that I wish she'd never run into Tommy Riley in the first place, never set us up on this wild goose chase. If nothing else, I've succeeded in making her as miserable as I am.

'What frustrates me the most is that we might well have figured out a piece of the enigma that's Jim Bulger and it's done us no good,' Murphy tells me as we sit over a beer in yet another gay bar. 'Whoever would've thought Rome would be filled with so many of these goddamn bars? We've been in so many of them that I'm beginning to feel like a gay myself and who knows, considering my lousy track record with women, maybe I'd do better with guys.'

After that comment, I stare at him. It's one of the few personal remarks he's made to me. Could it be that he's actually joking around with me? I'm still not sure if Murphy really has a sense of humour.

'Maybe,' I reply, giving him the answer as if his question to me was, well, straight.

'Not that you've got such a great record either,' he tells me, probably regretting he let his defences down for a minute. 'Shit, you've never even married that woman you talk to every night!'

190

But he must see the fury lighting up my eyes because he shuts right up and goes off to show Jimmy's photo to the bartender. A few minutes later he's back beside me, looking flushed and shaking his head. 'Take a look at that guy,' he tells me, pointing to a muscular figure wearing a baseball cap, no more than forty and sitting alone at the end of the bar. Before I can say a word, he says: 'I know he looks nothing like Jimmy but for one quick minute, my brain did tricks on me and I was sure it was him. What would that have been like to have it all end here? Not that I know how it would have ended, but I'm sure it would have ended.'

For a moment, he's quiet but then he starts up all over again: 'Every night I lie in bed, trying to figure out where he could be and what he's doing. When I finally close my eyes, I'm haunted by an image of him laughing at me, pointing his finger to my face like a little kid, sneering, "You can't catch me, you can't catch me!" Maybe I've lost my mind, I'm not sure but I can't give up. If he's not in Rome, I'll figure out something else. But for now, until we've exhausted every museum, every church, every hotel and every gay bar in this city, we're not leaving. You understand?'

I take another sip of the same drink I've been nursing all night. My head aches, my whole body aches. I can't help but feel sad for this guy: he's so over his head that it's not even funny. If that had been Jimmy, Murphy would be dead – a screwdriver slid into his throat so quietly, so easily, that no one, not even me, would have noticed until he slid to the floor a few seconds later.

Finding Jimmy, I want to tell him, is not even half the problem: subduing him, killing him, is what keeps me up at night.

'Yeah,' is all I say, 'I understand.'

Chapter 45
Cathy, Fiumicino Airport, Rome

I don't know what's wrong with me but I'm just not myself. Strangely, Jimmy's been sleeping well these past two weeks but I'm up almost all night long. For the first time in my life, everything around me feels dark and gloomy – I can't seem to shake off the dreariness. Even though I'm so groggy in the mornings, I force myself to get out of bed and take long walks while he's still sleeping, certain the exercize and stopping at my favourite little market will restore my good spirits but nothing seems to help and I come back to the hotel as sad as when I left.

This morning, I'd just left the hotel when I got this weird feeling that someone was following me – that's been happening a lot lately. Two days ago, I was convinced that a man in a black raincoat, with a big yellow umbrella by his side, was tailing me. I took a sharp turn and he did, too; I managed to duck into a small bakery. He kept on walking and when I came out, fifteen minutes later with two long breads and a large box filled with *cannoli, pasticciotti* and ricotta tarts, he was no longer there but I was so nervous that I dropped the box, spilling the desserts all over the sidewalk. It's not like me to be so paranoid. I've known since Jimmy and I took off, especially when we were placed on the Most Wanted List, that people were looking for us but I used to be able to shrug it off. I know Jimmy's smart, probably smarter than anyone who might be looking for us, but now I can't get my mind to stop playing these awful games.

This morning starts out very bad: when I turn around to check if anyone's following me, all I see is a mother walking her two little girls to school. The children are chattering away and of course, I can't understand a word they're speaking but I realize right away that they're twins, identical twins like Karen and me. And the homesickness gets so overwhelming that I can't stop the tears – I have to stop walking and lean against a building, where I stand like a crazy woman, sobbing into my hands.

A few people stop and then go on their way but one little old lady, dressed in black, touches me lightly on the face. She's such a tiny thing, barely able to stand up straight herself, but her touch feels warm and soothing. Before I know what's happening, she's wrapped both her thin little arms around me, murmuring words I don't understand into the back of my head. Finally, after I've exhausted my supply of tears – for the moment anyhow – she lets go and stands beside me, gently patting my arm. I tower over her, but that doesn't matter; she's soothed me.

'Grazie, grazie,' I keep on saying as she stares at me kindly and I swear if she'd asked me to come home with her, I would have. But she doesn't: she just leans over, kisses me on both cheeks and with one last sad smile, turns around and leaves me. I stare at her retreating black shape until she vanishes from sight and when she's gone, I feel so hopeless that I think I'll crumple to the ground. Instead I just walk away, understanding then, as I haven't quite understood before, that I'll never see my sisters and mother again; that it's just a matter of time until whoever's hunting us down catches us.

While I'm walking, I force myself to get a hold of my emotions. This is not like you, I tell myself: you're a strong, capable woman, not some meek girl who can't take care of herself. You've always been a streetwise lady and you understood what you were getting into when you started your relationship with Jimmy; also you knew what you were letting yourself in for when you took off with him. I take a deep breath and feel a little better. And I know why I'm acting like this – it's homesickness at its worst. I haven't had a single female friend to chat with since we left that nice family in Shreveport, but that doesn't matter: I made the decision to follow Jimmy to the ends of the earth and that's exactly what I'm going to do.

Later in the morning, I decide to go to the church that I love. There's a funeral going on and my priest, Father Dante, is officiating. Naturally I have no idea what he's talking about since it's all in Italian but I watch four beautiful children – girls – do the readings: each one small and delicate, with thick, black hair and eyes as blue as Jimmy's. They must be sisters, maybe a year apart.

When the service is over and the church has emptied, I sit there, just staring at the altar. I'm waiting for Father Dante to return, but he doesn't appear: I want to go to confession but I can't move from my spot. Morning turns into afternoon and congregants and visitors come and go. A few sit next to me and we exchange greetings. 'Peace be with you,' I say to each one and they all smile in return. I'm wearing a veil over my face and feel protected from the world by this small piece of lace; I'm not even hungry or tired.

It's after four o'clock when Father Dante comes out and sees me. I wait for him to call out to me, to offer some sort of greeting, but he's in a hurry and walks by, his long black robe swishing across the floor like a dark wave. My heart sinks when he lowers the lights and leaves. I slump down into my seat and fall asleep for two hours – more than I could have imagined on the hard pew. When the street lights starts to seep through the stained-glass windows, I glance at my watch and I'm stunned to see that it's six o'clock in the evening. I want to wait and see if Father Dante comes back, but I need to get up and stretch … and try to put my head on straight.

When I realize that Father Dante has gone for the day, I return to the hotel. There, I have a quiet dinner with Jimmy and tell him all about the funeral and the church. He's glad that I'm taking an interest in the local culture – keeps me out of trouble, he says, jokingly.

The next day I'm out of bed very early. Jimmy's still sleeping and I'm trying to pull myself together to go back out again and get us some fresh bread. When I start to think about the man who I know is out there, I realize that I don't fear him anymore. Maybe he'll be the one to end this nightmare and to me, that doesn't sound such a terrible thing. Jimmy's still stretched out on his back, wearing blue cotton sweatpants and sweatshirt. Soundly and peacefully he sleeps, undisturbed by the usual nightmares. I stare at him for a long time before taking off my clothes and crawling

194

back into bed beside him. In his sleep, he reaches over and pulls me closer to him; I'm glad my sobs don't wake him.

I'm pretty good the rest of the day. When Jimmy and I do get out of bed, I act like I'm just fine and while he takes care of a couple of errands, I have a lovely time at the little art museum at the end of our street. Unobtrusively, I join a group of Americans who are part of a tour and in one hour, learn more about Italian Renaissance art than I've known in my whole life. At dinner, Jimmy listens carefully as I repeat as much as I can remember. There's no subject in the world that doesn't interest that man: he even surprizes me by already knowing the names of two of the artists whose works I saw.

Later that night, long after Jimmy's fallen asleep, I'm awake and sitting up in bed: I stare at him for a long time and I know from the sounds of his breathing that he's about to have a horrific nightmare. I also know that I won't be there when it happens, I'll be gone – I do love him more than I love anybody else in the world, but I can no longer be with him for I'm becoming a liability. Why, I nearly attended confession the other day. I've always prided myself on being a strong woman, someone who can handle whatever comes her way, and I'm certainly not one of those silly, over-protected women who just can't fend for themselves but lately I'm just not so sure of myself and that scares me. I don't know what I'm going to say or do and I'm terrified that somehow I'll compromize Jimmy. I'd rather die than do that, so I'm going home. And when they arrest me and question me, I'll tell them so many lies that I'll help him in ways I can no longer do. Jimmy will be better off if I'm behind bars than out beside him, hindering him and holding him back.

Besides the money I have hidden away, I take nothing with me and I'm gone before his first nightmare scream fills the air. I take a taxi to the airport, but all the ticket windows are closed and I learn that it will be six hours before I can take the next plane back to the US – I'm thinking of going to New York.

So, I walk all around the terminal, back and forth like some crazy woman, unable to sit still even for five minutes. At one point, I sit down next to a lovely young Italian couple who are holding hands and looking at each so lovingly that I want to die with jealousy.

'You are American?' asks handsome man, who must be no more than twenty-five.

'Yes,' I answer, trying to smile and act as if I'm just calmly waiting for the airport to open, as they are.

'We were in New York last month,' the woman, who seems even younger than the man, her beautiful thick black hair pulled back at the neck with a gorgeous red-and-blue Hermès scarf, tells me. Her English is better than the man's. 'We love New York. Are you from there?'

'No,' I say, 'I'm from Florida.' I've no idea why I said that, but the two of them begin to smile at me as if I just told them they won the lottery.

'Our best friend move to Florida,' the man tells me. 'Do you know the Miami Beach?'

'Oh, yes,' I say and then continue to talk to them, aware that Jimmy would never approve of the conversation. It's all right when he talks to someone but he never likes me to get involved in a real discussion, like he's afraid I'm going to reveal some important detail that will break our cover. We talk about the weather in Miami and the humidity and the best restaurants for ribs. I love talking with these people – they're so glamorous and yet so easy to talk to – and I can tell they like me just as much as I like them.

'Can we have your telephone number in the States?' asks the young woman, whose name I now know is Gina, as she opens her Palm Pilot and waits to take it down. Before I realize what I'm doing, I'm giving her my old phone number in South Boston (from the Squantum condo, where I lived with Jimmy). I try to change the area code from 617 to what I think is the Miami area code, but I just can't figure it out in time. I'm sitting there, too stunned to say another word, when their plane is called and they're gone ... with my old phone number in their Palm. There's no doubt that I'm falling apart. I sit in the same spot for another few hours,

196

knowing I must leave Jimmy, that I have to get on the next plane to the States, no matter where it goes. So, I check my money and I have several thousand dollars; I can buy a ticket for any US city that I want to go to.

When I finally summon up the nerve to walk to the nearest Alitalia ticket window, I know I'm unable to do this, that I can't leave Jimmy as a life without him would not be worth living. No matter how he treats me or what's in store for the two of us, I need to be by his side. I sit back down in another chair, close my eyes and surprize myself by falling asleep for three more hours before I take a taxi back to the hotel.

Before I can put my key completely in the lock, Jimmy flings open the door to our room and the rage on his face makes me gasp. His face is literally purple, his eyes so wide open that they seem unable to close. When he pulls me in and grabs me by the throat, I know he really wants to hit me but he can't – he's afraid of leaving a bruise that will draw attention to my face when we're out in public. When he releases me, I fall backward, hurting my back on the coffee table as I go down. He pulls me back up again, holds me by my shoulders and shakes me like I'm a rag doll. I can feel my head flop back and forth. If he kills me now, he'll be doing me a favour.

I hear him screaming, calling me awful names, telling me how he searched the city for hours, that he should kill me right then and there. But he doesn't. I don't say a word when he disconnects the phone and takes away my cell phone. Nor do I say anything when he locks me in the bedroom and tells me I'll be going nowhere without him.

'I don't want to go anywhere without you,' I whimper through my tears, uttering the first words I've spoken since the door opened. 'Don't you understand why I came back?'

And then he stops and sits down on the bed beside me. He looks at me and says in a low, hushed tone: 'You must understand, Cathy – there's only you and me, we have only each other so we can't afford to make mistakes or the two of us will end up in prison and never see each other again.'

'I'm back, Jimmy,' I repeat, over and over. 'I'm not going anywhere.'

At this, he reaches over, grabs my shoulders and pulls me towards him, holding me, neither one of us wanting to let go.

Chapter 46
Whitey, Villa Borgehse, Rome

The night before we leave, I stop off at a gay bar near Villa Borgehse. It's one of the more popular spots in Rome, just the sort of place I'm sure Murphy and Joey would be looking for me. Since my call to Bobby, I've made it a point not to frequent any gay bars, certain these guys could be looking for me there. I've given a lot of thought to the idea that Joey is tracking me: I'm almost a little proud of him for having the guts to try and hunt me down, it's like someone I've trained is showing me what he's made of. But I wouldn't be at all surprised if, when we met, Joey turned round and finished off Murphy, then he'd join me and Cathy and it'd be like old times. Anyway you look at it, things are getting more exciting every day.

Once I make sure neither of the two sleuths is there, I walk over to the bartender – a pencil-thin, good-looking Italian who speaks perfect English – and strike up a conversation with him.

'So you've enjoyed your time in Rome?' he says, after we've been chatting for a few minutes.

'Yeah,' I say, figuring out this is as good a time as any to get my point across, 'but I'm leaving here tomorrow.'

'Oh, yeah?' he says, looking disappointed, his arms folded across the counter. 'Where you going? Back to the States?'

'Actually, I'm heading for Amsterdam,' I say, moving a bit closer to the counter. 'I hear they have a great night life there.'

'They sure do,' he smiles. 'I've been there myself three or four times. It's fabulous.' He looks at me a bit more closely and adds, 'It's weird, but I feel like we've met before – you been in here before?'

'Yeah, several times,' I lie, now suspecting Murphy or Joey has recently shown him my photo. I finish off my beer and hand him a hundred bucks. 'Keep the change,' I say as I leave, and he smiles broadly.

A half-hour later, I'm seated in another well-known gay bar, this time on the Piazza de Popolo. Our conversation goes pretty much the same way as it did at the first bar, only a bit slower since this guy's English is not quite so good. But it doesn't take me long to add the fact that I'm leaving Rome into the conversation.

'Too bad,' the bartender says. 'Where you going?'

'To Amsterdam,' I tell him. 'I've never been there but all my friends tell me it's great.'

'You won't be sorry,' he smiles. 'It's very good there.'

He too looks at me a little funny and I have to hand it to Murphy and Joey: they've hit both these places and I wouldn't be at all surprised if they came back. But the bartender's funny look turns to all smiles when I give him a hundred dollars for my beer and tell him to keep the change. I hit two more bars and blow two hundred more bucks before I go home to tell Cathy we're taking an early-morning flight to Amsterdam the next day. Since I got her the anti-depressant pills I had no trouble buying here, she's pretty much snapped out of the despair that was making her crazy. Women are always more trouble than they're worth, but Cathy's too valuable to me to do without her. Not that I haven't considered doing that more than once. For the moment, she's doing just fine and I intend to do whatever I have to do to keep her that way.

I sleep well that night, certain my Boston buddies will return to those bars and this time when they show my photos, the bartenders will remember me. No one forgets the face of someone who leaves a ninety-dollar tip, nor will they forget what I told them. John Murphy and Joey Donahue will be in Amsterdam very soon – and I'll be waiting for them both.

Chapter 47
Joey, Forno del Ghetto, Rome

I'm standing outside the trattoria where we just finished a nice lunch. Inside Murphy's struggling with the bill, the way he does after every goddamned meal. It makes me crazy to watch him take out his little calculator and sit there forever, struggling to translate every last euro into dollars. As if it matters: everything goes on his credit card, paid for by the FBI. And I hate the feeling I get when he pulls out that fucking card and hands it to the waiter after every breakfast, lunch and dinner we have together, like I owe him. Jimmy paid for every meal, huge bills at some of the finest restaurants in Boston, and it never bothered me: we were business partners but this arrangement is far sicker than that. I'm Murphy's prisoner; he's my warden – though all too often lately I feel like his fucking therapist.

I glance inside and see he's still staring at the bill. I wish to hell he would hurry. The sky around me is threatening to spill a downpour our way any second. And then I see them, coming out of the Forno del Ghetto bakery across the street. I'd recognize them in a second. She's holding a sleek, pink plastic bag that looks like it's from some ritzy clothing store. He's got the long, thin paper bag from the bakery. Knowing him, it's filled with some healthy loaf of fresh baked bread. She's wearing a stylish black raincoat and starts to pull the hood over her long black hair. It doesn't surprise me that she's traded in her shot-blonde head of hair for this black one: smart move. She's got on long leather boots that disappear under the hem of the raincoat. From a distance she looks pretty good but the way she's holding herself, she doesn't look quite so confident. There's a new fragility about her that I can sense despite the stylish clothes.

She's saying something to him and he's nodding. He looks exactly the way I would have expected: black leather jacket over what looks like designer jeans. Black boots and a wide-brimmed cap, sort of a small version of a cowboy hat, and black gloves. I watch them walk away, her arm locked in his. But her exuberant bouncy step is gone: he's holding her arm tightly, moving her forward. Something's wrong with Cathy. Maybe she's ill or sad, I'm not sure.

But there's nothing wrong with him: he looks as strong and in control as ever. And if and when we meet face to face, I know he'll never surrender peacefully. I will have to kill him or he'll kill me but not today, not now.

When Murphy emerges from the restaurant, they've disappeared from sight. 'That damned waiter was trying to trick me,' he's saying, holding up the bill for me to take a look. 'Charged us for three glasses of wine and you didn't have any. I swear these waiters are robbers, all of them.'

'I had a glass of wine,' I tell him simply. 'And you had two. That makes three.'

He looks at me as if I'm crazy. And at that moment I am: I just let the couple we've spent all these months looking for slide out of our grasp. Frozen to my spot on the sidewalk, I watched as they left the bakery and slowly made their way down the street. And I've no intention of telling Murphy what I just saw, of precipitating a mad dash down the street in pursuit of Cathy and Jimmy. I'd wondered what I would do when I finally saw them. Well, I just learned the answer to that question: nothing; for today, nothing at all.

'To hell with them!' Murphy mutters at my side. 'I've been cheated so many times it's about time I did it back to them.'

I say nothing as the rain starts to fall heavily and begin to walk slowly down the street in the opposite direction to where the object of our chase just headed.

Chapter 48
Joey, Bar San Caliso, Rome

I come close to not going into the bar: I'm tired and cranky, also feeling completely miserable with my existence these interminable past weeks. I've tried to stop calling Jeannie every night, doing her a favour by removing my bad-tempered personality from her life. Besides, I have nothing to say to her, or even to Rosie. What could I tell them anyhow? That I'm sick to death of eating with Murphy, talking with Murphy, sleeping in the same room as him?

What makes it all the worse is that the bastard's enjoying this absurd crusade, certain we're going to run into Jimmy around the corner or in the very next bar. Yet the only ones we run into are creepy bartenders or the half-deaf old lady at the desk of our hotel. I'm tired of walking through the streets of Rome, looking for Whitey or Cathy, wondering what I'll do this time if I ever see them again, watching couples pass by, arm in arm; bumping into families with kids, moving through the Eternal City, all filled with joy and a sense of purpose.

In an absurd attempt to restore my defeated sense of purpose, I walk into a series of churches, accompanied of course by my Siamese twin, who seems incapable of leaving me alone for even a second – certain, I'm sure, that I'm about to take off and disappear into the crowded streets, leaving him alone to face his nemesis. Ignoring his bulky presence beside me, a presence that grows larger each day as he downs plate after plate of pasta while I munch listlessly on little more than bread and wine, I enter each church feeling every bit the outsider that I've been for my entire adult life. Inside the high-ceilinged, ornate candlelit buildings, I try to pull out a memory of a rare childhood day, sitting in a pew between my mother and aunt, anything to break up the monotony of the dull, unproductive days I now face.

No one among the uniformly black-adorned crowd of the faithful so much as glances at me as I light my candle and sit down. I feel nothing but emptiness as I sit there, gazing at the crimson draped altar and row upon row of flickering white candles. In such an edifice, there's no sense in thinking of my mother and aunt, both long dead, or my sister, married so miserably. How has this happened? I wonder. How have I, saddled with the unwelcome character alongside me, become so alone? At this moment I realize that I've become strangely invisible, much as the man I once knew so well, only he has made an art of this skill and I am yet again learning from the master.

But now far from the church, I walk into the bar, buoyed up by my new partner's refusal to give up. 'It's going to happen,' he's told me so many times, drunk on too much vino, his defences down. 'I can feel it. I'm going to find Whitey Bulger and my life will be changed forever: this case will make me the envy of every agent. All these years in the Bureau will have been worth it, all the mistakes, all the problems ... This time things will be different.'

And I glance at him, red-faced and spluttering, and feel a mixture of revulsion and pity. 'It *will* be different,' I agree. 'I promise you that.' But he's too far gone to understand what I'm saying and the chances are, he won't survive that life-changing encounter. And me? I have no idea what will happen to me.

'Yeah, I've seen him,' the bartender tells us in perfect English as he looks at the photo Murphy is showing him, 'just last week. Nice guy, heading for Amsterdam. Why are you looking for him?'

'He's a friend of ours,' I say, before Murphy can mess this up, world's most intrepid agent that he is. 'We were supposed to catch up with him but he left before we got here. It's a ridiculous mix-up. So, did he tell you exactly where he was going in Amsterdam? What hotel or anything?'

The bartender stares at me for a few minutes before answering. 'No,' he tells me dully and then turns around and begins to walk to the other end of the bar.

'You sure?' I call after him, practically hurling a twenty-dollar bill at him.

He turns back around to face me again. With sleekly combed, shiny black hair that reaches the shoulders of his heavily muscled torso, he exudes the perfect combination of macho man and pretty guy.

'Yeah, I'm sure,' he says.

I'm getting off my stool when he adds, delicately tucking the twenty into the pocket of his tight pants, 'I don't think you're his friend.'

'Why would you say that?' I ask.

''Cause your friend tips a hell of a lot better,' he replies.

Murphy practically skips all the way to the hotel, talking to Boston on his cell the whole time. Back in the room, while he goes over our arrangements to fly to Amsterdam in the morning with Berman, I head for the phone booth on the first floor to call Jeannie. It's been a few days since we last spoke but as always, she takes me back in her arms. No questions asked. The second I hear her voice the dark cloud lifts and I ask myself, for the millionth time, how did I get so lucky?

'We're going to Amsterdam,' I tell her. 'Got a strong lead he's there.'

'I want you to find him so much I can barely stand it,' she tells me, 'but I don't want you to find him even more strongly.'

'Yeah, I'm pretty much on the same road,' I say, tempted to tell her that I already saw him once, but instead I hold my tongue. Lately I've begun to wonder if that whole scene was just my imagination playing tricks on me.

'What will you do when you find him?' she asks.

'Tie him up and haul him to the nearest taxi and then to the airport.'

'You're worried, aren't you?'

'Yeah,' I say, 'but I'll figure it out.'

'I know you will, Joey,' she tells me. 'But that doesn't mean it's going to be easy. I remember the last time you saw him and Cathy in New York, you said he was so different that whole day, like he knew it would be the last time you saw each other. He's not usually wrong, is he, Joey?'

'No,' I answer, remembering that late afternoon at Grand Central Station and how he shook my hand for longer than usual.

Also, the strange things he'd said that day, like, 'If they come for you, Joey, give me up.' Which ended up being just what I'd done. There was a weird feel to the day – like he was telling me he was taking off for good. 'But that time he was wrong,' I tell her. 'I'm going to see him again, Jeannie, and it's going to be soon.'

'Please think about it, Joey,' she says, her voice hoarse and sad. And I feel a stab of guilt for what I'm doing to her. 'You're every bit as smart as him but I can't even imagine how he'll react to seeing you, what he'll think, how you'll feel …'

'I've got it all figured out, baby,' I lie, needing to hear her cool and reassuring voice again. 'I'm gonna do what I have to do, that's just the way it goes. Murphy and I have a plan.'

'Will you kill him, Joey?' she asks bluntly.

'If it's him or me, it'll be him,' I tell her.

'That's all I wanted to hear,' she says, her voice filled with what I know is false enthusiasm. 'Get some rest, big guy. I'll call Rosie and Lucy to let them know you're fine.'

And those final words say it all: no matter what happens, Jeannie will be there for my sister and niece.

'Bye, baby,' I say, and quickly hang up the phone.

Chapter 49
Cathy, Amsterdam

I've had the worst headache of my life since we landed in Amsterdam, three days ago. It started yesterday during our six-hour flight from Rome and just won't let go. Jimmy's been so busy checking out of the city he's barely noticed that I haven't left the apartment since we got here. He did find us a beautiful place actually called the bridal suite in the Hotel Schiphol, one of the prettiest places I've ever stayed in. It's huge, with two full bedrooms, a large kitchen and a wrap-around balcony overlooking a charming little courtyard. Everything in the suite is blue and white, like a Dresden china pattern. The weather's been beautiful and from the little I saw of it during our ride from the airport, the city's even more so. Right now, I'm determined to make good use of the hotel's indoor swimming pool and see if it eases the ridiculous pain in my head.

Lately I've been talking to myself a lot, trying to shape up and stop moping around like a sick cow. I hate the way I feel, and I know I don't look much better, so I'm determined to stop this nonsense. So far my pep talks haven't done me much good but maybe getting out of the room will do the trick. I'm so pleased to see that I have the pool to myself and dive right in. Sure enough, within five minutes of vigorous swimming, my head feels better. I've always loved it and I'm delighted to think that I can swim every day we're at this beautiful place.

I swim laps for a good fifteen minutes, amazed I've got the energy for this exercize. While I'm going up and down, I try and think only good thoughts, like the time Jimmy and me took his boat up to Gloucester for the day. We left it in a marina and had lunch at this adorable fish restaurant. He had scrod and broccoli, while I had the fisherman's platter. The clams were thick and plump, not greasy at all. Jimmy never eats fried foods but he took a couple off my plate, dunked them in tartar sauce and loved them. I remember the way he looked, a small spot of sauce still on his upper lip as he sat back in his chair and studied the ocean, his beautiful blue eyes hidden behind sunglasses, so handsome, so relaxed.

After lunch, we walked around the Rocky Neck area and checked out the darling art studios. An artist was sitting outside one of the studios and asked if I'd like my portrait painted. Before I could answer, Jimmy said, 'Definitely,' and he stood there and watched while I sat on a stool and the artist drew my likeness. The face on the sketch was much prettier than mine, but Jimmy loved it and gave him a hundred-dollar bill even though he only asked for $25. When we got back home, Jimmy went out and had the picture framed and kept it in the bedroom of our condo. Every time I looked at the picture, I remembered that special day we spent together in Gloucester. And I try not to think about where it might be now, if maybe my twin sister Karen came by and took it to hang in her place. Or gave it to my mother. After all, we're identical twins and it might as well have been Karen's face in the portrait. Maybe that's what happened.

So I keep swimming and thinking about the fun that Jimmy and I always had with Nicky and Gigi: the long walks at Cunningham Park in Quincy, the way the dogs slept on our pillows and how the four of us would all fall asleep, snuggled up together. How Jimmy would lie on the floor and let the dogs crawl all over him and they would cover him in kisses. Even in the water I can smell their sweet doggy aroma, feel their warm breath and sand-papery tongues on my face.

For a moment, I stop swimming and sit on the edge of the pool, letting my feet dangle in the water, now remembering the time we went hiking up the New Hampshire White Mountains on a beautiful September day. We drove up from Boston on Friday night and put on our hiking shoes the next morning, then hiked all day on this trail off the Kangamagus Highway. I wore the expensive designer turquoise sweat-suit that Jimmy bought me for my birthday and felt like a million dollars. Jimmy had amazing stamina, but I managed to keep right up with him. I remember the two of us finally exhausted as we reached the summit overlooking the valley, but the view was worth it.

After we were through for the day, we went back to the bed and breakfast place and took a nap for a couple of hours, then used the Jacuzzi, showered and went out for dinner. We ended up at this nice little restaurant in Lincoln, NH. In Boston, it would have been a five-star but up there it was so reasonable, I couldn't believe it. I even remember the name – The Common Man – something Jimmy got a kick out of. 'Yeah, that's me – the Common Man!' he laughed. We came home Sunday after another short hike and a delicious brunch at the Woodstock Inn, feeling just so very, very good.

When I jump back in the water, I pretend that I'm swimming beside Karen, the way we did when we were at the Y pool. No two little girls could be as silly as we used to be, and still were when we grew up. I picture us sitting beside one another in the little luncheonette that we loved in Southie, laughing so hard that the poor waitress had to come over and ask us to keep it down 'cause we were bothering everyone else there.

At the funeral of one of our uncles, just before Jimmy and I left, Karen and me got this terrible case of the giggles and had to leave the church, hugging our sides and each other, staggering out like total lunatics.

Everyone felt bad for us, certain we'd both been overcome with sorrow. Ma couldn't understand it, though. 'I never knew you two cared so much for Uncle Eddie,' she observed after the funeral and that just cracked us up again. Nobody can make me laugh like Karen.

By the time I get out of the pool, my skin is shrivelled and I'm exhausted, but the headache is gone. I go back to the suite, shower and wash my hair, then wait for Jimmy to come back.

'Hey, you look great,' he says when he sees me. 'Hungry?'

'Starved,' I tell him and wait patiently while he showers and gets changed. I'm fine during dinner and I'm enjoying myself until a large man walks into the restaurant and starts to approach our table. My hands begin to shake so badly I spill my red wine all over Jimmy's plate and it flows onto his lap. He gets up quickly to avoid the mess and practically bumps into the man. And then I hear myself shriek.

Jimmy walks me home, saying nothing, then changes into jeans and a black sweater and leaves to go back out, just the way he has every night we've been here. I know I'm acting paranoid, but I can't help it. I go to bed with a terrible headache, wishing Gigi or Nicky was lying beside me and feeling nothing but an empty, tear-stained pillow.

'I hate this life,' I tell myself over and over, unable to sleep. 'I hate Amsterdam, I hate Jimmy; I hate myself ...'

Chapter 50
Joey, Amsterdam

I'm shaving when Murphy barges into the bathroom, waving his cell phone in front of his face. I have less privacy, living with this guy, than I had in a cellblock – and I liked my warden there a hell of a lot more than this one.

'Your girlfriend's on the line,' he growls at me, 'Joanie or whatever. This better be important – you know how we feel about you using my cell phone for personal matters.'

Oh, I know all right: Berman and Rogers couldn't care less, but this guy's so anal with the minutes on his phone that I practically have to beg to use it. Initially, the Bureau issued me with one, but Murphy in his infinite brilliance decided I'd most likely use it to contact Jimmy to keep him informed of our progress. He just doesn't get it, and so he decreed that I should only use my cell phone when we're out canvassing together and might need to call one another for help. Like I'd ever call him for help! As a result of his brilliant micro-managing, I'm stuck using payphones whenever I can find one to keep in touch with Rosie and Jeannie. But I let Rogers and Berman know that I gave Rose and Jeannie the number for Murphy's cell phone and they understand that it's for emergencies only. This is the first time I've had a call from one of them on his phone.

'Give me the fucking phone,' I say, ripping it out of his hand. In one quick motion, I shove him out the bathroom and slam the door in his face. I'd do a hell of a lot more damage if I wasn't so anxious to hear what Jeannie had to say – it can't be good.

'I hate to bother you, Joey,' she tells me and I know from the tone of her voice that there's bad news. 'Lucy's in the hospital and it's serious: she had a severe asthma attack last night. Her breathing suddenly got tight as could be and in seconds she was wheezing something awful. Rosie called 911 but by the time the paramedics got here, Lucy had stopped breathing. They got her incubated right away but there were two or three minutes when she had no oxygen. Rosie called me from the ER at City Hospital and I raced over here. Joey, Rosie's hanging on by a string – she looks worse than Lucy.

'The doctors have Lucy on steroids and antibiotics and they're running tests on her now – an EEG to see if there's anoxic encephalopathy (like a heart attack of the brain), to see if there's normal or reduced brain activity. Rosie told me to call you right now. She wants to talk to you while Lucy's off for the EEG. Can you hang on for a minute while I get her?'

Jeannie's words are clear and easy to understand but spoken quickly and without emotion. I've seen her in action during medical crises before – when her brother was in a horrific car accident and her mother was dying from cancer – and no one has that woman's strength and intelligence when it comes to medical jargon; there's no procedure she doesn't make sure she gets explained in the simplest terms so she can understand exactly what the doctor is saying and doing. God help the physician who mumbles in front of Jeannie or fails to give her every piece of information she needs.

'Get her,' I say, my mind filled with images of my tiny niece all hooked up to machines, the fear showing in her big green eyes; and Rosie, all alone with no living relative except me to help her. And where am I? Locked in the bathroom in a hotel room with a total asshole, looking for a man who can't be found, more than 3,000 miles away: I'm trapped in yet another cell while those who I love and who need me are forced to struggle without my help.

'Joey, *Joey* …' Rosie says. After that all I hear is the sound of hiccupping sobs, like a small child crying in pain, helpless and abandoned.

'Lucy'll be okay,' I tell her, forcing the anger, the total frustration and my own helplessness away from my mind. 'You're in a great hospital – and you got her help right away. She's a tough little kid – she's going to be fine, I know it, Rosie. And you've got to be strong for her. You know that, don't you, baby?' Memories of all the times when Rosie got hurt or was sick when she was little and I was pretty much on my own to take care of her flood

212

my mind when the anger takes flight. And now she's in the same situation with her daughter. I wanted so much more for my baby sister – she never had a childhood, she never got a break and it was my fault – and so is this.

'Jeannie knows how to talk to the doctors,' I go on, keeping my voice even and calm. 'She'll make sure Lucy's taken care of. And she says ...' There's some noise in the background and I can hear a nurse calling Rosie's name.

'I love you, Joey,' she says, but she's gone and Jeannie's back.

'I gotta go, Joey,' Jeannie tells me. 'The neurologist just came in to talk to us. I hated to call you like this but Rosie insisted. Just hearing your voice helped her, I know. Are you going to be okay?'

'I'm coming home, Jeannie,' I tell her. 'Right away.'

'No, you're not,' she says forcefully, my redheaded spitfire in full military armour. 'You're finishing what you have to do in Amsterdam so you can be freed from this mess. I'm here and I'm a thousand times better than you in this kind of situation. I'll call you with updates. She wasn't deprived of oxygen for more than two or three minutes, Joey – that's not a danger for a kid. She's got an excellent chance, you have to believe that: we all do. Okay, honey?'

'Okay, Jeannie,' I say, 'but I'll be home as soon as I can. I'll call you with my flight information.'

'I've got to run,' she says. 'Please stay where you are. I'll call you as soon as I hear anything – and I'll cover Lucy with kisses from you.' And then she hangs up.

I'm standing there, shaving cream dripping from my chin and right cheek when the bathroom door opens and Murphy storms in.

'You're not going anywhere,' he announces, pulling the phone from my hand. 'And did you have to get shaving cream on the phone? Disgusting!' He wipes it off with a towel and sinks it into his pants pocket, right on top of his fucking little notebook. 'Don't even think for one second that anything your girlfriend tells you is a reason for you to take off – you're here until we find Bulger, and that's that!'

All the anger I've been suppressing so far pours out of me like steam bursting out of a boiling teakettle. 'You motherfucker!' I scream. 'Who gave you the right to listen to my conversation? I'll break your fucking head!' But the bastard doesn't flinch, just stands there in front of me, shaking his head like he's a teacher giving me detention, blocking my freedom for yet another infraction of a dumb rule. Who the fuck does he think he is?

I ram him against the bathroom wall, one hand on the wall above his head, the other on his chest. He's solid, but no match for the furious energy I'm feeling at this moment. 'When it comes to my family, you have no say. Do you understand? *None*! I'll gladly go back to prison rather than listen to you tell me what I can do with my sister or niece.'

My hand is pressing deeper into his chest and his eyes are getting wider but they also tell me he's not backing down. Struggling to control my fury, I release him and start to walk out the bathroom door. Jeannie's right: I need to finish this job and then I'll be home for good. But the bastard puts his arm out to block my way. Like I'm going to let that happen. Breathing hard, feeling the anger grow stronger like a balloon inside my head that this asshole is blowing up, I shove his arm away.

'Stay the fuck away from my family's business!' I say, glaring at him. 'Don't ever mention their names or tell me what to do. Do you understand that?'

At this, he puts his arm back out again to stop me and says, 'Fuck you, I own you!'

Breathing much harder now, I propel him equally hard out the bathroom. As I turn my back to walk away from him, the prick tackles me from behind, grabbing me around the waist and driving me towards the far bed. I snag him around the neck and as we tumble over the bed, I hit the lamp on the end table with my foot, smashing it to bits. I feel the pain in my foot but the adrenaline is flowing now and I'm too mad to acknowledge any discomfort. We've ended up on the floor in between the two beds when it hits me that I'm at a disadvantage. As if to prove my point, the towel around my waist falls off and I'm on the floor, completely naked, wrestling with this maniac.

But the old instincts, the old techniques come back quickly. As always, my head is completely clear when I'm fighting. Since I was a kid, it's always been this way for me: I have the ability to relax and methodically plan what I'm going to do next, like a fight is developing in front of me in slow motion. It's pretty obvious that Murphy doesn't share this trait, though. With one hand wrapped around me, he starts to claw at my face with the other, struggling to get at my eyes. This fucking asshole actually thinks he's going to beat me – and by fighting dirty at that. I can barely process that insane thought when he surprizes me again. With the hand that was wrapped around my waist, he grabs me by the balls and starts to squeeze. Now I know he's trying to do damage.

Immediately I release his neck and stick my two thumbs deep inside the corners of his mouth. With both hands, I extend my fingers, latching onto his jaw on both sides of his face. It's an old move but growing up in Southie, we all learned the double fishhook early on. I've got it going perfectly today as I apply pressure to the corners of his mouth, pulling my fingers tighter and tighter so I'm practically ripping his mouth wide open on both sides. But just as fast as my fingers move, I realize this is a fight I can't win. Yeah, I can win the battle but I can't win the war. This asshole holds my freedom in his hand. I could kill him right now if I wanted to, but with no money and no resources I wouldn't last long on the run.

I have no choice but to end this confrontation by inflicting as little damage to him as possible. Quickly lifting up his head, I turn it to the side and wrap my left arm around his neck, inserting that arm inside my right elbow. Then I put my right arm just as quickly behind his head, bending it forward. He'll be choked out in about twenty seconds. With anything longer than that I'll either kill him or he'll have brain damage. I know he can't breathe and then I can't help but laugh as he begins to tap on my thigh with his hand, like this is an Ultimate Fighting cage match and he's given up and I'm supposed to let him go, but I do release him.

I stand up from the floor and look down at him. What a sight this would be if someone barged in: Murphy's lying on the floor and I'm standing over him, completely naked. Shaking my head, I walk back to the bathroom door, pick up my towel and wrap it around my waist. When I get into the bathroom, I stare in the mirror and I can't believe what I'm seeing: I look like I've been in a fight with a bobcat, with bright red scratches all over my body and face. I run the tap and throw cold water on my face before heading back out into the bedroom. Murphy's sitting on the edge of the bed, his pants and shirt dishevelled, a couple of scratches on the inside of his mouth from my thumbs, marks no one can even see but I know are there. Anyone looking at the two of us would think I was the one who took the beating; he could change his clothes and comb his hair and look fine. Instead, he gazes up at me, looking a bit dazed and says simply, 'You could have killed me.'

I gaze down at him, smile and say, 'Nah, I like you too much.'

For one of the first times since we've been latched onto one another, I see Murphy actually laugh but it's only for a second.

'I'm truly sorry about your niece,' he says seriously. 'I'll make some calls back to Boston to ensure she gets the best medical care.'

It's funny, but it's kind of automatic that I extend my hand out for him to shake and say, 'Thank you.'

Murphy looks back at me and says, 'You know I'm 0 for 2, but I'm getting better.'

The funny thing is, he's still a dickhead but there are times when I genuinely like the guy. Reminds me of a kid I knew, growing up in Southie: every time you fought him, you beat him and he knew you were going to beat him, but he just kept on coming back. Grudgingly, you had to give him that respect. I smile at Murphy and say, 'Now I've got to take a shower all over again.' Then I look at the hotel room: I see the beds are tipped over, two lamps smashed, the end table wrecked and a broken ashtray lying on the floor, even though neither of us smoke.

'Come on,' I say, 'let's put the room back together. We don't want this to look like a gay lovers' quarrel.'

I start to replace the mattress on top of one of the box springs. Murphy goes to the other bed and begins to do the same. I then get the wastepaper basket from the bathroom and start putting pieces of the broken lamps and ashtray into it.

Murphy finishes making his bed. 'Don't' worry about it,' he tells me, tipping his head towards the mess. 'The damage costs go on the credit card. If Boston asks what happened, I'll just say the room was broken into and ransacked while we were out looking for Whitey.'

I smile and say, 'Don't forget they stole my Rolex, too.'

He shakes his head and says, 'Always the criminal.'

Chapter 51
Whitey, Amsterdam

I see him eight days after we arrive in Amsterdam. I'm sitting in a dark corner of the first floor of the bar, nursing a beer when he walks in, wearing khaki pants, a short, black long-sleeve collared shirt and brown penny loafers. He looks a bit thinner than when I saw him in Rome but I recognize him immediately and smile at the thought of how close we are to one another; he seems tired, moving more hesitantly than the last time I saw him strolling confidently through the streets of Rome.

He looks around quickly, not even glancing at the far corner where I'm sitting at a table with two other Americans that I've struck up a conversation with. I'm wearing a black cap and jeans with a black sweater and blend in well with the rest of the crowd, I'm certain. Then he shows a photo to the bartender, who barely glances at it before shaking his head. Murphy hesitates and looks as if he might sit down at the bar but instead ends up putting the photo back in his pants pocket; he then heads up the stairs leading to the next two floors.

There are so many gay bars in this one area that I'm not surprized it's taken us so long to end up at the same one. Right away, I learned there were four main gay areas in this city: Amstel, Kerkstraat, Reguliersdwarsstraat and Warmoesstraat. The Reguliersdwarsstraat is Amsterdam's main gay street, filled with bars and cafés and the only gay coffee shop in the city. Most of the leather bars and shops are located on Warmoesstraat, while Kerkstraat has several smaller gay bars and gay-friendly cafés, the most famous being the heavily occupied Thermos night sauna.

Altogether, I mapped out twenty-eight gay bars and cafés that I plan to visit. In just eight days, I've already found twenty-five of them. While I've only been inside fifteen, I've stood outside the other ten, mostly in alleyways, noticing who goes in or out. When I go into the bars and cafés, I have as little contact as possible with the bartenders, instead finding guys to talk to and I've no trouble looking like a typical American tourist. In fact, I'm so focused on the search for Murphy that my usual distaste for gays barely registers.

So here we are, Murphy and me, together at the Exit in Reguliersdwarsstraat 31, but only one of us is aware of that crucial fact. There are three floors in this club, each one playing different music, as well as one large dance-floor on the first floor. I've been told it's mobbed here on a Saturday night and while the first floor is filled this Tuesday evening, I doubt the other two are. It doesn't take more than five minutes before Murphy comes back down the stairway and without a glance in my direction, leaves the Exit.

Minutes later, I take off and catch a glimpse of him walking into the Downtown bar, a few doors down along the Reguiliersdwarsstraat. It's a little smaller than the Exit but serves good food and it's always packed. I stand in a narrow alleyway, waiting patiently until he comes back out, ten minutes later, and note he looks even more tired now; I produce what I would imagine might be described as a demonic smile when I think of how foolish and discouraging his attempts thus far to find me have been.

He moves only a few feet and stands idly outside Café April for a few minutes and then walks away, heading down an alleyway so narrow only one person can pass through at a time. But he's walking slowly, dispiritedly, and I have no trouble following him for fifteen minutes until we reach a garage outside of the Red Light District, where as luck would have it, his rented white Peugeot is not only identical to mine but parked a mere twenty feet away from it. Fascinating how intertwined the two of us are, too bad he has no idea of this remarkable coincidence.

I let him get in and drive off before I get into my own car and follow him back to his hotel. It doesn't surprize me that an FBI agent is so clueless about being followed by the person that he himself is supposed to be pursuing – I was always miles ahead of any of the agents on my trail back in Boston. I think about how easy it would be to get Murphy right now as he sits in his car. If I had a gun with me, I'd shoot him on the spot. I've done that before, executing not one but two rats as they sat in their car – and with a large crowd on the busy Boston Harbor sidewalk to boot. But that wouldn't be half as much fun as what I have planned for this guy, nor would it be quite so safe. After all, I intend to continue my life on the run, enjoying it as much as ever minus this little nuisance. Actually, he's not bothering me all that much, but he's driving Cathy nuts and for that, he'll pay dearly – and soon.

When he drives his car into a small yard set aside for the Hotel Amstelzicht, I pull over to the kerb and watch as he gets out and wearily walks a few feet into the hotel. He looks worn out. Maybe he got here this afternoon and he's exhausted from his flight, perhaps he's just plain tired of the chase. And he doesn't even know how the game has changed: he's no longer the hunter, now he's the prey – and I know exactly where he is and I'll snag him when I'm good and ready.

I watch him enter his hotel, make a mental note of the name and I'm ready to return to mine when I see him. Up until now, I tried to put him out of my mind, to convince myself the idea that Joey Donahue might be connected to this FBI agent was absurd, but there's no reason to play this game of pretence any longer. There he is: walking into the hotel less than two minutes after Murphy.

I lean my head back against the headrest of my car and take a deep breath. So, this is what it's come to. Never in my wildest imagination did I think I'd be tracked down by the one guy I trusted most of any of my associates, a tough kid for sure, but with no direction at the time. But there he is, looking none the worse for his six years in the can – strong, confident … the only guy I wanted to watch my back in a score. For a moment, I feel the need to race out of my car and grab him, to let him know how good it is to see him, to sit down and talk with him till dawn, just the way we'd do around the South Boston waterfront. But I hold back and remember what's just happened: this isn't the Joey I knew and trusted – it's someone out to get me. For whatever reason, he's clearly made a pact with the devil. Or, I laugh as I think it over more clearly: he's made a pact *against* the devil.

'Joey,' I say softly, 'this isn't what I wanted to happen, this isn't how I wanted to see you again, but you of all people will understand that it's just business and I have to do my job.'

From a phone booth outside my hotel, I find the number of the Hotel Amstelzicht and have no trouble getting through to their room. First, I describe Murphy to the clerk who answers and then explain that someone who is in this hotel left his cell phone in the Exit bar where we just met and I need to return it to him. I'm sure the clerk assumes I'm gay and looking to score with this guy. He has no problems connecting me to Mr Tom Silver. Not a bad phony name. Who knows, I may use it myself some day in the not-too distant future, has a nice ring to it. Besides, it'll be retired in a short while.

If Joey answers the phone, I'm prepared to hang up but luck is with me and Murphy picks up on the first ring.

'I think you just came into the bar,' I say, using a flat voice devoid of any Boston accent. Not that Murphy would recognize me, anyhow. I've always had a good knack for imitating voices and I'm pretty sure I have the bartender's down pat. Besides, it was loud in the bar and most likely Murphy barely heard his words. 'I'm the bartender from the Exit,' I continue. 'I couldn't talk to you earlier tonight. You gave me your card with the hotel name. I know where the man you're looking for is staying. How much you offering for this information?'

It's so easy it's almost no fun at all.

Chapter 52
Joey, Hotel de Roode Leeuw, Amsterdam

At first I think I'm dreaming. When I get back to the room, I'm so exhausted that I fall onto my bed, grateful Murphy's already sleeping, and sink into an immediate deep sleep. The next thing I know the phone is ringing and Murphy is saying, 'Three thousand Euros. I'll give you three thousand Euros to tell me where my friend is staying.'

I open my eyes and sure enough, I'm back in yet another miserable hotel room with Murphy, only this time his eyes are bulging with excitement, his voice filled with barely contained hysteria. I watch from my bed as he grabs a pencil from the drawer beside his own and begins to scrawl on a pad of notepaper. 'Yes, I have it,' he repeats several times, followed finally by a breathless, 'I'll be there.'

When I get out of my bed and approach him, he's still staring at the phone. I take the phone from his hand and listen to the dial tone before placing it back on the receiver. 'It was the bartender,' he tells me, his voice quieter now, more subdued, as if he's run out of breath. 'He knows where Jimmy is.'

'Oh,' I say, calmly. 'Really?'

'*Really*,' he repeats sarcastically, looking at me as if he's seeing me for the first time and not liking what he's seeing.

'Which bartender?' I ask, as always not liking what I'm seeing either.

'From the Exit,' he tells me and then grabs his pad of paper as if I might steal it. 'I figured you'd have a problem with all this when it came down to the final wire.'

'And you're so sure this *is* the final wire?' I ask, barely getting the words out before he explodes into a rage, jumping off the bed and pushing his face way too close to mine. Any peace treaty we'd created the night Lucy got sick has been trampled to pieces. Without hesitation, I grab his arm and bend it behind his body, using all my restraint not to break it.

'What the hell are you doing?' he yells, and for one long moment, I see myself flinging him onto the floor again – and this time beating him with my fists until there's no more colour in his already-pale face. But just as quickly as the rage comes, it leaves. And so I release his arm and sit down in a chair near his bed.

'I'm sorry,' I say, and truly, I am. I don't know how I want all this to end, but I do know that I want it to end as soon as humanly possible.

'So, where are you meeting him?' I ask.

Murphy grabs his arm and rubs it briskly – we're both of us relieved I didn't break it. He stares at me for a while. 'His shift ends at 10.30 tomorrow night,' he finally says. Then he grabs the pad of paper and reads from it. 'I'm meeting him in the Vondelpark by the second water fountain from the Eegenstraat entrance. When I give him the money, he'll give me the address.'

He stops talking and just stares at his pad of paper. Neither of us speaks. I have nothing to say 'cause I see it all now: this guy was no bartender and Murphy was talking to Jimmy. The thought that he doesn't understand leaves me more than a little stunned. But what was I thinking: Murphy versus Jimmy?

'What do you think?' he asks, the first to break the silence. His eyes leave the pad of paper and gaze earnestly at me. 'Is it a ploy to extract money out of me?'

I simply shake my head: I've always known Jimmy was a genius. The guy's got to be plotting this whole transaction with Murphy. I want to say, 'Hell, you're the big-time FBI agent, you figure it out – I'm just a criminal,' but instead I say, 'I have no idea.'

He looks at his watch and then back at me before saying: 'I hope I can remember what the guy looks like.'

'I'm sure you will,' is all I can say.

'I'm pretty good with faces,' he continues, his voice more confident now. 'I think he had a moustache and blond hair. 'Course everyone here seems to have blond hair, but I'm pretty sure about the moustache – it was blond, too. But just in case there's a problem, I'll be well-armed. I'll be situated in a good spot so I can see him before he sees me. If I don't like what I see, I'll hightail it out of there, you can be sure of that.'

He's talking fast now. I want to get back into bed and back to sleep, but he's all wound up – I couldn't shut him up now, even if I tried. I watch silently as he walks around the room, clasping his hands in front of his chest as he talks. There's a noticeable reddish glow on his face, like he just opened a wonderful present and he can't stop thanking the giver. Am *I* the giver? Have I given him something? Does my silence mean something to him? But I'm too tired to try and figure it out – it's enough to stay awake and listen.

'Look,' he says, stopping his mad march for a minute, unconsciously rubbing the arm I twisted, 'if it turns out to be Whitey, I'm not stupid. I know what to do: get out of there and call the Bureau for help. But I at least I would be the first one to see him. If that sounds dumb, then call me dumb – I want something out of this. Just facing this madman alone, although at a distance, would be enough for me. I don't expect you to understand but I'd be mighty grateful for your not calling the Bureau, for trusting me to do this part of the job.' At this, he starts marching again, slower now. 'Hell, it's probably *not* Whitey! But if it is, I'll stay far away. I won't go near him, I promise. Okay?'

'Sure,' I say, nodding. 'And now I need to get some sleep.'

Then he smiles at me and it's the smile of a grateful little kid. I guess I did give him the present and it might be the worst one he ever got. And this could be the worst mistake of my life, but hell no, I'm not his father: he's a big boy. This time I'm stepping out of the ring – I just hope he has a better match tomorrow.

Right before I drift off, after telling myself that I'll try talking some sense into him tomorrow, I see him studying maps of the city and making notes in the small notebook he keeps in his pants pocket. He's concentrating so hard he doesn't notice the moon seeping through the window, lighting up his face even more. I've never seen him look this happy … except maybe in the picture with Mia.

Chapter 53
Murphy, Amsterdam

I'm on the phone to the Bureau a little after nine in the morning, telling them that nothing has happened and that we're getting ready to head out to the hotels and bars when Joey surprizes me and walks out the bathroom. I'd heard the shower start up ten minutes ago but the bastard was obviously standing by the door, listening to my every word. And I'd thought we'd come to some sort of an understanding last night: fat chance of that ever happening. Same old Joey, doing everything he can to screw me over.

'You can't overcome this single-handedly, man,' he tells me when I hang up, standing there dry as can be, a towel wrapped round his waist. 'You've never realized what you're up against: this man lives and sleeps crime, murder is his specialty and I guarantee he has every step of your murder figured out. That was no bartender you were talking to, that was Jimmy, and he's setting a trap you'll fall right into: an horrific, indescribably painful trap.'

'Oh yeah, you're really scaring me,' I say, unable to suppress the smirk that I know is lighting up my face. 'If that's Jimmy, terrific, bring it on – I'm ready for him. But you've never wanted me to get him, and why would you? You're nothing more than a common criminal, you wouldn't know how to speak the truth if someone paid you a million dollars, which is another big deal here – the million-dollar reward. You can't tell me without lying all over the place that you're not thinking of the reward. It's just what you need to buy some houses for your pathetic sister and her kid, not to mention your supposed girlfriend.'

Yet again, he surprises me by answering calmly rather than taking a pop at me – which wouldn't have bothered me one bit. This time I'm ready for him. If necessary, I'd shoot him right this minute, here in this room, and afterwards concoct a story to the Bureau to clear myself. Nothing's going to keep me from going after Whitey myself.

'I don't want the money,' he tells me. 'They'd never give it to me anyhow: you're not thinking clearly. Just give it a rest for a few hours and you'll understand what I'm ...'

'Oh yeah,' I say, laughing in his face, 'just give it a rest, so once again you can let him know I'm onto him. Well, I'm onto *you* – I know you're still connected to him, that you've never stopped worshipping the man and that he's like a father to you.'

'You couldn't be more wrong,' he says.

'And you couldn't be more obvious,' I tell him, practically spitting the words out now. *Come and get me one more time, big boy – you standing there yet another time with a towel around your waist.* 'And if you do anything to ruin my chances of handling this alone, I swear I'll do everything in my power to get you back to jail for the rest of your fucking life – and make your family and friends suffer right along with you! I'll leave no stone unturned to make that happen. Hell, I know how you feel: you'd love to see someone else come in and take this away from me. Or scare the guy off and make me fall on my face again, like we did in St Barts, but it's not going to happen – not this time. This is my case, I've made it all happen and I'm going in there tonight.'

'I thought you said you'd let the Bureau know if it's Jimmy and then come back for him,' he persists. 'What happened to that promise?'

'You're in no position to get any promises from me,' I say. 'But I'll give you one anyhow. If I see you anywhere near the park tonight, I'll shoot you on the spot and worry about the consequences later. That's another promise I'm gonna keep.'

'Don't do this, John,' he tells me, calm as can be, like he didn't hear a word I just said. 'You're signing your own death warrant.' And when I turn and head towards the door, he says, 'She's not worth it.'

For a second I stop, but then I just shake my head and leave. My plan is simple: I'll be ready for my man, guns drawn. I don't need anyone to help me do what I need to do: all my life, I've waited for this chance. And if I fail and end up another one of Whitey Bulger's victims, so be it. Hell, wouldn't that be something, adding an FBI agent onto his list? First time he ever went after the law, that's taboo. The FBI would have to pull out all the stops to take revenge on the murder of one of their own. Bet they'd raise the reward to two million. I'd be famous anyway you look at it. Besides, I've got nothing to lose and everything to gain.

Chapter 54
Cathy, Vondelpark, Amsterdam

Jimmy has been positively euphoric all day. He was up early before me, which is unheard of. And he's insisting on coming with me to the little cheese store when I go to buy our breakfast. At the shop, he orders more food than we could possibly eat and wants to buy the cheese in a whole block, something I never do. As a result, we have to find a special cheese cutter. He isn't satisfied with just any old cheese cutter, but makes us go into two different cheese shops until he finds the one that he wants: the one with a thin wire connected by two wooden handles. And he likes it so much that he even buys two of them.

'Just in case one breaks,' he tells me, as we leave the shop. 'I'm telling you, the cheese will taste so much better when we buy it this way and slice it ourselves.'

After we get our whole breakfast together, he decides that he wants to go to the park and eat outside. It isn't such a gorgeous day, but it seems there's no stopping him.

'You need some outdoor activity,' he tells me as we walk into the Vondelpark. 'You've been doing way too much swimming and not enough walking. After we eat, we can walk around the park and even go into the Van Gogh Museum – you'll love it.'

And he's right: the park's incredible, filled with people dog-walking, jogging, roller-skating, listening to music or just lazing about in the grass. I'm entranced by all the different play areas, loaded with adorable kids, their mothers and nannies. Jimmy sits with me right on the grass, spreading out a blanket he's carried from our hotel, and we eat our breakfast right there. He's so careful with his new cheese cutter, which he happily announces is more than sharp enough to do the job; you have to see the way he cleans the silly thing with his handkerchief, treating it as carefully as if it were his most prized possession. Me, I'm just happy sitting there beside him, nibbling on the yummy cheese, cut so very thin and listening to the children's cries of delight as they climb over the jungle gyms and stumble down the slides.

After breakfast, we walk around the park and Jimmy's particularly interested in a statue of the Dutch poet Joost van den Vondel, for whom the park was named. He's so filled with energy that we walk for hours. When he sees I'm having trouble keeping up, he insists I rest a bit. Despite my protestations, Jimmy settles me on the blanket with the plentiful remains of our breakfast and my book, ordering me to rest while he does some more exploring. He's gone nearly two hours but I'm so relaxed and delighted with the park that I barely notice how long he's been gone. When he eventually returns, he's still in his upbeat mood, anxious for us to roam a bit longer. It's after four when we return to our hotel and we're both exhausted so we settle in for a nice long nap before dinner.

When we get up from our nap, I'm still a bit groggy but Jimmy's raring to go. Already he's decided what restaurant we're going to. It's one we have to drive to, and again he surprizes me by having me drive there. Our little white Peugeot has a shift, which is no problem for me, but he wants to be sure I can drive it in case I need to. Dinner is romantic and delicious; I love the restaurant he's chosen, too. It looks like a little farmhouse, surrounded by a wraparound white fence and a garden filled with white tulips. Both our plates are filled with fresh vegetables from the garden. Our table is set in a charming little corner, where we have total privacy – it's as if we have the entire room to ourselves. Jimmy's thoughtful and considerate the whole meal, making sure my wine glass is always filled, though he doesn't take a sip himself.

When I think he can't please me anymore, he gives me a blue velvet box containing a beautiful diamond bracelet. He just hands it to me across the table, along with the sugar for my coffee. I'm stunned into silence but he's uncharacteristically full of words.

'I know you've been having a hard time, Cathy,' he tells me, as he gently slips the bracelet onto my wrist and adjusts the delicate clasp, 'but I don't want you to worry about anything. Just trust me that there's nothing to worry about, okay?'

Too overwhelmed by emotion to speak, I just nod.

When we leave the restaurant, around 9.30, he has me drive again and just when I think there can be no more surprizes this evening, he adds one more. 'Drop me off at the edge of the park,' he tells me, 'and pick me up at the same place at midnight, all packed and ready to take off.'

I nod, leaning over to give him a kiss on the cheek, and watch silently as he pulls a small black bag out of the trunk of the car and disappears into blackness of the park. I finger my bracelet for a long moment before I drive off: the diamonds are icy-cold.

Chapter 55
Joey, Gauchos Spuistraat, Amsterdam

After Murphy leaves, I forget all about my shower and head back to bed: my head's banging away with far too many thoughts to process. Too exhausted to think clearly, I pull the pillow over my head and promptly fall into a deep sleep. Jeannie insists no one can sleep away their problems like me and no matter what's going on, I always get a good night's sleep. And she's right. Even after the most gruesome murder I'd witnessed, I could put the scene out of my head and sleep like a baby. Maybe there's something wrong with me, but it's the way I'm wired. Everything's a chapter to me and when it's over, it's over.

Jimmy had his own post-murder routine. Immediately after his victim exhaled his last breath, he'd head off to take a nap while I disposed of the body. It wasn't that he was tired – he was a terrible sleeper and suffered frequent and violent nightmares. But a good murder was the perfect sleeping pill for Jimmy: it relaxed all the tension in his body and he'd reward himself for a job well done with a thoroughly enjoyable nap.

But this morning, I need to sleep: I have to have an escape from the decision lying ahead of me. Do I call Rogers and Berman to let them know what that moron plans to do? Should I follow him to the second fountain in the park and do whatever I can to save his sorry ass? Or do I convince myself he's meeting the bartender, not Jimmy, and forget the whole fucking thing?

I'm in the midst of a terrific dream about a beautiful summer's day with blue skies, puffy white clouds and a 32-foot Chaparelle cruising across Lake Winnipesaukee, heading into a secluded cove with a sandy beach. A small fleet of boats are anchored in the cove, four or five hundred yards from the shore, the water no deeper than five feet. Then I look out over the bow of the boat and see the bottom of the lake, a stretch of soft brown sand shimmering in the bright sunlight.

I dive off the boat and slowly pull my body out of the cool azure water to see I'm the only male here. All around me lying on the shore are gorgeous women, dozens of them with perfect bodies, all wearing the skimpiest, brightly coloured bikinis. Just as one of those bikini-clad beauties is walking towards me, her long golden-blonde hair swinging languidly across delicate, tanned shoulders, I hear noises that have nothing to do with the women or the boat, or the gentle slapping of the waves on the shore. It sounds like the slamming of drawers. And then light fills my dream and it's not the light of the sun bouncing off crystal-blue waters: it's a dull sad sun, peeking through not clouds but most probably and most miserably, dark green curtains.

'Are you awake?' an unpleasantly familiar voice asks when I turn over and try to burrow my head under the pillow, desperate to return to Lake Winnipesaukee and my harem of half-naked girls. 'For Christ's sake, it's after one o'clock in the afternoon. You're working, you know, you lazy bastard!'

Surrendering my dreams, I leave the beach and turn over to face Murphy. Even in my half-conscious state, I note the unwanted intruder looks relatively calm and relaxed, unlike his usual warring states of deep anxiety or hyper-excitement. 'Okay, I'm up now,' I tell him, sitting up, all memories of the lake evaporating like steam in a glass of cold water. 'So what do you want me to do? Buy you a bullet-proof vest?'

'No reason to,' he says simply. 'I'm not going to the park, not tonight anyhow. I've given the whole situation a lot of thought and decided I'm not ready to face that killer alone. For once, I agree with you. But listen, I have another idea: how about you and me head over to the Exit around 10.00 and keep an eye on the blond bartender, see if he's heading for the park at 10.30? If he heads to there, we'll know it wasn't Jimmy who called me. And if he sticks around the bar or heads somewhere else, we'll know it was him. Then we'll head back to the hotel and do the right thing: call the Bureau and get reinforcements. Sounds like a sensible plan to me, don't you think? So, get the hell out of bed! Right now it happens to be a beautiful day out there, so let's start combing the streets.'

232

For a long moment, I stare at him: he looks completely unfrazzled, so drastically different to his normal state – harassed and hacked off about everything. I wonder if he's lying, but I've a whole day to figure it out. 'Okay, boss,' I say. 'Let me take the shower I didn't get to take earlier and get ready.' He nods, sits down in a chair and begins to read one of the picture books about Amsterdam lying on the coffee table.

An hour later we're doing our thing: Murphy on one side of the street, me on the other. There's no word to describe how much I hate this. By dinnertime, we've covered close to ten miles on foot – I've hit seven bars and two hotels, but he's beat me by two bars and one hotel. As always, he notes the names of each hotel and bar in the little notebook he keeps in his pants pocket. I'm ready to fall on my face but he hasn't broken a sweat. By now, I'm seriously wondering if he's on something – after all, this is Amsterdam and you can get anything you want at the local drug store.

Dinner is at an especially nice restaurant, a fancy steak house that we went to a week earlier and Murphy liked. He's so wrapped up in his sirloin, smothered in mushrooms and Béarnaise sauce, that he barely has time to talk to me; he's never looked quite so content. I'm more than happy to eat my steak in the unfamiliar silence that I enjoy as much as the food. It's only when he finishes his dessert – some ice-cream concoction covered in chocolate sauce and nuts, which makes me ill just to look at it – that he breaks the delicious quiet.

'You know, the more I've thought of it, the more certain I am that it wasn't Whitey,' he says, as he drains the last of his cappuccino. 'There was nothing sinister about that voice and no trace of a Boston accent.'

'I don't know if you realize this, but Jimmy's an expert at disguising his voice,' I tell him. 'Sometimes he'd fool around and call me, using one of those voices, and I had no idea who I was talking to – and I spoke to him pretty much every day for twenty-five years.'

'Hmmm,' he nods, as if he's taking my words seriously, something he rarely does, 'like you've always said, never underestimate him – but still, it's just a gut feeling I have. I'll bet you a hundred bucks when we get to the Exit tonight that the blond bartender working there last night will make a quick exit himself around ten. You know, I was just thinking about the bartender we saw in Rome in that bar near the Spanish Steps. Do you remember him? The guy with the long blond hair, who spoke perfect English and asked if we knew where Montana was? This guy could have been a relative of his, wouldn't have been impossible. So, are you on?'

Now he's confusing me and I'm beginning to wonder if that's his purpose. 'On for *what*?' I ask.

'Hey, are you drinking too much wine?' he asks, laughing lightly, something else he rarely does. 'The bet.'

'I'm in,' I say, looking at my watch – which, I now realize, he's been doing a lot of. 'It's nine-thirty now. Maybe we should head over to the Exit.'

'Sounds good,' he tells me. 'Why don't you take care of the bill for a change? You're always quicker at these things than me. I'd like to get this over with soon and call it a night.' He hands me his credit card.

'I'll get a head start and meet you at the Exit.'

'Okay,' I agree, more than happy to avoid another scene with Murphy doing mental gymnastics to convert Euros into dollars and see how much we really spent.

He's halfway out of the dining room when he turns around and walks back to my chair. I look at him and for the first time tonight, he seems tired. 'You know, I'm beginning to get discouraged,' he tells me, his hand on the back of my chair, his eyes not meeting mine, staring towards the window a few feet above my head. 'If this bartender thing turns out to be a false lead, I think we should call the Bureau and head back to Boston. We can honestly say we've covered this entire city and I think we could both use a break.'

No other words could please me more than the ones he's just spoken. 'Sounds good to me,' I say, and signal for the waiter as Murphy takes off again. For some reason there's a problem with the card and it takes forever to clear it up. Seems Murphy gave me the wrong one and the waiter has to check with the manager to make sure it's okay if I use this one. It costs me twenty bucks of my own money to make the problem go away or else I'd be there all night. I make a mental note to get it back from Murphy's petty cash envelope.

I'm about ten minutes from the Exit when it hits me: this is all too smooth, something's not adding up. Murphy wouldn't leave this city until he's worn the soles off yet another pair of my Reeboks; there's an entire section of Amsterdam we've never even entered and he never makes a mistake with his credit cards.

Without waiting another second I race to the Exit and sure enough, the bastard is nowhere to be seen. But the bartender and his moustache couldn't be blonder. Oh shit, that means it *was* Jimmy on the phone and now I know for certain that Murphy's heading to the park with a good thirty-minute lead over me. I try and grab a taxi, but there isn't one in sight. I can't believe I let this happen. Sure, Murphy did a good job in fooling me but I did an even better one of letting myself be fooled. I never wanted to get involved in the scene if it was Jimmy – which I knew it was all along. It's so much easier to let this jerk throw himself into the lion's den and be eaten up in one quick bite. Why the hell should I care what happens to him? If he wants to go out like some big FBI hero, who am I to deny him his pleasure?

I keep standing on the kerb, looking for a taxi outside the Exit, but I can't find one. And there's no way I can make it to the park on time by foot. Like a madman, I race back into the bar. 'Call me a taxi,' I order the stunned blond bartender. 'I'm an American FBI agent, this is an emergency!' It takes a good ten minutes, but the taxi finally appears: it shouldn't be more than a ten-minute ride, which would get me there at 10.15 but naturally, there's a traffic jam and the idiot taxi driver attempts some crazy detour, which doesn't work out at all. All the while, I'm cursing myself out, wondering how I let this happen ... and wondering exactly what I'm planning on doing when I get to the park. I have my stiletto in my jacket pocket, and I'm stronger and younger than Jimmy. Somehow I'll figure it out when I get there.

Suddenly I remember the cell phone in my jacket pocket and I can't believe I haven't thought of it earlier. Murphy and his miserable cell phone have been a constant source of trouble since day one. Like he's talking to an idiot, he reminds me every day just to use it for official business – and this is about as official as it gets. As I pull out the phone, I rip my pants pocket. I press the button to turn it on, but nothing happens: deader than dead. I wouldn't be at all surprized if Murphy had made sure the battery was dead when he handed it to me this morning.

'I need you to call the police,' I tell the taxi driver as he's manoeuvring his way around a route that takes us through a couple of backyards. But the guy speaks no English and is either too stupid or too disinterested to understand what I'm saying even when I use my hands to pantomime a telephone to my ear and scream the word 'police' over and over. Ready to tear his throat apart with my bare hands, I pull out the tiny English-to-Italian book that Murphy bought me, then throw it out the window because I'm not in Italy, I'm in Holland – so many Dutch people speak pretty good English, we never bothered to buy a Dutch phrase book!

Suddenly, the bastard jams on his brakes and orders me out of the car. 'No politie!' he shrieks at me. 'Ga weg!' I realize then that he's a Muslim guy and obviously no fan of the police. Same here, brother, but now, maybe for the first time in my life, I need a cop – perhaps even an entire squadron. As for my friend Ahmed here, I consider killing him or at least knocking him out and taking his taxi but since I know nothing about these roads it would get me nowhere. So I'm standing here at 10.35pm in the middle of nowhere, as effective as my dead cell phone.

Chapter 56
Whitey, Vondel Statue, Amsterdam

Once I'd settled Cathy on the grass, I checked out the place. I'd spotted it a few days earlier when I was scouting out possible locations and I have to admit it's perfect. It's an abandoned shack that's surprizingly close to the park, down by the railroad graveyard where they keep the old freight cars and the ones temporarily out of service. I never saw a security guard any of the times I've been here and today was no different, but the car that I parked there a day ago was still hidden from view by a freight car. When I put it there, I figured it might be weeks before I used it, but I'm pleasantly surprized that the time has come much sooner than I expected.

It's been a long time since I've been filled with so much adrenaline. I know the exercize was a great way to keep the momentum going, but now I must conserve my strength for the big event tonight. I have every small detail planned, nothing will go wrong, and I intend to enjoy the rewards of my hard work. One of the problems with working with Stevie was that he always wanted to do the actual murder. Joey didn't care one way or the other, but Stevie actually enjoyed the killing just as much as I did, whether it was with a gun, a knife, a car, a rope, an ice pick or whatever. I can't think of anything else in this world that I've enjoyed as much as a murder – and I know John Murphy's death is going to be an especially satisfactory killing.

I've given some thought to Joey's involvement in this upcoming scene. I'd bet a million he'll be nowhere near the park tonight: he'll be around but he knows me well enough to understand what I'm doing. I'm not sure what his relationship is with Murphy or how tied he is to the agent. There's always the chance that Murphy will come with backup but I know the park well enough to know that it will be very difficult – I'd pick that up well before it became a problem.

Murphy's coming alone: the more I think about it, the more certain I am about this. He's so hungry, he's not going to risk losing this connection to me.; Joey, on the other hand, understands there's no connection, that there will be no bartender at the park, it's me his buddy will be meeting. If Murphy doesn't show up, then I understand a lot more about that relationship and I'll change my game plan accordingly. But I'm quite sure it won't happen, that guy's too hungry to get me – I've done enough scores to know how to do it all.

By the time Cathy and I finish dinner, I'm completely calm. When we leave the restaurant, she's surprised when I tell her to drop me off at the edge of the park and pick me up at the same spot at midnight. I see the fear in her eyes but she struggles to contain it, just like the old Cathy, and nods acceptingly to me. Obviously our day at the park and the diamond bracelet have wrought the changes I was hoping for; now she's steadier and more controlled than in weeks. I need her tonight and she knows it, but she'll rise to the occasion just the way I expect her to. When I tell her to pack up and put everything in the car before she comes to get me at midnight, that we're moving on, she just nods again, no change of expression on her face. Before I leave the car, she leans over to kiss me then waits patiently while I get my bag out the trunk: she'll be here at midnight, ready to go.

I'm standing behind the Vondel statue when Murphy enters the park and heads for the second fountain. Alone. I can't help smiling at that one. That a boy, Joey! You remembered everything I taught you. And I'm 100 per cent positive no one's following him. Seconds after Murphy reaches our appointed spot, I come from behind and whack him over the head with a 12" pipe wrapped in tape. He collapses to the ground, unconscious, and in less than five minutes, I have his hands tied behind his back, his ankles bound together and I'm carrying him to the car parked a few feet away.

The park is as empty as it's been every night that I've checked it out since we arrived in Amsterdam. I open the trunk, throw him inside and stand back up. Thanks to my daily calisthenics routine, carrying 180 pounds of dead weight is no big problem and I'm barely winded but I'm energized and thoroughly pleased with myself. Now the work's over, all the fun lies ahead.

When Murphy comes to, he's lying on the floor, neatly tied up. He takes one look at me and sees it all. I wish I could take a picture of that look so I could study it any time I wanted: it's pure unadulterated fear, mixed with a profound sadness. I can't take my eyes off his face – I just want to stare at it and revel in my own limitless power.

Chapter 57
Murphy, Cabin, Amsterdam

The moment I open my eyes, I know I'm a dead man. I'm lying on the floor, arms tied behind my back, feet bound tightly together at the ankle. I'm a calf being roped in the rodeo. It's over: all my efforts, clever intuition, dreams of money and fame are shattered. I'm about to die a terrible death, no different to any other victim across the world tortured by Whitey Bulger.

I want to scream, to shout to the heavens to help me, to beg this man to release me but nothing's going to work. I'm going to die here on the dirty floor of a deserted cabin. The death of a loser, tied up like a helpless animal slaughtered by a vicious butcher.

All I can see are the eyes of the man standing above, his eyes so icy-cold they make me shudder. No human can have eyes that cold, and when he speaks, the voice is equally inhuman.

'I'm Jim Bulger,' he tells me and somehow I manage to nod. 'And you are the late John Murphy.' I nod again. 'Well, I know you've been anxious to meet me so here we are, just the two of us. Now that we're together, is there anything in particular you'd like to ask me?' There is nothing to prevent me from speaking, no rag in my mouth, no fist over my face, but all I can do is shake my head again. No words can make it out of my parched throat.

'Well, I have a few questions to ask you,' he says. He stops for a moment, pulls a few tools from a small black bag beside him and neatly assembles them next to me. Unable to blink, I watch as surgeon-like, he removes what looks like two wire cheese cutters, straightens them out and places them gently on the floor. This is a dream, I try and tell myself: this is not happening. Any second, I'll wake up in my bed at the hotel. Joey will be sleeping and I'll wake him to tell him this incredible dream. He'll shake his head and say, 'Didn't I tell you this is just what will happen if you go after him, you fucking asshole?'

But this is no dream: I'm lying there, watching the monster prepare to inflict unbearable pain on me. This is no dream: I'm awake ... and soon I will die.

The man who will soon kill me now removes what looks like a road flare from his bag. He briskly slides the socks from my bound feet, his icy fingers touching my cold flesh. Like a terrified dog about to be beaten by a strap, I'm panting as Whitey carefully, oh, so carefully, removes the top of the flare, lights it and brings it near my right foot.

I struggle to remember the lessons learnt so long ago about surviving captivity and torture: the need to hold back information long enough to allow the affected agents to escape from the location the captive will inevitably give up. But there's no other agent to consider here: just me. And there will be no rescue. Unless, and I can't remove all vestige of hope from my wretched brain, Joey comes to rescue me.

The spitting magnesium illuminates the look of pure pleasure on his face as he moves the flame up and down the bottom of my foot. And then I see and think nothing. Pain. Searing pain. Oh my God! No light, just pain. I want ... I want to *die*! Oh God! There's the smell of burning flesh. Me. My flesh. Tearing my foot apart. Fuck! Just end it, end the pain.

'I have a few questions,' Whitey repeats as he removes the flare from my foot. 'You can either answer them on your own or with my assistance but you'll eventually answer them all.'

Oh my God, thank you, thank you for making it stop! So breathe, act like a man, I try and tell myself but the thought's too fleeting to grasp; I can't stand the pain tearing my body into shreds. I see that the flare is dangerously close to my foot, but it's not searing my skin and ripping apart my brain. It will return. Brief respite now – thank you, Whitey!

'So, who sent you on this mission to find me? And who's footing the bill? Who's involved in all of this?'

I want to speak but I can't find my voice. It's lost somewhere. Now it returns. Oh God, oh God, *please* help me! That smell ... a black hole, no escape, red-hot; flying through my arms, legs, feet, face, missing nothing. A voice shrieking – *my* voice. And then a screech.

'*Stop!*'

And it does. I don't want to die like this, like a … like a coward. Disgusting. But *please*, make it stop, make the pain stop, make the hurt go away! I knew those blue eyes … demonic. Going to die. Tonight. But *please* not like this, like a man – not a quivering coward. Breathe. Open my eyes. Find strength, somewhere. I stare into Whitey's eyes. They're happy. He's enjoying this. Fiendish. He wants to make this last, to watch the skin burn, *my* skin; to break me down, his victim – to break down my defences, one by one. Can't do it, can't let that happen. Need courage. Won't save me, nothing will. I'm going to die tonight. Die … with … dignity.

And so I talk – quickly, in a shivering voice that I don't recognize as my own: 'It's the FBI, following you since St Bart's. We got close.' I'm gasping for air. Between words, I hesitate and Whitey moves the flare closer. He is smiling.

'So, why did they choose you?' he asks conversationally.

Is there hope? Maybe I'll live.

'Good question,' I tell him, desperate to be heard – to say the right words, to feed the monster and melt the black ice in his heart. 'I have no answer for that one.'

'Actually, you did a pretty good job,' Whitey observes flatly, 'but not good enough. You became a nuisance.'

He stares at the flare in his hand. Here it comes. I try to prepare myself for the pain. Guess I said the wrong … Oh my God! No, oh *no*! The pain! Crashing … A hammer breaking my skull. And the stench – burning like a steak on the barbecue. Oh the sound, the sizzle! No steak, *me*! Smell getting worse … sweeter … metallic. Oh my God, the blood! Please let me die, please, please, *please* end it. Try. Not. To. Scream. But words: hate, pain – 'Fuck you, motherfucker!'

I'm done but the flare is gone. Just the pain is left. And Whitey … Whitey is laughing … at me. Oh God, what a monster! A monster. Won't let me pass out. Keeping me on the edge … of pain. Must take away his pleasure. He can have my life, but not my dignity.

'And Joey?' I hear him say. 'How did you get Joey to work with you?'

'We trapped him,' I whisper. Desperate, I give up. 'Either he helped ... or went to prison. Forever. He had ... no choice.'

'No choice,' Whitey repeats. 'There's always a choice. He made his and you would never have gotten as close as you did without him.'

He's quiet now. Motionless. Oh, to break through the ropes ... shove the flare in his face. Wonderful agony ... his mouth ... nose ... lips ... ears on fire. Serenity. A reason to draw ... another breath ...

But Whitey is ... dissatisfied? Did he read my mind? But this ... this is *bad*! There's more. I feel it ... I *know* it. But what else can he do? Can't take much more. Sweet Jesus, just kill me! Now. Quick. Don't let me die ... like a ... like a loser.

Oh no! I see it. Fear. Terror. Whitey's hand. In his bag. Blue handles. Pliers. Seen these in Home Depot. Channellock. Plumbers use them. For tightening fixtures, sinks. Whitey Bulger is no plumber. Grabbing my jaw now. Won't open my mouth. *No*! Remembering Joey's testimony – pulling teeth from dead victims. But I'm ... still ... alive. Clenching jaw tight. Lips sealed. Teeth together. Whitey Bulger is ... mad dentist.

Eyes twinkling now. Laughing. Whitey – pliers – upper lip. *Nooooo*! Squeezing the pliers shut ... pulling. Oh shit, oh shit. oh shit! Ripping off top lip. It's in the pliers. Blood flowing. Down my chin ... across my lip, what's left of it. Searing agony ... going down ... but not out. He shows me. The bastard. Chunk of ... my upper lip attached to pliers. Pain, oh God, the *pain*! I can't. I won't. I have to ...

'Agggggggggghhhhhhhhhhhhhhhh!'

Mouth open. Screaming ... like a woman. Oh no, *big* mistake! The pliers – click open, now on two front teeth ... halfway up. No don't, oh *please*! Oh fuck! Snaps them ... snaps front teeth ... in half. Nerves exposed. Oh my *God*! Suffer ... worse ... than flare

... can't shut mouth. Air on nerves ... a gaping hole ... no lip ... blood gushing down my throat. Going to choke, can't swallow. Sweet mother of God, release me! Eyes shut. Must die ... end the pain.

Eyes open. Whitey's face ... joyful. Can't deny him ... his pleasure. Should ... have ... known ... better. *Please* Whitey, God, Jesus, let me pass out!. But no ... Air, exposed nerves keep me awake. Won't release me. No more, can't take more. How much longer?

My eyes ... on his face. Whitey Bulger ... smiling. Hate. Deep hate. Motherfucker! One last act ... before I go. Act like ... like ... a man. *Do* something! Make him ... kill me. I spit. Blood. Saliva. Phlegm. In his face. Smiling Whitey. No one has ever done that. Grimacing, trying to smile. Blood dripping down his forehead, eyes, nose. It feels ... great.

Whitey, standing over me now, wiping his face with his hand, looking at me strangely. He says, 'It's been a pleasure to meet you.' Beyond pain now. Head clearing. Very slowly, slow motion, reaching down for the cheese cutter. Whitey standing behind me, I know. It will finally be over. Won't beg for mercy. Already said what I wanted to say.

Whitey yanks me into a sitting position. Kneels in back of me. 'Who the *fuck* did you think you were?' he's shouting. The ice is gone. Raging fury. I fall back to the floor. Surprized ... by his rage. His ... words. He rips me back upward, tearing at my hair. A large chunk ripped out.

'Did you think you could just come here, capture me and try and collect a huge amount of money for your efforts? Like an FBI agent could collect a reward! So what was it – the fame, the glory of bringing me in? You fucking idiot! You thought you could use Joey, my closest associate, to help you in this mission. Don't ask for mercy – you wanted to kill me, using Joey's brilliant mind that I helped create. But where is he now that you need him? As far away as possible!'

No more words. The cheese cutter – a garrote! Moaning. Can't help it. Trying to stop. Hopeless. I look around at the room, the last view I'll ever have of this world. How right he was, how stupid I was – going up against this monster … on my own. Everything I heard was true, everything I read: Joey was right.

I will sit absolutely still. I won't move, I won't fight. I will not give him that one pleasure. He won't see me squirm. What a time to grow a backbone.

Boston Herald. Front page. I see my name: 'BULGER KILLS FBI AGENT'. At last, people will know who … Now the wire's around my neck. Tearing into my flesh. No agony, just the wind being cut from my throat. Gasping for air. Hot liquid, my own blood, runs down the front of my chest … no pain. Dark fog. I understand. Whitey Bulger … has … cut off my … oxygen … Being strangled. A tunnel. Mia running towards me … arms open. No light at the end. I'm dying. So tired. No reason to fight it. Don't want to. Fight it. Accept it. I want … I want … Mia.

Yes! Go to sleep – finally, a good night's sleep.

Chapter 58
Whitey & Murphy, Amsterdam

He's pathetic now – crying and sobbing, making moaning sounds in his throat … but only for couple of minutes. I check my watch: it's already 11.30. Cathy will be here in a half hour. Time to get the job finished. I wrap the wire around his neck and with all my strength, pull the handles until it tears into the skin on his neck, ripping through the layers. I keep pulling even when the blood is covering my hands, unable to stop even if I wanted to … which I do not. I'm not sure exactly when he's officially dead but I've pretty nearly decapitated him.

And then I hear it: a tiny sound outside the cabin. And I know what it is: he's there. I knew he would be. But he won't stay around, he'll take off – and I understand why. He'd never try to bring me down, and he'd never take off with Cathy and me. He has no choice – at least that's what he believes.

I let go of the handles of the cheese cutter, wrap the body in a blanket I've left here and carry it out to the car parked behind the cabin. Now I open the trunk, dump the body inside and slam it shut. I take off my shirt and put on the fresh one I have in my bag, place my tools back in the black bag, along with the bloodied shirt and walk out of the cabin.

I'm trying to ignore it, but I can't: the sonofabitch denied me one of the things I enjoy most in life. It was a good murder. He's dead and I'm alive – and it'll be a long, long time before the FBI sends someone else in his place. But I saw clearly what he was doing: he gave it up too quick, he made it too easy for me and there was nothing I could do once he did that. I could have prolonged the agony but for what reason? He'd receded into a place no amount of torture could pull him out of.

All I wanted to do then was to get it over with and get the fuck out. Like a cat plays with a mouse before he kills it, I was denied the pleasure of watching my prey suffer, of screaming for mercy. Maybe the bastard was a lot smarter than I gave him credit for.

Chapter 59
Cathy, Cabin, Amsterdam

When I drop him off at the edge of the park, I know without him saying another word that something bad is going to happen. But I refuse to think about it: I can't think about it, I have to pack up all our belongings and bring them down to the car without making it obvious what I'm doing. Jimmy never likes us to announce we're leaving – he always pays our bill in advance so there's no reason for anyone to know we're taking off.

It takes me a good hour to get everything together and another half-hour to bring it to the car in small loads. I don't have to pick him up until midnight and it's barely a fifteen-minute drive to the park where I dropped him off, but I can't sit in that empty hotel suite one minute longer – I have to get out of there. And so I drive to the park. It's an hour early but I'll wait in the car until he comes. Who knows? He might be through early. Through ... that word sends shivers down my spine. It is not as if I don't know what Jimmy's capable of, or what he has done: he's wanted for nineteen murders and I know there are many more. But this is different, this is happening now, maybe a few feet from where I'm parked in this car. I have no fear that Jimmy could be in danger: still, I have a sudden urge to scream. Instead, I place my hand over my mouth and sit there.

At 11.15, I can stand it no more. I'm jumping out of my skin. So I get out of the car, just stand beside it for a few minutes and then I start to walk. I don't know where I'm going but something's propelling me forward. Before I know what I've done, I can see the small, broken-down cabin in the distance. And then I hear it – a bloodcurdling scream, barely human. It's short but so horrific that it knocks me to the ground with its agony.

Like a creature in a horror movie that has lost its mind, I pull myself up and move forward, zombie-like and unable to stop until I'm outside the cabin. There are no sounds now but still, I move towards one of the two windows. I am ice-cold inside, colder than the diamonds still around my wrist. When I glance through the broken pane of glass, I see it all: Jimmy leaning over the body of a man whose head has nearly fallen off, his hands pulling savagely at the remains of the bloodied neck. I don't know how I do it, but I turn around and race back to the car, running faster than I've ever run in my life, and the vomit rises up in my throat like a rogue wave from deep inside my stomach. And I'm sick all over the grass in front of the car. Through the corner of my eye, I see a figure – perhaps a man, though I'm not sure – walk by, glance at me and continue walking. Perhaps like me he is nothing more than a zombie, the walking dead.

I have vomited violently three times when Jimmy walks over to me, wiping his own hands with a handkerchief. He's smiling, but it's not a good smile. I'm sweating and shaking, and I know my lips are stained with vomit.

'I think I may have a stomach virus,' I mutter weakly. 'I haven't felt right since dinner.'

He looks at me for one awful minute, puts the handkerchief in his pocket without offering it to me and says, 'I'm sorry to hear that. Let's get going now – we have a long drive ahead of us.'

I nod silently and get into the car. I'm struggling to keep my head up and not to vomit again. Finally, he speaks without looking at me. 'You shouldn't have gotten out of the car,' he tells me, his voice like ice.

And I understand that everything awful that has been said about him is true: he will kill me right here and now without a second thought. 'I wasn't sure if I was in the right place,' I say in a normal voice – my shaking has stopped and I'm sitting upright in my seat now – 'but I realized I was.'

He glances over at me now, but says nothing. 'So where are we going now, Jimmy?' I ask, straightening my sweater firmly around my shoulders. And this time when he looks at me, he's smiling. But I see his eyes move and I know that he too has noticed the figure moving down the path, away from the fountain. A sad smile forms across his mouth as he waves towards it.

'Anywhere you want,' he shrugs.

Chapter 60
Joey, Cabin, Amsterdam

It's after 11.30 when I finally get a taxi to drive me to the park. As I walk towards the small overlook with a full view of the tiny shack on a remote spot beyond, I'm certain it's all over. This time, I just know I've missed the action. Not that I haven't witnessed it all before: I've seen the way Jimmy took care of Dirty Bob. And Smitty. How he tortured those poor bastards till they begged to die. They'd turned on Jimmy, tried to give him up, made deals with the Feds ... and he got them. Sometimes he killed his victims mercifully, one quick bullet to the head or a sharp thrust of the knife, but Bob and Smitty were spared no mercy. Their murders were long drawn-out, meticulously planned affairs involving intricate forms of torture carefully constructed by Jimmy.

I also know Murphy was spared no mercy. Jimmy was probably aching inside for a good murder – most likely hasn't enjoyed more than one or two since he's been on the run. That's not nearly enough to satisfy him. And Murphy's been pestering him, thinking he could take him on. I wouldn't be surprised if Jimmy had already figured out he was an FBI agent and that made things even worse.

So what do I really want from this confrontation, if I can call it that? Murphy versus Bulger – it doesn't even qualify as a skirmish. Whatever you might call it, I could have easily been convinced to root for Murphy to crack Goliath's skull and sink a stone into his brain with his pathetic slingshot. That stone might have set me free from the relationship with Jimmy that I seem doomed to carry around with me for the rest of my life.

But there's no sense in hallucinating over this one-sided scuffle. Murphy, the poor motherfucker, never stood a chance in this one. And in a way, neither did I. I'm feeling sorry for myself now, while Murphy is probably chopped to pieces in that cabin. Nobody, especially some outclassed ridiculous FBI moron, is gonna change my past or my future. My link with this monster, with pure evil, will never end and any chance I've got of a normal life, of seeing myself as a decent man, can never last. Somehow Jim Bulger will find a way to pull me back to the darkness, no matter where he is, no matter where I might be.

As I stand behind a tall tree with thick dying leaves, thinking equally ridiculous thoughts, I notice a figure stumbling away from a spot outside the shack. She's got blonde hair and can barely walk a step without swaying. It's Cathy and she looks far worse than when I saw her walking out of that bakery in Rome. She falls to her knees and throws up behind a bush. Oh boy, she's seen it all – her boyfriend at work! Minutes after, she stands up, wipes her mouth with a Kleenex and slinks away, I watch him come out of the cabin and I know for sure that Murphy is now 0 for three.

But I also recognize the look on his killer's face and it's not a satisfied one: I smile despite the sick feeling that fills my stomach. Something happened – or better yet, something *hasn't* happened during the murder – and it's left Jimmy still hungry. Perhaps Murphy died too quickly. Or didn't suffer enough. Maybe he finally found himself a set of balls and refused to beg for mercy; perhaps, after all, he wasn't reduced to the disdainful shrivelling wretch Jimmy had hoped for. For Jimmy, it was never enough just to kill – the killing had to offer more than a dead body, it must satisfy his need to reduce any bothersome human to a subhuman creature. Only in that way could he feel superior.

My guess is Murphy hadn't conformed to Jimmy's idea of the perfect victim: he simply hadn't grovelled enough. Good for him! I'd feel proud of him if I wasn't so nauseated by the knowledge that I'm directly responsible for letting this happen.

Minutes later when I see Jimmy walk to the car where Cathy has withdrawn, I wonder if he'll kill her too. But no, even a weakened Cathy is too valuable for him to lose. When I hear the engine turn over, I leave my secluded spot behind the tree and stand in the roadway. It wouldn't matter if he shot me now but just before the car gets onto the access road to head out the park some sixth sense makes him turn his head in the direction where I'm standing. Our eyes meet and his mouth turns up into a small smile.

I want to hate him, I want never to see him again but we'll meet again, I know that for sure. And when he waves, I wave back as the car and its two occupants vanish from my sight.

Acknowledgements

I would like to acknowledge the following people: Chris Murphy, business agent, Laborers Local 609, who took a chance and gave me a job when no one else would. Al Stone and Billy James, thanks for all the laughs. Pam, Kevin and Brian Weeks, who have made everything worthwhile in life; Phyllis and Jack Karas – open the champagne I gave you four years ago. And a special thanks to the late Joan Mazmanian, who always had a kind word and a helping hand whenever I needed it. I will miss her greatly.

Kevin Weeks

For Jack, the love of my life: the one who makes the sun shine every day. For my beautiful children, Adam and Amy, Josh and Chalese, Belle and Danny, each one too precious for words, too special to describe. For Toby and Larry Bondy, Eddie and Mel Karas, with all my love. For my friends: Sheila Braun, Barbara Ellerin, Karen Feldman, Ali Freedman, Barbara Gilefsky, Sharda Jain, Arlene Leventhal, Karen Madorsky, Barbara Schectman, Risa Sontz and Sarah Woolf, who sustain me every day, each one so dear, bringing fun and warmth into my life. For my loving nieces, Sheryl Perlow, Charissa Bondy, Julie Hoffman and Beth Speciale, with all my gratitude.

My writers group listens and understands and I gratefully thank each one: Anne Driscoll, Florence Graves, Melissa Ludtke and Judy Stoia. For Gail Borden who never gives up trying to teach me how to breathe. Without my brilliant agent Helen Rees there would be no book and worst of all, no laughter. And for KJW, yet one more ride on the endless road – never dull and always full of surprizes.

Phyllis Karas

More From Tonto Books

Please feel free to browse more from Tonto Books at
www.tontobooks.co.uk

Fiction

Dirty Leeds	Robert Endeacott
Disrepute: Revie's England	Robert Endeacott
Scandal FC	Robert Endeacott
9987	Nik Jones
Run For Home	Sheila Quigley
Johnny Lonely	Pete Tanton
Everything You Ever Wanted	Rosalind Wyllie
Being Normal	Stephen Shieber
Make It Back	Sarah Shaw
Tonto Short Stories	Various
More Tonto Short Stories	Various
Even More Tonto Short Stories	Various

Crime Fiction

The Road to Hell
Sheila Quigley
Hardback, £9.99, 9781907183034

DI Lorraine Hunt is back in the next installment of Sheila Quigley's gritty crime dramas set in Houghton-le-Spring.

When a woman's body is found mutilated in a field outside of Houghton-le-Spring, it's more than just another case for DI Hunt. Not only does the body show evidence of violation and human bites, it transpires that Hunt knows the victim. But she also knows that this is an exact replica of a crime that occurred more than fifteen years ago, on an evening that changed her and her friends' lives forever.

With flashbacks to Lorraine's past, *The Road to Hell* is a charged, fast-paced page turner with appeal to Quigley fans old and new.

Crime Fiction

9987
Nik Jones
Paperback, £7.99, 9780955632662

To him, the shop is everything; always neat and tidy, safe and reliable. The rental DVDs carefully categorized, alphabetized and memorized. But when one valued member starts to leave bloodstains on the fresh new carpet, handing back porn still sticky with gore and paying in blood-smeared banknotes, his careful existence is compromised and uncomfortable.

Then the girl arrives, with her pale skin, green eyes and fresh scarlet slashed beneath her thin cotton blouse. He wants to rescue and protect her. He wants to be with her. Forever.

Tragic and dark, *9987* is a story about a wholly jagged and at times disturbing, uncaring world where only three things are constant: fantasy, loneliness and love. A tale of a crime that only one person seems to care about.

Non-Fiction

Run For Home:
The Geordie Who Ran Across America   Mark Allison

Riverside:
Newcastle's Legendary Alternative   Hazel Plater &
Music Venue   Carl Taylor

Riding On The Granzwagon:
My Life With The Greatest Jazz
Producer In The World   Dennis Munday

Carpet Burns:
My Life With Inspiral Carpets   Tom Hingley

Him Off The Viz   Simon Donald

The Fifth Pillar: The Extraordinary
Pilgrimage Of A Muslim Convert   Duncan Lyon

We Are Not Manslaughterers   Martin Knight

The Change Agent:
How To Create A Wonderful World   Andrew Crofts

Mr Music Man: My Life In Showbiz   Mervyn Conn

Slimmer Charlie   Charlie Walduck

Sin Cities: Adventures Of A Sex Reporter   Ashley Hames

Non-Fiction

Slimmer Charlie
Charlie Walduck
Paperback, £8.99, 9780955632686

Growing up in Barrow-in-Furness, painfully shy as a child and oversensitive for as long as he can remember, Charlie Walduck was drawn to food as an escape. He went from being an obese child to weighing nearly fifty stones by the time he was in his mid-thirties. Working as a bingo caller in Manchester, the catalyst for change came when one day he was up on stage and the chair he was sitting on collapsed. The shame of that moment sent him to rock bottom.

It was at this time that his best friend took Charlie's life in her own hands by penning a letter to Fern Britton on *This Morning*, asking for help. With the nation watching and with the immeasurable support of the programme's GP, Dr Chris Steele, Charlie began his weight loss quest, eventually losing thirty stones in less than two years.

Slimmer Charlie follows Charlie's weight loss journey in his own words, recalling with insight his struggles with food and the associated problems of low self-esteem, lack of confidence and shyness. With vivid recollections of growing up in a working-class family in the north of England, this is as much a memoir as a self-help guide.

Non-Fiction

Shakespeare and Love
Raymond Scott with Mike Kelly
Paperback, £8.99, 9780955632693

The Shakespeare First Folio is one of the most revered books in the English language and worth millions. One is owned by billionaire John Paul Getty; another was in the hands of Raymond Scott, who lived with his mum in their modest Tyneside home until his arrest.

When he tried to sell the folio to fund the good life with his young Cuban dancer fiancée, Raymond sparked an international investigation involving the FBI, Interpol and the British police. Did he steal it from Durham University ten years ago, or was he just an innocent middleman for the real owner, a former bodyguard to Fidel Castro?

Shakespeare and Love lifts the lid on this real-life crime mystery, told by the man at the centre of the extraordinary tale – Raymond Scott himself. As he says: 'There are two Raymond Scotts – one who lives quietly at home with his mother, the other who people think is some Raffles-type international thief.'

Non-Fiction

Sin Cities: Adventures of a Sex Reporter
Ashley Hames
Paperback, £7.99, 9780955632600

With a weakness for women, good times and binge drinking it seemed inevitable that Ashley Hames would turn cult hero with *Sin Cities*, blazing a toxic trail through a minefield of debauchery and fantasy across the globe.

As clown prince of L!VE TV, he happily changed his name by deed poll to News Bunny and produced such lowbrow classics as *Topless Darts*. A few months down the line his career had him hoisted up on meat hooks, tortured, clamped and generally trampled on in the name of entertainment. It was only when the cameras stopped rolling that it got messy.

In this book, Ashley investigates the sexual habits of some of the most extraordinary people on the planet – from the bizarre to the unimaginable – and somehow helps it all make perfect sense.

Non-Fiction

We Are Not Manslaughterers: The Epsom Riot And The Murder Of Station Sergeant Thomas Green
Martin Knight
Hardback, £12.99, 9781907183140

Derby Day 1919 was a day of celebration, it being the first Derby Stakes to be run in Epsom since the First World War. Yet only 15 days later 12 Epsom policemen found themselves defending their quiet station against a 400-strong rioting mob in a vicious hour-long battle. By the end many were injured and the dependable Sergeant Thomas Green lay dead. However, the rioters were not drunken revellers or incensed locals: they were Canadian soldiers, many of whom had seen action in France and Belgium, bent on releasing their comrades, arrested earlier in the evening following a minor disturbance in one of the town's pubs.

This book traces the events of 17 June 1919 and explores the reasons why the Government was so keen not to allow the case to become a cause celebre. Future King Edward VIII was scheduled to tour the colonies, including Canada, to thank them for their extraordinary sacrifices during the war. To do this while Canadian soldiers were being hung in prisons across Britain did not bear contemplation. Prime Ministers Lord Rosebery, Winston Churchill and David Lloyd-George are among the historical figures who were faced with the murder's potential fall-out; the worst-case scenario being the disintegration of the British Empire.